Notes & Apologies:

✭ Subscriptions to *The Believer* include four issues, one of which might be
themed and may come with a bonus item, such as a giant poster,
art object, or free radio series. View our subscription deals at
thebeliever.net/subscribe.

✭ This issue's cover depicts, clockwise from the top left, Creed Bratton,
Darth Maul, Eileen Myles, and Olúfẹ́mi O. Táíwò.

✭ The illustrations of Green Men in this issue are by Niv Bavarsky.

✭ Appearing on pages 14, 22, 23, 26, 51, 71, 90, and 114 is a microinterview
with Devon Price, conducted by Emerson Whitney. Price is the author
of *Laziness Does Not Exist*, *Unmasking Autism: Discovering the New
Faces of Neurodiversity*, and *Unlearning Shame: How We Can Reject Self-
Blame Culture and Reclaim Our Power*. For this issue, they spoke about
autism, transness, activism, self-help books, Goop, and the pitfalls of
psychiatric medicine.

✭ In case you missed it, we are once again publishing online exclusives!
Follow along on our website as select guest columnists explore, in weekly
installments, a variety of themes. Our first column, by Katie Heindl, is about
women's professional basketball. Future columns will consider books written
in exile, film set design, and maybe beekeeping. If you would like to stay
au courant with our online offerings, you can also sign up for our recently
launched newsletter. Dispatches will arrive on a monthly basis and will
include, among other things, announcements, archive highlights, and special
deals. Visit thebeliever.net/newsletter for more information.

✭ Last issue's "Close Read" by Veronique Greenwood was, quite lamentably,
published without footnote references. Head to our website to read the full,
corrected piece.

THE BELIEVER

TWO DECADES OF THE BEST ESSAYS, INTERVIEWS, JOURNALISM, AND MORE, RIGHT AT YOUR FINGERTIPS

Subscribe now and get exclusive access to
The Believer's entire twenty-year archive.

SUBSCRIBE NOW AT
thebeliever.net/subscribe

DEAR THE BELIEVER

849 VALENCIA STREET, SAN FRANCISCO, CA 94110

letters@thebeliever.net

Dear Believer,

As someone who has happily wasted many hours wandering through used-book stores, I felt very seen by Ken Howe's essay in the Fall 2023 issue, "What Henry James Has Done for Me." His reflections on book collecting resonated with me in spite of the differences in our reading lives. Unlike Howe, I am not much of a collector, nor am I a completist. I have only a fraction of the complete works of Henry James on my shelves, and the books are mismatched: a patchwork of Penguin editions and sketchy old Riverside editions and a couple versions of *The Golden Bowl*, neither of which I've opened. (Sorry, Henry.)

But now that I've read Howe's essay, I'm questioning everything. Maybe I really *do* need to hunt down all sixty-eight of Ursula K. Le Guin's books without going on Amazon. Maybe I *do* need to find a first edition of *Pedro Páramo* somewhere in Mexico. If this sounds like a fool's errand, well, that's because it is: it's also what makes book collecting a meaningful and maybe even a beautiful pursuit. Howe writes movingly about a yearslong quest to find all the volumes from one edition of James's works in an era before the internet. "All that time spent looking kindled desire…," he writes. "All those afternoons when I found nothing—and that I regarded as futile and wasted—were in fact forging value."

It would be easy to mistake book collecting for just another form of fetishism. But Howe, I think, is getting at something deeper. I was reminded of the sentiments of the critic-philosopher Walter Benjamin. Near the end of his essay "Unpacking My Library," Benjamin writes, "For a collector—and I mean a real collector, a collector as he ought to be—ownership is the most intimate relationship one can have with objects. Not that they come alive in him; it is he who lives in them."

This is the language of religion; this is a higher form of metaphor. By collecting books—and collecting them with passion—we take a leap of faith that these objects, these bundles of paper and ink and glue, are worth our investment. I'm not talking only about time or money, but about meaning, which always runs the risk of being misplaced. After all, most books are disappointments. Even Henry James has his duds. But if you believe, like I do, that literature is a force of good in the world—or, at the very least, that it's not a net negative—then there isn't much difference between a reader and a collector. It's all a matter of suspending one's disbelief. The rest is magic.

Michael Southard
Watertown, MA

Dear Believer,

Like Jordan Kisner, I am "working on a few too many things at once," so I found her "Underway" column (Spring 2024) both fascinating and reassuring. It inspired me to reflect on what's on my own creaky, hand-me-down desk: a bundle of pens, half of which are out of ink; a framed photograph of my grandmother, because she's my muse; a vase of wilted flowers that really need to be composted; my trusty pink keyboard. Before reading the piece, I looked at all these items as a bunch of clutter, but maybe now I'll see them as relics. Hopefully the Shakers were right, and my icons and I will be able to conduct a little divinity through our labor, here at my desk, my own place of worship.

Thanks for the new outlook,
Helen Broder
San Francisco, CA

Dear Believer,

I was so glad to see Greer Lankton's life, art, and legacy celebrated in your last issue ("Uncanny Valley of the Dolls," Spring 2024). Especially in these times when avenues of identity expression are being outlawed, it is so important to continue commemorating fearless, boundary-pushing LGBTQ artists like Greer. For those who enjoy the themes of her work, and those of the equally incredible Nan Goldin, I'd recommend checking out Catherine Opie, Félix González-Torres, Zanele Muholi, and Nicole Eisenman, among so many others.

Sofia J.
Placitas, NM

> "I STOOD THERE LIKE THIS AND ALL OF A SUDDEN *BAM!* KUNDALINI SHOT UP MY BODY THROUGH MY FEET." *p. 33*

> "THE CONTROVERSY AROUND THE STONE WAS ONLY THE LATEST IN ALMOST A DECADE OF TENSIONS BETWEEN UKAI AND BECKWITH." *p. 61*

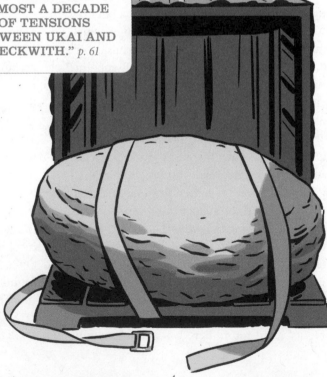

Compiled by Natalia Borecka; portraits, rock, and pigeon illustrations by Kristian Hammerstad

OT: I'm not speaking metaphorically. When I say we should change the world, I mean it literally.

> "THIS IS A PLACE WHERE IT WAS ONCE A LIABILITY TO HAVE SKIN, LUNGS, A BODY." *p. 19*

"BAM." *p. 80*

Photo by Laura Marris; bicyclist illustration by Lane Milburn

THE ROUTINE: ANDREA BAJANI

AN ANNOTATED RAMBLE THROUGH ONE ARTIST'S WORKDAY

9 p.m.

Baby 2 on my chest in the dark, my wife sleeping next to me.

9 p.m.–1 a.m.

10 p.m.–12 a.m.

Counting syllables for a poem, writing emails on the phone.

5 a.m. ⤳ **5:10–6 a.m.**

Baby 1 screaming that he wants to get up. *No.*

Writing down the poem I was thinking of in the dark, thinking it was better in my mind.

5–6:30 a.m.

6:15 a.m.

Baby 2 screaming that he wants to get up. *OK.*

8 a.m.

Dropping off Baby 1, promising soccer after school.

8–9:25 a.m.

8:30 a.m.

Driving to campus talking to my Italian editor and other Italian friends, who are already seven hours in the future. Optimism.

Baby 1 asks me to set up the soccer field in the meantime. I say "I can do that for you."

9:25–11:40 a.m.

9:25 a.m.

Entering class. Teaching students "Candor" by Anne Carson and A Man's Place by Annie Ernaux. Telling them either you have a secret and some pain or it's better to not write.

11:40 a.m.–5 p.m.

2–5 p.m.

Changing diapers, rocking the baby, asking my wife's help in revising translations of my poems (Geoff Brock), and a sample from my novel (Jamie Richards).

12 p.m.

Fifty laps in the pool to get rid of tiredness and melancholy.

5:30 p.m.

Playing soccer in the living room with Baby 1.

5–8 p.m.

6:15 p.m.

Cutting fish, preparing pasta, showering Baby 1.

8 p.m.

Asking my wife how she is doing, telling her I love her, wishing her a good couple of hours of sleep.

8–9 p.m.

8:30 p.m.

Reading Kafka in the dark on the phone. Baby 2 on my chest. ✶

Photos by the author

RESURRECTOR

A ROTATING GUEST COLUMN IN WHICH WRITERS REEXAMINE CRITICALLY UNACCLAIMED
WORKS OF ART. IN THIS ISSUE: *THE PHANTOM MENACE*

by Alejandro Varela

The most well-known resurrection in recorded history has had arguably dubious consequences for humanity, so you'll understand my initial hesitation about publicly unearthing anything, least of all George Lucas's millennium-capping galactic boondoggle, *The Phantom Menace*. But this long-awaited *Star*

halcyon originals and the sleeker but still not great J. J. Abrams–conceived sequels. Usually over the course of two weeks; often with my kids beside me.

It's little more than comfort viewing, but over time, I've come to appreciate the artistic and sociological value of the first chapter in Darth Vader's origin chronicles.

backdrop for introducing Vader prime, a.k.a. Anakin Skywalker—Ani, if you're nasty—a little blond engineering savant, who, along with his mother, lives on Tatooine, a planet with more moons than paved roads. Qui-Gon, played by high-end yoga-retreat concierge Liam Neeson, senses that Anakin is the One, not

Wars installment, panned by critics and audiences alike, isn't without merit. In fact, in the quarter century since *Phantom*'s release, its ambitious story has only grown in my esteem.

First things first: the movie—in 1999, Rita Kempley, in *The Washington Post*, described it as "joyless, overly reverential and impenetrably plotted"—retains its standing as not particularly good.

I watch it nonetheless.

Every year, in a traipse through the long-ago, far, far-away timeline, I revisit *Phantom*, along with the next two endearing clunkers, followed by the

Possibly because I watched the first *Star Wars* films as a child, there's a neurological wire-tripping that occurs as soon as John Williams's brass section blows, and that intensifies when the opening crawl travels across the screen and galaxy. The *Phantom* prologue tells us there's a Trade Federation, disputed tariffs, a blockade, a Supreme Chancellor, two Jedi knights, and, for some reason, an attack on Naboo, but how and why these pieces fit together remain a mystery to me.

It doesn't matter, because the film's political wonkiness is primarily a

unlike Jesus and Keanu before him, and so commences the journey of a human destined to bring balance to the Force. And we begin to understand Vader.

Ironically, it was the easy moralism of good versus evil in *Star Wars* (and a low-key crush on Mark Hamill) that first captured my youthful imagination. *The Phantom Menace* disappointed because it veered away from that simplicity; the most recent trilogy veered back, resulting in fun, unambitious stories. Twenty-five years ago, it didn't occur to me that

Illustration by Kristian Hammerstad

COLLEGE

by Monica Sok

She senses that I'm surviving so she doesn't want to bother me.
When she calls me, I whisper, *I'm in the library*,
and we don't talk for days. It's my fault that I forget to call.
Mother, I'm not prepared for college.

In Economics, I'm learning the invisible hand theory
but scribbling poems in the margins. In World Politics,
I scour the textbook but find no Khmer faces, no Khmer names.
My mother is not an academic and cannot help me.

When grandma falls in the hallway, nobody wants to tell me.
I drive home on a whim, and my parents take me to the hospital.
In bed, surrounded by grandchildren, she reaches for my hand.
She knows that I'll be the one missing when she is on her deathbed.

Spring semester. Final exams. My mother calls me to break the news.
Everyone told me not to tell you, but I wanted to tell you, my daughter.
I walk the tree-lined campus to History and Film: Vietnam & Cambodia.
Is it no longer true that genocide survivors may live forever?

In the hall, Professor Kuznick asks about my lack of attendance.
And it came as a surprise? Such callous words for a woman grieving
her grandmother, a survivor of the genocide he isn't teaching in class.
Excuse me, Professor. What do Cambodians call the Vietnam War?

I've watched the films, bought the books, which I'll never finish reading.
In one small paragraph, the word *sideshow* as in a *circus*. 540,000 tons
of bombs, in a span of six months, dropped in Cambodia.
I try to answer my professor's question.

My grandmother had survived everything except for her own death!
My grandmother's death should've been impossible!
But in college, I do not say these words. Still, I tell him the truth.
She was 92 years old. Yes, it came as a surprise.

Lucas was taking a risk with *Phantom* by exploring how one of cinema's most iconic villains became a monster, in the process complicating our sympathies and giving us something that's often missing from art (and life, and most military conflicts): a reckoning with the past that doubles as a primer for the present.

George Lucas shot his shot and sorta missed, but kudos to him. Not for the rampant Tolkien-like racism in his gimmicky characters—Jar Jar, Sebulba, Watto, I see you—but for his willingness to upend a facile narrative and contextualize the motivations of a severely damaged protagonist. Yes, Darth Vader was a planet-incinerating tyrant, but he was first a floppy-haired child mechanic who had a fine-enough life on a beige-colored desert planet, until a well-meaning, albeit impulsive, Jedi used the Force to cheat at dice and take little Anakin away from all he'd ever known, leaving his mother to suffer a terrible fate, and instilling in him a fear that led to anger that led to suffering. Oh, you get the point.

Frankly, it's a shame J. J. Abrams didn't go further with the more recent films, instead spotlighting another megalomaniacal cosplayer whose motivations are without roots, trauma, or plausible explanations. I say: bring Lucas back for another trilogy that explores Palpatine's rise, or the midi-chlorians and whether their concentration was elevated in Anakin because he was reared in a high-stress household on a planet whose denizens had been dispossessed of culture, land, and dignity, where wealth inequities and social hierarchies abounded, facilitating his seduction by the dark side. ✶

THE BELIEVER

CONGRATULATIONS
TO *BELIEVER* EDITORS

ANDREW LELAND AND ED PARK

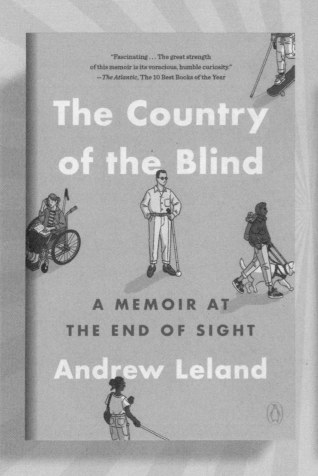

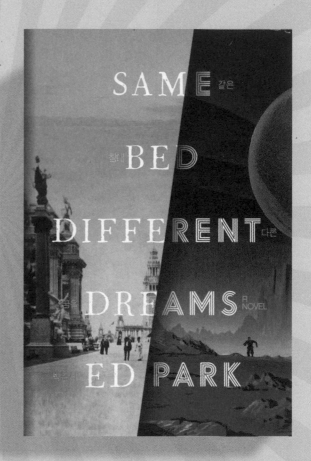

FINALISTS
FOR THE
2024 PULITZER PRIZE

UNDERWAY

WE ASK WRITERS AND ARTISTS: WHAT'S ON YOUR DESK? WHAT ARE YOU WORKING ON?

by Ruth Madievsky

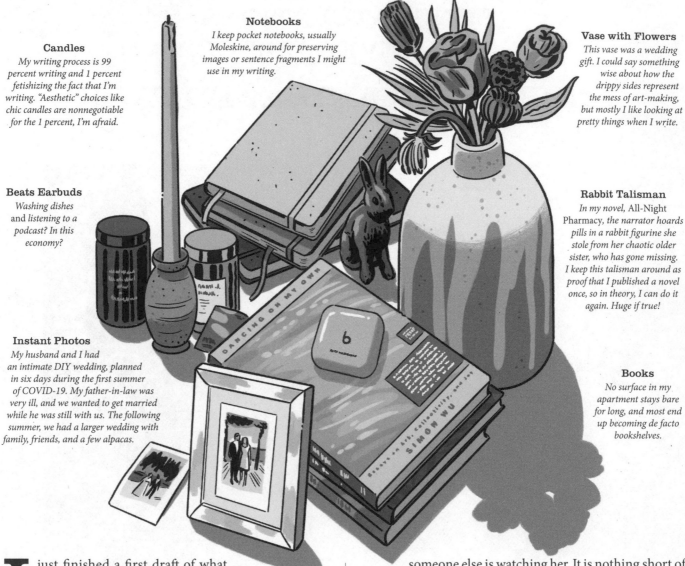

Candles
My writing process is 99 percent writing and 1 percent fetishizing the fact that I'm writing. "Aesthetic" choices like chic candles are nonnegotiable for the 1 percent, I'm afraid.

Notebooks
I keep pocket notebooks, usually Moleskine, around for preserving images or sentence fragments I might use in my writing.

Vase with Flowers
This vase was a wedding gift. I could say something wise about how the drippy sides represent the mess of art-making, but mostly I like looking at pretty things when I write.

Beats Earbuds
Washing dishes and listening to a podcast? In this economy?

Rabbit Talisman
In my novel, All-Night Pharmacy, *the narrator hoards pills in a rabbit figurine she stole from her chaotic older sister, who has gone missing. I keep this talisman around as proof that I published a novel once, so in theory, I can do it again. Huge if true!*

Instant Photos
My husband and I had an intimate DIY wedding, planned in six days during the first summer of COVID-19. My father-in-law was very ill, and we wanted to get married while he was still with us. The following summer, we had a larger wedding with family, friends, and a few alpacas.

Books
No surface in my apartment stays bare for long, and most end up becoming de facto bookshelves.

I just finished a first draft of what I hope will be my second published novel. My debut, *All-Night Pharmacy*, came out in July 2023 and took nearly a decade from first conception to publication. There's this vulgar analogy about two types of writers—bleeders and pukers. I was always a bleeder, revising as I went, bleeding over every word like the insufferable poet I am. Then I had a baby, and suddenly I'm a puker, expelling everything I can in brief but intense spurts while someone else is watching her. It is nothing short of mortifying to put career-ending prose on the page and hit SAVE. But, hey, I have a full draft of material to mess with, and no one other than my precariously placed iced coffee can take that away from me. I've also been working on a second poetry collection—my first since *Emergency Brake* came out in 2016. It's wild to see eight years of poems in the same manuscript, like bumping into different versions of myself at a party. ✷

Illustration by Kristian Hammerstad

HERE COMES EVERYBODY

WHY IS NO ONE READING DAVID BOWMAN'S *BIG BANG*?

by Andrew Lewis Conn

1. THE CANON

It's right there in the title. A declaration of intent, a self-creation myth, a promise or threat to deliver something epochal. With *Big Bang* (2019), David Bowman makes naked the writer's wish, with trumpets blaring, to shoot himself from a canon of his own making. That he succeeded so spectacularly is doubly miraculous, given the author's backstory and premature death over a decade ago.

Bowman's six-hundred-page last novel is a great big cabinet of wonders: a cartographer's mapping of all the years of postwar American life leading up to President Kennedy's assassination. It's an encyclopedic work, a Here Comes Everybody doorstop in the spirit of James Joyce, or peak Pynchon, or the Don DeLillo of *Underworld* (1997), or the Norman Mailer of *Harlot's Ghost* (1991)—only it wears its erudition lightly. And, similar to much of Joyce and Pynchon, for all its structural complexity, Bowman's book isn't difficult at all. Its surface is pure pleasure; on a page-by-page, sentence-by-sentence level, the reader is skipping stones.

Rather than following a single protagonist or several strong leads, *Big Bang*'s collective antihero is baby boom America; the book's hundreds of short scenes shunt between its mid-century, *Hollywood Squares*–caliber cast members. Stretched across the book's canvas is not just the totality of 1950s and early-'60s national political life—JFK and Jackie, E. Howard Hunt and Robert McNamara, Khrushchev at Disneyland and Castro on *The Ed Sullivan Show*, Pat Nixon cringing through Tricky Dick's Checkers speech—but the nation's cultural dream life too.

11

Illustrations by Peter Oumanski

Bowman gives us Monty Clift wrapping his Chevy around a tree trunk, and a young Jimi Hendrix inadvertently carjacking Bruce Lee's Silver Hawk. In the novel's pages we have Carl Djerassi creating the Pill and Dr. Spock spooning out parenting advice; Willem de Kooning slugging critic Clement Greenberg at the Cedar Tavern; William Burroughs playing William Tell with his wife; not to mention Howard Hughes juggling three women on New Year's Eve; and Saul Bellow and Arthur Miller in a Nevada grocery store awaiting their divorce papers, talking about girls.

If *Big Bang* is a book of anecdotes—some of which have the rollicking feeling of tall tales—none of it feels extraneous, thanks to the phenomenal, propulsive energy of the prose. The set pieces are spectacular, and, here's the thing, this book is *all* set pieces. It's the *Raiders of the Lost Ark* of contemporary American fiction—one trailer-worthy jaw-dropper after another. (I'll suggest about Bowman what Pauline Kael wrote about Mailer: "His writing is close to the pleasures of movies.") Bowman gets his who's who company of players up and moving with a minimum of brushstrokes. The portraits are swift, witty, psychologically sharp. There's no winking at the reader, not a caricature in the mix. The world-devourers on display think, move, and talk in ways that feel exactly right—like Bowman had some magic walkie-talkie plugged into the astral frequencies of his novel's fifteen-year span.[1]

Our emotional engagement never lags. A work collaged from scenes no more than a few pages in length, over its many hundreds of pages *Big Bang* never flounders or spins out of control. Rather, one of the amazements of the novel is how its flywheel narrative approach allows it to achieve a kind of self-generative centripetal power.

The historic scholarship wedded to strutting fanboy confidence is dizzying, delightful, and, in this reader's experience, unique in our literature. How does Bowman know so much? How does he keep his dozens of plates spinning with such confidence? How does he pull off the trick with such a sense of cool, never slipping into embarrassment or excess, purple prose or parody? How come you and the person who recommended this book to you are the only ones who've ever heard of it? Why isn't everyone reading *Big Bang*?

2. DOUBLE EXPOSURES AND TOP FIVES

David Bowman died of a cerebral hemorrhage at age fifty-four in 2012, seven years before *Big Bang*'s publication. It's in that knowledge—Bowman posthumously gracing us with a work of this kind of artistic fulfillment, and in considering the book's beautiful and worrying introduction from his friend Jonathan Lethem—that one's reading experience gains a special, uncanny valence.

The Bowman that emerges from Lethem's portrait is a heartbreaker. "Marvelously charismatic," with ambition that might singe paint from walls, Bowman is also deeply troubled: a person of "stark limitations," curdled with qualities that—in the absence of the

affirming success he'd envisioned—rendered him incapable of engaging in the daily humanity business. The tribute is especially wounding because Lethem at the start of the relationship was something like the junior partner. During the *Motherless Brooklyn* author's early innings, Bowman had already won some notoriety for *Let the Dog Drive* (1992), his high-octane, hallucinatory debut about "searching for the plastic heart of America"[2]—but ultimately Lethem felt the need to distance himself from his troubled friend. For all the quirky specificity Lethem provides about Bowman, his is a classic portrait of the difficult, brilliant people you know whose lives and dreams don't work out as planned. Read this way, the essay suggests a double portrait: Lethem's loving resurrection of his friend in the form of an apologia, and a kind of there-but-for-the-grace-of-God confession.

This backstory puts a semi-tragic topspin on your reading of the book. Insofar as every novel is an act of curation—each word filtered through the writer's experience, sensibility, and linguistic sieve—to say that *Big Bang* offers a kind of veiled autobiography is syllogistic. What's especially moving here, however, is how blatantly Bowman sets up his conceit. If the book has an organizing principle, it's

---

1. If the author is a star, baby, is not "David Bowman" the name of Keir Dullea's astronaut character in Kubrick's *2001*? Yeah, well, exactly.

2. In this first novel one finds the imagistic uncanniness that will allow Bowman to pin to the board *Big Bang*'s murderers' row. Here, roadkill is described as "pancaked mammals, snouts pressed into grins," while a dog resembles "a waddling loaf of bread." The youthful narrator considers an older woman "a rocket dropping its stages from higher atmospheres of womanhood than I understood," while another character is thumbnailed as "a terse Dashiell Hammett sentence on wheels." Great stuff!

the author's *taste*—the posthumously delivered novel gaining a special, spectral urgency, as if Bowman were pointing to the reader from beyond and saying, *Look at* this! *Watch* this! *Pay attention to all the good stuff here!*

The game of selection and emphasis—the flipping of tarot cards to reveal the picks that Bowman believes are most indicative of the age—is one of *Big Bang*'s deep pleasures. But, similar to a beachcomber sorting through sea glass to find pieces from which to fashion jewelry, Bowman's sifting through the cultural detritus of American life is discerning, rapt, intuitive. For example, we get John Huston making *The Misfits* instead of David Lean clomping through the desert in *Lawrence of Arabia*; Lucille Ball hanging tough while getting grilled by the House Un-American Activities Committee rather than Elia Kazan naming names. There's a lot of Warholian pop in the book, Bowman's approach to history finding its corollary in Pauline Kael's sentiment from her 1969 essay "Trash, Art, and the Movies"—the idea that "movies are so rarely great art that if we cannot appreciate great trash we have very little reason to be interested in them." The national cake won't rise, the author seems to be telling us, if the batter doesn't account for crap culture.

Viewed this way—as a chronicle of its author's obsessions and the story of an aesthetic education—*Big Bang* serves as a kind of serendipitous bildungsroman. As a result, the book makes you think deeply about your own pantheon—the things you love, the artists and works that make life worth living—and invites you to chisel your own Mount Rushmore, to compile your own top fives.

Page by page, however, Bowman convinces us that it was *this* particular bitches' brew of pop culture and politics, this unconscious pressure cooker, that led to the uncorking of that November day in Dallas. In attempting to capture a comprehensive "psychic X-ray of the century previous to this one, an enlivening dream voyage into the mystery of the world that made ours and which still haunts it" (per Lethem), *Big Bang* is a half-mad book—half-mad in the way of Oliver Stone's fever dream movie *JFK*, half-mad in the way of much of Mailer,[3] half-mad in the Boy Scouts–meets–torture–porn way of David Lynch at his best and most unsettling. And, similar to those touchstones, it catches the American vapors in ways that feel exactly right.

3. TWIN PEAKS

If *Big Bang* is Bowman's answer to *Harlot's Ghost*, Mailer's thrilling, immersive, 1,300-page alternative history of the CIA, and to *Underworld*, DeLillo's monumental "wake for the Cold War" (in Martin Amis's perfect net-catch), those books' authors are his twin peaks. Bowman pays loving tribute to these literary lodestars; in his pages, Mailer gets shafted by George Plimpton for a night on the town with Hemingway, while DeLillo, a young advertising copywriter on the make, catches a Lenny Bruce set at Café Au Go Go.

Blistering, funny, loving—as inflated with hot air as a Macy's float—the wild-man-years portrait of Mailer

that emerges here is among the book's glories. In *Big Bang*, Mailer is American lit's own cosplaying Dostoyevsky, insisting on his own messianism,[4] the artistic imperative of his own stardom, and the necessity of his centrality in the American circus. By contrast, DeLillo is the modest, media-shy observer, the quiet man in the corner. One senses that Bowman inherited in equal parts the former's grandeur and sense of destiny and the latter's crosshatching facility with plot and the ability to tune in to the pitter-patter hum of conspiracy.

These writers have a yin-yang relationship to history. In this regard, it's intriguing to see how Bowman stays in dialogue with his literary forebears as *Big Bang* catapults toward its defining historic event. Though DeLillo, in *Libra*, places Cuban exiles on his grassy knoll, one senses he's just as interested in the Warren Report as infinite text as he is in resolving the question of whether Oswald acted alone. (Indeed, DeLillo refers to that much-disputed historic document as the novel "James Joyce would have written if he'd moved to Iowa City and lived to be a hundred.") In *Oswald's Tale* (1995)—another of the author's big, late, not-crazy books—Mailer, who'd always had "a prejudice in favor of the conspiracy theorists," ultimately and touchingly comes out on the side of the assassin having acted alone. This fascinating nonfiction novel finds Mailer

---

3. When the genius is responding in erratic ways, the observations are incandescent and half-cooked in equal measure, and Mailer mistakes raising the temperature under the Bunsen burner for cognition.

4. This from the author who, upon receipt of a poor review in *Time* magazine, wrote: "The enemy was more alive than ever, and dirtier in the alley, and so one had to mend, and put on the armor, and go to war, go out to war again, and try to hew huge strokes with the only broadsword God ever gave you, a glimpse of something like Almighty prose."

pushing his muscles against his existential reflexes, working through an idea scarier than any conspiracy. "If such a non-entity [as Oswald] destroyed the leader of the most powerful nation on earth," he writes, "then a world of disproportion engulfs us, and we live in a universe that is absurd."

If I'm reading the ending of *Big Bang* correctly, Bowman concedes as much about the murder of our thirty-fifth president. And, movingly, it's Bowman's *novelistic* impulses that deliver him to that conclusion. The book's insistence on the individuality of Bowman's historic actors—the care he lavishes upon the specifics and sloppiness of their human fallibility—mounts a powerful argument against the kind of mass cunning and coordination that conspiracy requires. That *Big Bang* resolves this way is doubly poignant, given the writer's gloomy descent into crankdom and 9/11 conspiracy thinking that Lethem charts in his introduction.

4. THE CANON, REVISITED

Big Bang is a ballsy book, but joyously, generously so. It's ballsy like Scorsese pulling off the three-minute Copacabana Steadicam sequence in *Goodfellas*, psychologizing the camerawork so the viewer viscerally understands the excitement of being a young gangster; ballsy like *Sign O' the Times*–era Prince, when the artist could seemingly pull from the air perfectly formed, genre-defying pop songs every five minutes; ballsy like Sondheim making gorgeous, jaundiced musical theater about throat-slitting barbers and American assassins; ballsy like Pauline Kael overturning

the critical establishment, and the very notion of what a critic's voice might be, by championing *Bonnie and Clyde* and Brian De Palma over *The Sound of Music* and Merchant Ivory.

If, at the time of writing this celebration of everything he knew and loved, questioned and despised, Bowman—a semi-obscure, no-longer-young author—seemed to be self-consciously bucking for the big time, it wasn't in a desperate, vaudevillian way, but out of a determined sense of joy. The reader feels in the novel's pages the exultation of a writer scoping out the furthest reaches of his talent, delighting in the discovery as new vistas open—and you're held aloft in the grip of Bowman's confidence, knowing that at this particular moment, rocketing along at peak inspiration and instinct, the ground is solid and our guide cannot put a foot wrong. And something more. If you know the book's backstory, it's

as if you're right there with the author, cheering him on, grinning in admiration. Can the dude who didn't live to see this triumph through actually bring the thing off?

Reader, Bowman lit out for the territory and took the trouble to map it; let's do him the honor of planting a flag in that loamy soil. *Big Bang* is a blazing, signal work of American literature—a great book. A stunt and a dare, a howl and a history lesson, a prayer and a party, it's a novel that leaves one's eyes bloodshot, nerves crackling, and fingertips smudged from flipping pages, come two in the morning.

As the book's title suggests, every literary work of art is a potential conflagration, but it takes a community to light the fuse. In other words, cult status is fine and all, but sometimes canonization is what's called for. So—look! Here Comes Everybody! Why aren't you reading *Big Bang*? ★

MICROINTERVIEW WITH DEVON PRICE, PART I

THE BELIEVER: One of the main through lines in your work seems to be an offering for us to collectively heal shame. Can you talk about how your books link back to this idea?

DEVON PRICE: My first two books were about particular kinds of shame. *Laziness Does Not Exist* is about the shame of being useless under capitalism, and feeling like you can never actually earn the right to be alive. *Unmasking Autism* is about the shame of trying to hide autism, of feeling fundamentally broken or evil or fucked up. So you try to conceal, to fit in, and to overcome some stigma that you can't ever actually overcome, because who you are has been marked as defective. That book is so much about how trying not to be who you are is never going to be an answer to that. In *Unlearning Shame*, I'm putting all that into the container, along with the shame of being closeted, of living under capitalism and trying to make a difference, of not being a good enough activist. They're all part of the same conversation for sure. ★

STUFF I'VE BEEN READING

A QUARTERLY COLUMN, STEADY AS EVER

by Nick Hornby

BOOKS READED:

* *Super-Infinite: The Transformations of John Donne*—Katherine Rundell
* *Small Mercies*—Dennis Lehane
* *Now Is Not the Time to Panic*—Kevin Wilson

BOOKS BOUGHT:

* *Super-Infinite: The Transformations of John Donne*—Katherine Rundell
* *Small Mercies*—Dennis Lehane
* *Now Is Not the Time to Panic*—Kevin Wilson
* *Doppelganger: A Trip into the Mirror World*—Naomi Klein
* *Happy All the Time*—Laurie Colwin

"**P**eople couldn't sit still for so long, so there was moving, rustling, eating. Rowdy episodes could break out: it was recorded that one of the aldermen… suffered when 'somebody most beastly did conspurcate and shit upon his gown from the galleries above… some from the galleries let a shoe fall which narrowly missed the mayor's head'… Boys peed on the floor and used the slippery surface as an ice rink, adults scattered food or turned up drunk."

Welcome to the seventeenth-century churches of England, as described in Katherine Rundell's brilliant book about John Donne, *Super-Infinite*. I think we can all agree that these are services we can get behind, right? Lively, fun, funny? Well wrong, clearly. Americans don't agree. You couldn't cope. You all threw a hissy fit, sailed away on the *Mayflower*, and had no fun whatsoever. And there is a great irony in this, when you think about it. Within a few hundred years, our enjoyment of mob scenes and shit-flinging produced, to name just a few notable Britons from history, A. S. Byatt, Percy Bysshe Shelley, Vivien Leigh, Declan Rice of Arsenal, Lord Nelson, Winston Churchill, Emily Blunt, all four of the Beatles, and Princess Diana. I could go on. But the only notable Americans I can think of are Donald Trump and Barbi Benton, ex–*Playboy* bunny and onetime star of *The Love Boat*. (I don't actually need to tell you who she is, of course. You haven't got anyone else.) Weird how things turn out.

Super-Infinite (and the compound adjective was one of Donne's, used by him frequently) is a book by a superfan. Of course, Rundell is intimately familiar with Donne's poems and sermons, but there is a chance she has read both *Pseudo-Martyr*, his 1610 smash hit arguing that Catholic recusants were effectively committing suicide, *and* his book about flattery, *Ignatius His Conclave*. *Pseudo-Martyr*, says Rundell wearily, is "so dry and relentless that it has a dust-storm quality to it"; in the bibliography, she says it's "difficult to recommend that anyone read *Pseudo-Martyr*, except under duress." So at least he has a couple of blurbs for the paperback. But this kind of bafflingly impenetrable obsession is part of Donne's mind, too—an important part—and one of the joys of Rundell's book is that she captures his unique, extraordinarily complicated and conflicted mind with sympathy and acuity.

His was a remarkable journey. I knew only that he wrote strikingly original love poems, difficult to prize apart, super-imaginative, and that later he turned to the Church; I did not know he had been imprisoned for

Illustration by Kristian Hammerstad

a socially inappropriate relationship with a young woman who was not of age, or that he had fought against the Spanish Armada as part of Sir Walter Raleigh's fleet. And I didn't really understand that joining the Church was not quite the act of repentance for past worldliness that it appeared to be. The deanship of St Paul's Cathedral was "a fantastic piñata of a job: hit it, and perks and favours and new connections came pouring out."

And an incredible thing: Donne's poems were carelessly preserved. We have only one written in his own hand. "When you quote a Donne poem, you are in fact quoting an amalgamation, pieced together over four hundred years from various manuscripts of varying degrees of scrappiness." His poems effectively went viral, passed from hand to hand. There are more than four thousand copies of his individual poems, and many of them differ from one another. Textual precision is therefore impossible, and the titles of the poems—"The Flea," "The Anniversary"—are likely to have been bestowed by fans rather than by Donne himself. It is extraordinary to think it is only the appetite for

---

PROFANITIES AND INSULTS EXPRESSED BY THE FREMEN IN FRANK HERBERT'S *DUNE*

✶ "Shai-Hulud's tooth"
✶ "Muad'Dib's beard"
✶ "Water-fat"
✶ "Sietch-leech"
　　　—*list compiled by Milly Hopkins*

his work that has kept it alive. *Super-Infinite* is a joy: fresh, smart, human, and genuinely illuminating—not just about Donne and his times, but about life and, especially, death.

This column and its proprietor (although he could easily be tempted by a best offer—DM me) are huge fans of Kevin Wilson. *The Family Fang* and *Nothing to See Here* are two of my favorite novels of the twenty-first century, and *Now Is Not the Time to Panic* is another modern classic. I cannot be alone in wishing that more people wrote novels like this: smart, accessible, unusual, with narratives so fresh and unexpected that if someone pitches you a one-line synopsis, you laugh and want to read it. *Nothing to See Here*: two children repeatedly and spontaneously burst into flames, without harming themselves but causing chaos everywhere they go! *The Family Fang*: the adult children of two committed performance artists have to deal with the fallout of their long, over-imaginative careers!

Wilson is drawn back to the subject of art—why we make it, and the profound effects it can have—in *Now Is Not the Time to Panic*. It's a good subject for him: he writes with such simplicity and humor that it feels like he's doing something nobody else has quite done before. Who, after all, can write about the profundity of art without sounding like an arse, at least sometimes? (I experimented with both spellings of *ass/arse*, but it seems clear to me that the English variety is the mot juste. The American spelling refers to either a backside or an animal, I believe, whereas here in the UK it can be used to refer to an idiot or a pretentious art critic.) Anyway. Wilson is decidedly not an arse.

Now Is Not the Time to Panic is about a specific panic—the Coalfield Panic of 1996. You won't have heard of it, because Wilson made it up, but it's so singular that you may be tempted to wiki it at some stage during your consumption, not least because the author himself refers to its Wiki entry at one point in the book. It's a complete world that he has imagined, which is one of his many strengths: the Panic is so strange, but so carefully constructed, that its reality is both eerie and indisputable.

Wilson's central character, Frankie, now a writer and a mother, is jerked back to the summer of 1996 by a journalist's phone call: the journalist has discovered Frankie's key role in the Panic. Frankie is sixteen and geeky—she can name-drop Dorothy Allison, Bobbie Ann Mason, and Lester Bangs, and she is writing a book about a girl criminal mastermind and spends that dead-end Coalfield summer with an equally geeky boy called Zeke, who is an artist. There are some teeth-clashing make-out sessions, but really they are bound by their creativity, and eventually they arrive upon an art project they can do together. It's a poster, with drawings by Zeke and words by Frankie, words that come to her in a moment of mystical inspiration: "And then I wrote. *The edge is a shantytown*—and I took another deep breath, realized I hadn't been breathing that whole time. My vision got all fuzzy. Zeke touched my shoulder. 'Are you okay?' he asked, but I was already writing more—*filled with goldseekers*." Eventually, she adds another sentence: "*We are fugitives, and the law is skinny with hunger for us*." One wonders how long Wilson spent on these words—whether they came to him quickly, as they do to Frankie, or whether he was working on them throughout his entire writing process. Either way, they work perfectly. The Coalfield Panic requires him to repeat them many, many times—I have only a hard copy of the book; otherwise, I would be able to confirm that the author has broken the record for the most uses of the word *goldseekers* in a single volume. I'm not going to count them. I'm not paid enough.

Zeke and Frankie start to copy their posters on an old copier Frankie has in her garage at home and then put them up all over town, and the results, eventually, have a baffling and profound effect on the people of Coalfield. Some of these people are quite literally driven mad by them. They're advertising a satanic metal band. And then they are the product of a satanic sex drug cult. And then the police get involved. And people die (accidentally, but nevertheless it's an indication of the scope and depth of the panic). The posters are everywhere, more and more and more of them, and the mystery is too much for the people of the town—which is in itself a kind of tragedy for the smart and imaginative young people who have to live there, surrounded by parents and teachers who cannot accommodate a couple of Blakean lines into their everyday lives. And the journalist's discovery—because nobody can believe it's a couple of awkward teens who are responsible, so it remains a secret—provokes a sweet, sad reunion between grown-up Zeke and grown-up Frankie. I suppose *Now Is Not the Time to Panic* is a coming-of-age novel, but you've read plenty of those before. I suspect you won't have read anything quite like this.

Dennis Lehane's hard-as-nails, uncompromising *Small Mercies* also deals with the subject of frightened locals reacting with anger and incomprehension to a change in their environment. The novel is set during the Boston busing crisis of 1974–76; the crisis went on much longer, but this period was particularly intense. The Great Coalfield Panic, the Boston busing crisis… It's almost as if *Small Mercies* were the evil twin of Wilson's novel.

I am (as I might have mentioned at some point in the last twenty years) English, and though I knew about busing, I hadn't known how bitter, divisive, and violent the protests against it were. Maybe you don't, either, although you might have seen an iconic photograph that captures the shocking bigotry of the times. Stanley Forman's *The Soiling of Old Glory* shows a white teenager using an American flag to attack a Black man, and if you are interested enough, as I was, to investigate the crisis, you will learn that this photograph is totemic rather than definitive—by which I mean that Forman might have captured this ugliness at any point in

those two years. Interracial stabbings, a three-day fight at South Boston High in 1975, a white mob chasing a group of Black Bible salesmen off a beach with pipes and sticks, a pitch battle between Blacks and whites involving six thousand people… The scale of the hatred is shocking. (And if you are prone to romanticize the 1970s, with its punk rock clubs and its smart New York City discos and its enthralling independent cinema, *Small Mercies* is a useful reminder that those 1970s happened to about twenty-three people.)

What makes *Small Mercies* both admirably brave and sour is that we are inside the heads of the white bigots in Southie (South Boston) for the duration of the novel. Lehane's people are poor, desperate, old before their time; their endemic racism is an inevitable product of their environment, as are the drugs and the organized crime that disfigure their lives and their neighborhoods. Lehane's *Mystic River*—which remains, I think, the best crime novel this column has read since we started this malarkey—has already proved he has chops, and this novel reminds you of them: his depictions of social deprivation, and the minds and mores that result, are almost Dickensian in their detail, but that's only the beginning of it. This is still a crime novel, with a gripping, if devastating, narrative, apocalyptic in its almost complete lack of hope. Lehane is very good at combining what is normally the preserve of literary fiction with the genre excitement of an airport thriller. And if you think that sounds like eating vegetables and dessert at the same time, then I suggest you rethink your entire biblio-culinary diet. ✶

SACRIFICE ZONE

*A SEMI-REGULAR GUEST COLUMN ABOUT REGULARLY
IGNORED PLACES. IN THIS ISSUE: LITTLE BLOODY RUN*

by Laura Marris

*In its heyday, the run helped create an
international mystery: Canadian officials
wondered why so many lake trout in the
Niagara border region were dying before
they reached adulthood.*

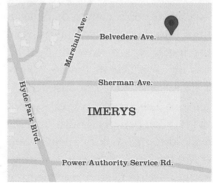

To arrive at Little Bloody Run, you have to come at it sideways, from the scenic road that skirts the Niagara River. My husband, Matt, and I drive from Buffalo, where we live twenty miles upstream, though it feels closer with the current at our backs. We wash up in an overflow parking lot for a fishing platform, run by the New York Power Authority.

As we park, I'm talking about seasonal depression, how deep my dread has grown in the last few weeks, as the afternoons have almost disappeared—though if I'm honest, I'm not sure the season's the problem. Matt listens as clouds rise over the water, and I want to hurry up and reach this place before snow and darkness fall on the landscape and flatten its

Photographs throughout by the author

gradations. Because the stream itself has almost entirely been buried—what's left runs just below the surface, underground.

Even in the best light, Western New York's industrial scars have a way of hiding. Most people have never heard of Little Bloody Run, because it was overshadowed by a famous cousin. In the '40s and '50s, Hooker Chemical created Love Canal, a leaking dump that would become one of the earliest toxic disasters in the US—the so-called "cradle of the Superfund." But when Hooker ran out of room at Love Canal, they began to pile their waste here. The new dump was called Hyde Park, and it received a slurry that was even worse than what went into the ground upriver: some eighty thousand tons of chlorobenzenes, volatile organic compounds, dioxin, and mirex, an insecticide developed for fire ants. For almost three decades, Little Bloody Run served as the natural drainage for this area. The chemicals stained the sediment a reeking orange-red.

In its heyday, the run helped create an international mystery: Canadian officials wondered why so many lake trout in the Niagara border region were dying before they reached adulthood. After a fifteen-year study, biologists realized that during the years of heaviest pollution, the Western New York chemical industry had released enough dioxin to kill all the eggs the trout laid. Because of their sensitivity to pollution, lake trout are sometimes called a "sentinel species." Their deaths were a warning that Love Canal and Hyde Park weren't contained—the waste had traveled miles upriver, winding up in Lake Ontario.

The start of Little Bloody Run is now buried under the cap of the dump itself. I stand in the street that passes over the old streambed, peering through swaths of chain-link fence. When you live in Western New York, this is the kind of second sight you develop when you find yourself on an empty road between man-made knolls and boarded-up factories and realize this is a place where it was once a liability to have skin, lungs, a body, never mind the sweetness of the air and the warmth of the afternoon sun on your face.

We keep walking. The swale of the invisible river makes a grassy dip under a factory that once built chemical drums, mainly for Hooker, mainly for shipping and waste. Everything gets renamed in these places where toxicity is big business—Hooker became Occidental became OxyChem—and while this factory is now owned by IMERYS, I know it was once called Greif. A trailer parked in the lot still boasts the old logo, a *G* with an arrow protruding from its lip. These barrels are buried all over the county—in woodlots and minor landfills, places that have never been mapped. Nearby factories sometimes paid their workers a little extra to take home a few drums and dispose of them. Which is another way of saying that "sacrifice zone" is too bordered a concept. No one fully knows, now, where all the chemicals are.

At the back of the Greif factory, oily liquid drains from a pipe, and the asphalt is greened with moss. A thick line of phragmites marches north, signaling the course of the river. In 1980, after the journalist Michael Brown helped break the story of Love Canal, he wrote about the people who lived next to Little Bloody Run, in "a cluster of about fifteen houses, set among fields of goldenrod and stands of cattails." Some residents worked nearby, and some had been there longer than the dump, in multigenerational households, with established gardens and vegetable crops. Over the years, those who were nearest the run fell ill, suffered lesions and miscarriages, and these blocks quietly emptied—a total chemical displacement.

Not even the rivers here get to keep their names. Once, Bloody Run and Little Bloody Run were known as two distinct rills, a thousand feet apart, that both tipped into the Niagara Gorge. In 1763, Bloody Run got its name from a battle between the Seneca Nation and the English settlers, who had named a white man "Master of the Portage," and routed wagon trains between the forts, putting Seneca porters out of their jobs moving and trading goods along the river. The Seneca fought back and won the battle. Sensational accounts say the water flowing into the gorge ran red, blood suspended in water. Nearby sites remain sacred to the Seneca Nation, Keeper of the Western Door, a member of the Haudenosaunee Confederacy, whose traditional territories extend across the whole region.

The portage trail became a paved road, and then a scenic parkway. When construction began along the river, as local author Scott Ensminger told me, it created drastic changes in hydrology that "wiped out the route of the run." After Bloody went dry, and Little Bloody was in the process of being dredged and buried, the EPA mixed up their names in reports, conflating the two places—and the gore in the water mingled with the red of chemical slurry. The remediation of this area ultimately cost Hooker's parent company some forty-seven million dollars. The state chipped in eleven million more. But the groundwater is still contaminated. To make money, Hooker borrowed against the long-term health of this area, but the chemicals in the ground are a debt that can never be fully repaid. In her visual essay on landfills, my friend Ariel Aberg-Riger calls this the "gutted future."

We cross the scenic parkway and stand at the cliff's edge. A cold wind rises from the gorge. We can see the Niagara River now, the pale teal of the rapids, the gulls massing by the hundreds, fishing the intakes of the hydropower plant. Matt goes to get the car while I hike down to the river in the last of the light, following a trail toward what was once the base of Little Bloody Run's cascade. I've been told this area is off-limits now, covered with riprap, loose rock that prevents erosion and keeps people away from contaminated sediment.

On the trail I pass two men carrying reels and nets, fishers out for a day in the rapids. Little Bloody Run ends in a steep cut of rock, and I know I've reached the right place because it's enveloped by chain link. That's when I realize water is pouring out of the

culverts high above me, enough that I can hear it racing under the crumbling slide of the cliff face, the stones tinged red with traces of algae or contamination, and as I step from rock to rock, I feel a liquid kind of lurching, as if I've lost my balance, thrown off by just how much river I have been walking over and alongside, all the way from the road outside Greif. The stream hits the open air for just a second, just as it joins the Niagara. As I watch, a golden-crowned kinglet slips under my elbow, his wings so close I can feel the wake of them in the evening air, see the trace of orange feathers sprouting from his yellow racing stripe. As babies, these birds are naked and defenseless, no bigger than bumblebees. Yet they survive. A birder once told me that kinglets like to follow people because our footsteps disturb insects in the leaf litter. And a pack of them does tail me along the edge of the contamination area, which is porous to them, their tiny beaks squalling as they dart through the overgrown fence.

This close to the border, my phone pings me "Welcome abroad." It's forgotten what country it's in. I no longer believe in neat boundaries of sacrifice, or in the salve of corporate penance—that money spent proves the land is clean. I'd rather think of these fenced-off zones as the seeds of a more-than-human country built out of everything industrial recklessness has forced us to abandon. Better to believe the kinglets eat from my leaf-rustle as I turn back against the river's course, as the night comes, as the winter sharpens their hunger. No way out but this body, climbing in the dark, buzzed by apparitions of mercy. ✳

FEAR AS A GAME

WHAT CAN THE PHILOSOPHY OF GAMES TELL US ABOUT OUR ODD IMPULSE TO SCARE OURSELVES?

by Elisa Gabbert

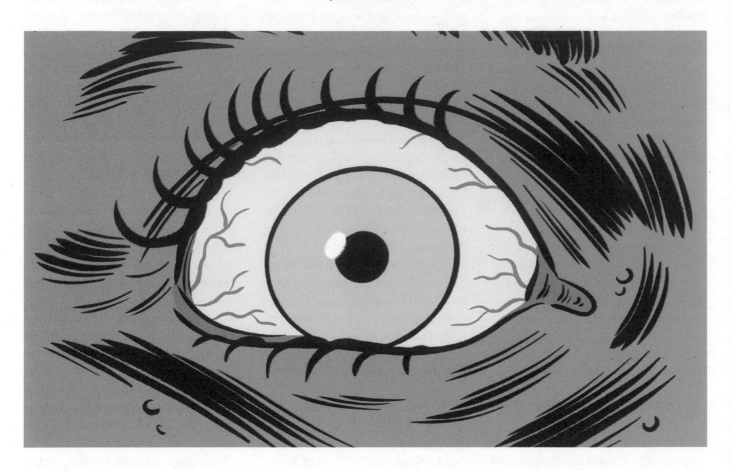

1.

My life in acrophobia: When I was eleven or twelve, I went with a friend to the pool at her family's country club and somebody dared me to jump off the high dive—or maybe I just felt implicitly dared because the other kids were doing it. It wasn't incredibly high, probably ten or twelve feet. I was not a good swimmer or diver, but I did have pride. As I climbed up the ladder, I knew I could not hesitate or I would freeze at the top. I'd seen a girl do this—she panicked and then had to crawl back down. A surge of adrenaline carried me off, and after I'd jumped (feet first, holding my nose) and survived, I felt such a thrill that I immediately wanted to do it again. The second time up, courage failed me. I'd become overconfident—I thought it would be easy. I climbed the ladder, walked to the end of the board and off into the water, but as I swam to the surface and then to the edge of the pool, I was shaking with fear. I hated the second jump, and I knew I would never be brave enough to go a third time.

During my first year of college, I often went to Six Flags in Houston with a group of friends. I wasn't afraid of roller coasters—I *loved* roller coasters—but I did fear one ride: the Dungeon Drop, a twenty-story "drop tower" that slowly lifted riders up a structure, something like a naked

Illustration by Kristian Hammerstad

elevator shaft, pausing for a terrifying moment and then plunging them back to the ground. My roommate was also afraid, but we agreed to try it once, together. It was nighttime, dark, our feet dangling freely, and I remember her saying the pause at the top felt "peaceful." Just as it had on the high dive, adrenaline got me through. Later I heard that the gondolas once got stuck at the top, and the riders had to sit there, 230 feet up, for over an hour. I never went on a ride like that again.

A few years later, I went skiing in New Mexico with a boyfriend. He was a good skier; it was my first time. We got on a chairlift, a metal bench without any kind of safety belt or bar to hold us in—something I did not have time to process before we were suddenly thirty feet high in the air. My boyfriend was six foot three, nonchalantly swinging his giant, heavy skis. A pure cold white fear of death overcame me. I began uncontrollably weeping, trying to wrap my arm completely around the metal bar that connected us to the cable. When we got to the top of the hill, I fell off and someone had to pull me out of the way of the chair coming up from behind us. I realized then that I would not like skiing, and that I was very, very afraid of heights.

For years, I avoided scenarios that might trigger that intense fear. But I sometimes caught glimpses, when crossing a high bridge on foot, for example—the footbridge in Harpers Ferry, West Virginia, or the Steel Bridge over the Willamette River in Portland, Oregon. I was safe on the bridges, I knew, but regardless, seeing the water far below through the gaps in the slats was a glimpse of the terror. Part of me liked those glimpses—the heart palpitations, my skin tingling. I felt a little more alive. I sometimes provoked this pseudo-fear vicariously, by watching films of people doing scary height stuff, videos of Philippe Petit tightrope-walking over Sydney Harbour or, most unbelievably, between the Twin Towers. Or of Joseph Kittinger, who parachuted from a helium balloon at an altitude of more than 100,000 feet. (It was actually closer to 103,000 feet—the extra 3,000 feet seem inconsequential, yet 3,000 feet in itself is already a terrifying height, an extra Twin Tower or so.)

I did not truly put my acrophobia to the test again until recently. On a work trip, my manager signed my whole team up for a ropes course. I wasn't required to do it, but everyone else was doing it. I had pride, still, and also curiosity. I wondered if maybe the ropes course could *cure* me. It was evidently safe—we were strapped into harnesses, attached to a cable overhead. Before going up, we had to participate in an hour-long training session, which was mostly an elaborate proof of the safety equipment. The ropes course was unlike a bridge, or the edge of a cliff or a building, where you fear l'appel du vide, "the call of the void," as much as falling. And so I was not *very* afraid, but I was very anxious, three stories up—it was hot, and we were all underslept and hungover—and when I completed each element of the course, I felt relief but not triumph, and the relief was short-lived. The segments were increasingly distressing, higher and more complicated, and the process did not get more fun. At the first opportunity to bail out, I did.

MICROINTERVIEW WITH DEVON PRICE, PART II

THE BELIEVER: I'm curious if—particularly as a trans and neurodivergent person—putting out public thoughts on the subject of shame can be shame inducing.

DEVON PRICE: I'm making things that are commodities. It really freaks me out. I'm working for one of the Big Five publishers, and sometimes they're like, *Oh, you should go talk to Goop about this.* There's this balance of, like, Am I reaching people and hopefully radicalizing them a little bit? Hopefully bursting bubbles for them? Or am I making books that are just helping privileged people feel better about where they are? That's a deep and abiding terror that in some ways is kind of good for me to have. I am very much not a perfectionist. I am doing it thinking I'm making positive changes. Even if my work doesn't connect in that radicalizing, abolitionist kind of way with every reader, I hope it puts people down that pipeline. And it's better to get these ideas out into the world so others can build upon them and improve them. And that helps me make peace with how sometimes I'm going to mess up and I'm going to cringe at something I wrote a year ago, because my politics get more and more radical each year. ★

2.

Fear is an oddly attractive force. Horror movies, haunted houses, bungee jumping—these are fear experiences we actually pay for. (My favorite tweet: "If I pay $40 for a haunted house I better die.") Why do we do that—why do we crave small doses of terror? Why do we like "safe" fear? In her book about the role of monsters in art and culture, *No Go the Bogeyman: Scaring, Lulling and Making Mock*, the scholar Marina Warner notes that "scariness has gained ground as a pleasure; it is perhaps a modern affect." A new feeling? Maybe not entirely, but according to Warner, writing in the late 1990s, "the ambiguous satisfactions of scariness have been cultivated more intensely during this century than ever before." This is in part because new technologies, from better special effects to computerized parachutes, enable us to terrify ourselves so successfully.

There's a theory in the science of emotion that the only innate human feelings are valence and arousal. *Valence* can be pleasant or unpleasant; *arousal* can be high or low. You can map any feeling on a wheel called an "affective circumplex," with the midpoint representing neutral valence and neutral arousal. The upper right quadrant contains feelings of pleasant valence and high arousal (like excitement), the lower left quadrant low arousal and unpleasant valence (like boredom). It's easy to tell if a baby is happy or unhappy, sleepy or wakeful. But as for more specific emotions—what does the baby *desire*—we have doubts. As neuroscientist Lisa Feldman Barrett explains in her book *How Emotions Are Made: The Secret Life of the Brain*, researchers have tried and failed to discover some underlying state in the body and brain that corresponds reliably to "fear" or "joy," or any of the seemingly universal emotions. There is no consistent physical difference between individuals who are "depressed" and individuals who are "anxious," and most psychiatric patients describe themselves as *both* depressed and anxious, or as neither, not one or the other. So how many emotions are there? As many as we can invent concepts for, and then claim to be feeling. We may need to learn a word for a feeling before we can feel it.

Kierkegaard thought anxiety arose from possibility—a reaction to radical freedom, the "dizziness of freedom." The ability to choose one's path in life, to *choose* an unknown among unknowns, is paradoxically paralyzing. This would make suicidality a condition of modernity, of fortune and "progress"—we did not always have so much choice. The philosopher John Kaag once said, "Existential crises are a luxury for those who don't have real on-the-ground crises." How strange, that life can seem pointless once survival is mostly a given. It's as though the survival instinct kicks in only at the last possible moment. I think of the people who, against terrible odds, survive jumping off the Golden Gate Bridge. These survivors almost always report having felt immediate regret. One said, "I instantly realized that everything in my life that I'd thought was unfixable was totally fixable—except for having just jumped."

Recently, researchers studying contemporary hunter-gatherer societies

---

MICROINTERVIEW WITH DEVON PRICE, PART III

THE BELIEVER: Western medicine's diagnostic way of interrogating personhood creates shame so distinctively. What can we do with this whole field if so much of it is harm based?

DEVON PRICE: The only way to work justly in an unjust field is to betray it at every turn, if even that. I don't know how much is worth salvaging in psychology. I really don't. I come to this as someone who, like you, was a young person at Barnes & Noble reading *The Sociopath Next Door*. This really dehumanizing stuff. I looked at it and I was like: I guess I'm a sociopath. I guess I'm evil. I guess I'm Hannibal Lecter. It's something I joke about, but it is a real shame that I carried in me, because I was autistic and didn't know it, and I was reading all these books that pathologize all these traits: BPD [borderline personality disorder] traits, narcissistic traits—those are my kin. I identify with those traits as much as I identify with the autistic community, but that kind of writing about people with autism and BPD did a real number on me and it does a number on a lot of people. All these posts online about narcissistic abuse: they do a lot of harm. This way of seeing things makes it seem as if "evil" deeds are done by a type of person rather than understanding that harmful behaviors are something we're all capable of. ★

were stunned to find that their metabolism is similar to ours—that is to say, to those of us who have pretty sedentary lifestyles, sitting at desks all the time and shopping in grocery stores. The Hadza people of Tanzania are nearly always walking, getting "more activity in a day than most Americans get in a week," as the evolutionary anthropologist Herman Pontzer has said. Yet they burn about the same number of calories as we do, between 1,800 and 2,500 a day. If anything, they burn slightly fewer than us, because they tend to be shorter. Pontzer calls this discovery "shocking" and "nonsensical." It goes against everything we thought we understood about metabolism. But it's true and verifiable. It's also true for monkeys in a zoo compared with monkeys in a jungle—they "need" the same amount of food. How is this possible?

It seems our bodies are incredibly efficient with the calories we have. If we need to, we can stretch two thousand calories to walk ten miles. With this new understanding, it does not make sense to say that walking a mile "burns" x number of calories. There is no fixed rate of burning. So what happens to the calories if you live in a modern society, in conditions of relative affluence and ease; if you work in a building and drive to work; if you're not moving much? As Pontzer explains it, your body finds other ways to use the calories. And they are not necessarily beneficial: Your immune system gets overactive, leading to allergies and general inflammation. Your stress responses spike much higher. Your body can *afford* the stress. You might say that comfort is the source of anxiety—this is not incompatible with Kierkegaardian

dread. When food is easy to get, and we move around in gas-powered vehicles, our brains have more energy than they know what to do with. The struggle to survive is old, but chronic stress is a modern feeling, much like the lite fear, the *fun* fear (high arousal, pleasant valence), we now use to alleviate stress. Even artificial fear can get the bad feelings out of our system.

Maybe after many centuries of facing constant natural danger, our bodies are built to expect some level of ambient danger. Too much safety and comfort feels wrong, so we go looking for some simulated threat. Or maybe it's just cathartic to scream, when you're pretty sure death isn't imminent. Maybe it's just good theater.

3.

Before I start watching a scary movie, I always turn off all the lights. It goes without saying that I watch scary movies at night. I want to be as scared as possible, of course—I want shadowy regions in the room that my mind can misinterpret, so I can think I see something moving and get spooked. This is all part of the ritual, like lighting candles for a

séance. (That's the first step of a séance, according to wikiHow: "Creating the right atmosphere." The second step, fittingly, is inviting some guests who believe that séances work.)

You might call it a ritual, or you might call it a game. In the philosophy of games, this sort of ritualized space is known as "the magic circle," a phrase that comes from a passage in historian Johan Huizinga's book *Homo Ludens: A Study of the Play-Element in Culture*. Huizinga believed that most of what we think of as *culture* is elaborate playing—sports but also war; theater but also religion. These specialized cultures have ritual settings—arenas and battlefields, stages and temples, card tables—"all in form and function playgrounds." And in these magic circles, "special rules obtain." The magic circle can be spatial—the dark couch in front of the TV, for example—but more so, the circle is a mindset we willingly step into, a space where we follow new rules and take leave of reality.

"To play a game," writes the philosopher Bernard Suits, "is to voluntarily take on unnecessary obstacles for the sake of making possible the activity of overcoming them." This is a neat summation of why we play games—for the pleasure of triumph over adversity, never mind that we introduced the adversity. The unnecessary obstacles can be very simple: the rules in a low-stakes game. The obstacles in *Tetris*, for example, are the random distributions of the different shapes of falling blocks (the seven "Tetrominoes") and their increasing speed as you advance through the game. The faster the level, the harder it is, and the more *fun* it is, to achieve a "*Tetris* line clear," or four lines of blocks at once. (What's unusual about *Tetris* is that you can't beat the game; the levels just keep speeding up until you "die.") But games might also have higher stakes, as in drag racing, or American football.

Looked at in Suits's terms, watching a scary movie is a kind of game. It's a way of taking on unnecessary *fear*. There is, for many people, some pleasure in the fear. We like the fear itself—the heightened physical arousal. But we also feel pleasure when we overcome the fear—by finishing the movie and going to sleep, hopefully not having nightmares forever. Haunted houses and roller coasters are also forms of games. A roller coaster isn't just formless fun, if such a thing exists; it's a kind of game, a finite engagement with fear, which offers both the pleasure of playing and the pleasure of winning. I like this kind of game—I like allowing myself to feel *just enough* fear that I know I can overcome it. The ski lift, the ropes course, those sheer-drop rides—for me those were too much fear, too much trembling, to be fun. I'm not Philippe Petit, who once said of his stunt at the World Trade Center, "When I see three oranges, I juggle; when I see two towers, I walk!" He saw those buildings, at that time the tallest in the world, and the gaping void between them, as a game he could win.

In order for something to feel like a game, we need to adopt what Suits called the "lusory attitude." This means we accept the arbitrary rules, "even though those rules often make the experience more challenging, in order to facilitate the resulting experience of play." The *lusory attitude*, the *magic circle*—I like how these terms feel like spells in themselves, like secret codes to skip a level.

I have a friend who approaches uncomfortable situations or difficult conversations, like asking for a raise, by telling himself, *Just win*—as though it's a game, as though the stakes disappear when you exit the room. That's the lusory attitude—also related to the suspension of disbelief, which is arguably more of an instinct than a skill. We use this ability to get lost in a movie, to convincingly pretend to believe in the movie's imaginary world. We're pretending for our own sake, of course, because caring about fake people and whether they find love, whether they live or die, feels good. This is how games work too. We convince ourselves that the world of the game, as defined by the rules, really matters.

In his book *Man, Play and Games,* the sociologist Roger Caillois describes four types of play: competition (or *agôn*); chance (or *alea*—the Latin word for "dice"); mimicry/mimesis; and vertigo (*ilinx*). In this framework, poker involves both chance and competition. *Ilinx* (Greek for "whirlpool"—I'm struck by how playful gaming jargon,

all jargon, can be) accounts for the fun of altered perception: for getting drunk as well as for roller coasters. But roller coasters also incorporate mimicry—the theater of screaming, screaming the way girls in slasher films scream, or the way we imagine we might scream in actual danger. For that matter, so does getting drunk. The alcohol gives us permission to laugh more theatrically, to act stupider, to take more risks, to be more violent—the rules of the game of getting drunk vary slightly by culture. But part of the game is mimetic. When I got drunk in college, I acted like my drunk college friends, euphoric, outlandish. Now I act the way my parents used to act, or I act like mildly drunk but sophisticated women in movies.

The philosopher C. Thi Nguyen, who has an interest in "Suitsian games," or games that involve (fake) struggles and (fake) obstacles, believes that in "striving play," winning is not the real goal. Rather, we convincingly pretend—again, for ourselves—to care about winning, but what we really care

---

NOVELS FEATURING CHARACTERS WITH SYNESTHESIA AND THE SENSES THEY BLEND

✮ *The Map of Salt and Stars* by Zeyn Joukhadar (sounds and colors)
✮ *Bitter in the Mouth* by Monique Truong (words and tastes)
✮ *Born on a Blue Day* by Daniel Tammet (numbers, shapes, and colors)
✮ *Ultraviolet* by R. J. Anderson (taste, sound, numbers, letters, and colors)
✮ *The Color of Bee Larkham's Murder* by Sarah J. Harris (sounds and colors)
✮ *The Color of Lies* by C. J. Lyons (sights and sounds)
✮ *The Moon Sisters* by Therese Walsh (sights, sounds, and smells)
✮ *The Beautiful Miscellaneous* by Dominic Smith (taste, sound, numbers, letters, and colors)
✮ *The Astonishing Color of After* by Emily X.R. Pan (sights, sounds, and colors)
—*list compiled Natalia Borecka*

about is the *playing*. The struggle is the point. Games are "morally transformative technologies," in that they alter the valence of struggle. Obstacles become opportunities for acts of creativity, of strength, of grace and beauty. The struggle is now aesthetic. In a game's magic circle, we develop new skills to help us overcome the arbitrary, necessary obstacles that make the goal elusive, and therefore attractive. Nguyen calls these game-specific skills "agential mindsets." These new types of agency can help us in the real world, too, even after we've dropped the lusory attitude. A good game provides a new mindset, a portable worldview.

Games can feel like a refuge or escape from our real-world problems, because we get to choose problems we know we can solve. There's a beautiful simplicity within the magic circle—even very complex games are less complex than real life, where we have many reasons to be scared. We likely fear death, our own death and other people's deaths; we fear incalculable loss. We fear personal pain and even inconvenience, and in the same day, the end of civilization. We fear cancer, microplastics, failing infrastructure, runaway AI, nuclear bombs. In fear games, we choose new objects of fear as substitutes for real fears. We can magically fear one thing at a time—falling, or ghosts. We need not even believe in ghosts to play at being-afraid-of-ghosts. We convincingly pretend. To "win" at a fear game, to conquer fake fear, the skill we need is fake courage.

The ropes course I partially ventured on was situated over a zoo. If you were "braver" than I, you reached a zip line extending over an alligator pit—ha ha. The course offered artificial fear, but also artificial safety. I don't mean the course was dangerous. On the zip lines, as on the rest of the course, there was no way to fall. I mean safety, in real life, is never that contrived. We don't have to *invent* threats so that we can then be protected from them. The real threats are already there.

4.

Not long ago I saw a news story about a man who was walking through an amusement park with his family when he noticed a "large crack" in a roller coaster that was actively carrying riders. It was a modern steel "giga coaster," meaning a coaster with drops of over three hundred feet. There was a GIF in the article—as the car runs by on the track, the two parts of a support pole come entirely apart for a moment, a crack you can see the sky through—looping over and over. For a few days I wasted all my free time watching videos of rides that had to be shut down after horrifying accidents. I read about a woman who lost both her legs when the car she was in slammed into another car that had been left standing empty on the track. I learned that multiple people have died after falling from drop-tower rides. I thought, Well, maybe I'll never ride a roller coaster again.

Around the same time, I read an unrelated story about airline "close calls"—near collisions of planes in the air, which are much more common than I'd realized. "On the afternoon of July 2, a Southwest Airlines pilot had to abort a landing at Louis Armstrong New Orleans International Airport," *The New York Times* reported in 2023. "A Delta Air Lines 737 was preparing to take off on the

---

MICROINTERVIEW WITH DEVON PRICE, PART IV

THE BELIEVER: Can you talk a little bit about how you see your work at the intersection of transness and autism?

DEVON PRICE: Every time I have conversations with people, I have new idols to knock down within these power structures. When it comes to the diagnostic process, we should not be working to reform it; we should be working toward phasing it out, in the same way that informed consent [the idea that those seeking care are able to choose the forms of support services they want] for trans people is phasing out gender identity disorder. You don't need to have a psychologist decide you're crazy with transness in order to get hormones in the US and some other countries. We can do the same thing with autism and so many other neurodiversities. I always get questions from people who are down with this, but are still learning. They ask things like *What will happen if there's no such thing as a diagnosis for a young kid who is autistic and needs services?* I always have to say, *Look at the services they're getting right now.* The services involve being taken out of the classroom and othered. What we need is community. ✷

same runway. The sudden maneuver avoided a possible collision by seconds." The *Times* investigation found that similar near accidents are happening, on average, multiple times a week. Sources in the article blame this disturbing situation on staffing shortages and extreme fatigue. "The margin for safety has eroded tenfold," one air traffic controller wrote in a report to the FAA. "Morale is rock bottom." A longtime captain and former fighter pilot is quoted: "Honestly, this stuff scares the crap out of me." In the comments section, which has thousands of comments, multiple people trace the blame back to Ronald Reagan, who broke up the air traffic controllers' union in 1981.

I collect this kind of story, the kind that reveals a crack in reality. They give me that skin-tingling feeling, a flutter in the chest. We tell ourselves that roller coasters are perfectly safe and that planes don't crash. I don't *want* it not to be true; I don't want to die on a plane. So why do I like the stories? It's like I want my sense of reality to be destabilized. It's like I'm playing some kind of game, a game in which the complex world falls away and I focus on a single threat. A single strange-but-very-real threat. I can stop riding roller coasters, obviously, but it's harder to avoid planes or other forms of transportation. Trains do get derailed. Bridges do collapse. So the threats are very real—but not *immediate*. Not *for me*, when I'm reading the news, when I'm sitting at my desk.

Is there anything useful about that feeling, I wonder? That artificial fear, or fear at a distance? Might *practicing* fear be a good idea? It seems more useful than anxiety—if anxiety is just the brain burning energy it doesn't really need, because you're not currently starving, or trying to outrun a lion. These may be just concepts, words I attach to agitation, but when I call the feeling anxiety, I'm mapping it alongside paralysis and existential dread. I associate anxiety with stasis, with insomnia, lying supine in bed. Fear, on the contrary, is a vertical feeling. It's activating. If I'm scared, I want to be moving.

What did I *learn* from the ropes course, if anything? I think it did make me slightly braver. At least I proved to myself I could perch in a thirty-foot tree without crying or throwing up. But what if the straps hadn't seemed so secure? What if there had been some crack in the system? (Surely, eventually, there will be, since there are cracks in everything?) Even "knowing" I was "perfectly" safe didn't stop me from sweating and clenching every muscle. Maybe the use of fear games is not to inure ourselves to danger so that nothing is scary anymore, but to embrace fear as a real state that sends us necessary signals. Maybe it's a way of taking fear seriously. Maybe what I learned from the ropes course was knowing when to quit.

Or maybe I'm projecting grand meaning where there isn't much, and I just didn't want to look pathetic in front of my work friends.

What I'd like to think—what I hope is true—is that I seek out fear because I seek activation. But at some point, in order to believe that story, I'd need to overcome real fear. That would be something outside the magic circle—fear of something I'm not sure I *can* overcome.

5.

There was a time when I couldn't watch horror movies alone—that was too hard a level in the game. I've built up my tolerance for horror movies over the years, and when my husband went away on a trip this past October, I watched several, including the original *Psycho*, which I had never seen. Its big moves are familiar at this point, too much to be truly scary. But it provided good atmosphere for thinking about fear. I had a lot of post-*Psycho* thoughts.

The thing about a horror movie is, I'm never afraid of the movie per se, not as an adult—the movie is fake. But there *is* some fear, some risk at play. What I fear is getting too scared for pleasure—too scared for the game. Usually, the fear is contained by the length of the movie. When I turn it off and turn on the lights, the fear dissipates, disappears. But there have been rare times when it hasn't—times when some mechanism tripped, and I stayed spooked for hours. That's what I'm afraid of when I watch a scary movie. I'm afraid of my own fear, that it might get away from me. What if I invite in more fear than I can handle?

What if I'm only pretending I'm not a coward? ✱

At a rehearsal, the conductor stops and shouts at the bass section: "You're out of tune. Check your instrument, please!"

The first bassist plucks all his strings and says, "My tuning is correct: all the strings are equally tight." The first violist turns around and shouts, "You idiot! It's not the tension. The pegs should be parallel!"*

*In this joke the bassist is just as wrong as the violist. Proper tuning of a stringed instrument is all about getting each string's sound right. Equal tension on all the strings won't automatically make that happen. You can't just make all the tuning pegs (at the top of the instrument's neck) parallel either.

How was the fugue* invented?

Two violists were attempting to play the same melody simultaneously.

*A fugue is a musical form, either part of a larger piece or a standalone work, characterized by "systematic imitation of a principal theme (called the subject) in simultaneously sounding melodic lines (counterpoint)," according to Encyclopedia Britannica. In a fugue, the counterpoint line is an interesting point of commentary on, or development of, the musical material in the subject line; the divergence is intentional. In the joke, the two viola lines are trying and failing to sound seamless and identical.

How do you get a violist to play a passage pianissimo tremolando?

Mark it "solo."

*Pianissimo tremolando is a performance marking in Italian. Pianissimo means to play "very quietly, and tremolando means to play with short, fast bow strokes. The idea of playing a solo is supposed to scare the violist so much that she trembles and stutter.

What's the best recording of Bartók's Viola Concerto?

Music Minus One's.

*Music Minus One publishes recordings by professional orchestras with the soloist part removed so hobbyist musicians can practice that part themselves. A "concerto" refers to any musical work in which one instrument gets a starring role, in this case the viola. Removing the viola line from Bartók's Viola Concerto would leave you with only the orchestral accompaniment.

Why is a viola called a Bratsche in German?*

Because that's the sound it makes when you sit on it.

*The word, which you often see on Teutonic composers' scores, comes from Germanizing the instrument's Italian name, viola da braccia, meaning an "arm viol" because you play a viola with your arms. This is as opposed to a viola da gamba, or a "leg viol," a forerunner of the modern cello that you brace between your knees to play.

A German orchestra travels to America for a two-week tour. An hour before the first concert is supposed to start, the conductor gets seriously ill and they have to find another conductor immediately.

The orchestra manager asks the orchestra if anyone is qualified to step into the role, and the only person who says yes is the violist sitting in the last seat of the viola section. The manager is nervous: "We don't have any time even to do a run-through practice. Are you sure you're up to it?" The violist replies: "No problem. I can handle it." She conducts the first concert, and it's a smashing success. And because the original conductor remains sick, the violist winds up conducting all the concerts on the tour. She earns standing ovations and rave reviews for each one. The orchestra travels home to Germany, and the conductor finally returns, and the viola goes back to the last seat in her section. Her stand partner nudges her and says: "Hey, where've you been hiding for the last two weeks?"*

*Two slightly mean sources of humor here. First, the "last seat" in any section is the lowliest performer in that section. If the first chair leads and defines the section's sound, the last chair follows the group. It's unlikely that any single performer would be virtuosic enough to conduct a two-week tour of music with no prior notice. The second part of the joke is the punch line delivered by her stand partner. String performers share a music stand with a player of equal stature; they flip the pages together as they play the same part. The stand partner is clueless about his friend's sudden success—and, it's implied, must have been pretty inattentive to any directions coming from the conductor.

HIGHLY SPECIALIZED JOKES

A fast and a slow violist both jump from a high rise together. Which of them hits the ground first?

They'd actually land at exactly the same time, because that's how gravity works. But it doesn't matter. The important thing is that they both jumped.

*It's possible this joke is mocking the supposedly lugubrious slowness that characterizes some violists' playing and can grate on listeners' nerves. But it's clear the joke turns on a more universal idea: minor differences between violists don't matter. The more violists are exterminated from the scene, the better off we'll be.

LONGEST VIOLA JOKE EVER

Harold in Italy.*

*Harold in Italy: Symphony with Viola Obbligato is an orchestral work by composer Hector Berlioz. He wrote it in 1834 at the urging of master violinist Niccolò Paganini. Paganini had just acquired a Stradivarius viola and wanted a virtuosic concerto-style piece to show it off. Berlioz, the man who composed the glittering, over-the-top Symphonie Fantastique, seemed the perfect person to ask. Harold in Italy turned out to be an extraordinary viola piece, but not in the flashy ways that Paganini had hoped for. A symphony in four movements loosely based on Byron's poem Childe Harold, the viola part represents the protagonist, Harold, who wanders melancholically from the Italian Abruzzi mountains and eventually into a small town. The whole thing turns out to be one big joke on the viola. It vanishes into the background. Paganini commissioned a concerto, a supposed star vehicle for his viola, which rarely earned the limelight. What he got instead was a piece where the viola often disappears for long stretches into the orchestra's larger sound, and which is not played up in predictable ways when it's onstage. Nonetheless, the work is true to the instrument's character: as a vehicle for human interiority, it is perfect for conveying a Romantic hero's budding inner life.

When I started dating a musicologist, I became friends with a lot of violists, who piqued my curiosity about the instrument. A viola is more or less a bigger violin. It was invented to fill out the middle register of the strings section's sound. If violins sound angelic, soaring, diva-like, violas are more earthbound, human, and interior. The viola's design makes its sound throaty and often constrained, qualities that are less "clean" than a violin's but that impart a depth and vulnerability to the entire strings section. From its place between the violins and the cellos and basses, the viola speaks of human frailty; its resonance draws us into darker thoughts but also helps us bear them.

Yet in a symphony orchestra's cruel hierarchy, violists are rarely stars. Instead, they're relegated to supporting roles, unfairly derided as failed or lazy ex-violinists. Violas have thus become the butts of so many jokes that they constitute a whole genre. My violist friends are resigned to all the jokes but also to their social role within the orchestra itself: not to embody sonic perfection, but instead to reveal the human struggle involved in music-making. If viola jokes help their colleagues blow off steam, so be it: they are happy to be of service.

—Jude Stewart

THE ALL-TIME SHORTEST VIOLA JOKE

A violist goes to a "master class."*

*Musicians often attend master classes with world-class performers of their instrument. It's a chance to learn from the greats in an intimate setting... provided you don't think "a great violist" is a contradiction in terms.

Thanks to my husband, the musicologist Seth Brodsky, as well as violists Justin Lee Mark Cauley and John Pickford Richards for their help and infinite good humor.

AN INCOMPLETE CONTINUUM OF VIOLA JOKES

JUST PLAIN MEAN JOKES

What's the difference between a bassist falling out of an open window and a violist doing the same? It's more technically correct to have them, but things feel a lot better without them.

The newspaper writes up the bassist's death as an obituary and puts the violist's in the "Better Living" section.

What do viola playing and condoms have in common?

A violist and a conductor are standing in the middle of the road. Which do you run over first and why? First the conductor, then the violist: business before pleasure.

Two violists are sitting in a pub. Then a musician walks in.

What do you call it when a violist falls into a vat of hydrochloric acid? A problem solved.

When rent is due, a masked violist brings her instrument into a bank and screams: "Give me all your money or I'll play!"

An airplane passenger is feeling chatty and decides to talk to his seatmate. Having noticed the fellow was carrying a black musical case at check-in, the passenger says: "I just heard a really good viola joke. Want to hear it?" The seatmate replies: "OK, but first you should know that I'm a violist myself." "No problem," says the passenger. "I'll tell it to you really slowly."

REVENGE ON THE VIOLINS JOKES

A violin is really not so much smaller than a viola. It's an optical illusion because violinists' heads are swollen.

Why don't violists get hemorrhoids? Because all the assholes sit in the first-violin section.

Why can't you hear the violas on CD recordings? Because all the screeching, unnecessary noises have been filtered out.

What do you call an audition for a violist? A scratch lottery.

Why can't you hear the violas on CD recordings? Because all the screeching, unnecessary noises have been filtered out.

A violist returns from work to find his house a smoldering wreck and his yard full of ambulances and fire trucks. The fire chief approaches him and asks, "Do you own this house, sir?" The violist nods. The chief continues: "Well, I have really unfortunate news. Earlier today the conductor came to your house and burned it. Your wife died, your three daughters died, your dog and even your goldfish died. I'm truly sorry." The violist receives this news like a body blow, staggers a few steps backward, struggles to speak. Finally he makes out a few words: "Let me get this straight. The conductor came to my house?"

What's the difference between a violist and William Tell? William Tell knew how to use a bow.

What do peeing your pants onstage and a viola solo have in common? Both are warm, private experiences that nobody can hear.

A violist and a cellist stand on a sinking ship. The cellist says: "Help, I can't swim!" The violist replies: "Don't worry, just act like you can."

How would you define a well-mannered musician? Someone who can play the viola but chooses not to.

NONSPECIALIZED JOKES

A violist forgot to lock her car and left her viola in the back seat. When she came back, there were two more violas there.

A violist and a hand grenade and a viola solo have in common? Once you can finally hear it, it's already too late.

How do you define a "tone cluster"? A group of violas trying to play in unison.

A violist dies and goes to heaven, where Saint Peter greets him: "Welcome! Because you were such a misunderstood genius on Earth and had to put up with so much teasing, I'm going to grant you one wish, without hesitation." The violist replies: "I wish for world peace." An angel slips a map under Saint Peter's nose, and Saint Peter studies it for a long time, sighing. "Hmm, so much war and conflict in so many places.... It's really impossible." He folds the map, hands it back to the angel, and apologizes to the violist: "I'm sorry, but I just can't do it—I'm not all-powerful, you know. Can you think of another wish I could fulfill?" The violist pauses, then says: "I do have one other wish that's followed me around my whole life. I would love, at least once, to play the C-major scale cleanly up and down." "Oh boy," says Peter. "Angel, let me take another look at that map."

CREED BRATTON

[ACTOR, MUSICIAN]

"I KNOW NOW THAT AS LONG AS I DO THE PROCESS OF A HUMAN BEING IN THE MOMENT—EXERCISING, MEDITATING, DOING ALL THE RIGHT STUFF—THEN I CAN LET THAT PONY DANCE, AS IT WERE."

Meisner method prompts suggested by Creed in this interview:
"Dad, I'm pregnant"
"I'm going to leave home right now"
"Something happened and I'm on drugs"

Creed Bratton is an enigma. As is the case with Creed Bratton, the character he played on the American version of The Office, his persona is bound up with incredible lore—some of it misinformation that threatens to become canon. There's a rumor that Jimi Hendrix once taught him how to play a guitar riff. (This is untrue; Bratton's former band, the Grass Roots, was on the bill with Hendrix at the legendary Newport '69 Festival at Devonshire Downs, in California, but that's as far as the connection goes.) There's the rumor that he authored NBC's Creed Thoughts blog. (Jason Kessler, a former digital writer for The Office, actually ghost-wrote the blog.) There's also a rumor going that Creed Bratton isn't even his real name.

That one happens to be true, or at least partially true, depending on the credence one gives to a birth name. Bratton was born William Charles Schneider in February 1943 in Los Angeles. Eventually, he went by Chuck Schneider, and then Chuck Ertmoed, incorporating the surname of his stepfather. At some point, he became Creed Bratton. In the 1960s, Bratton joined the psychedelic-folk-rock-pop band the Grass

Illustration by Kristian Hammerstad

Roots, but he left in 1969 because he wanted more creative control. In the aftermath, he had relationships, and children, and searched for himself. He acted in films, sometimes as a character actor and other times as a stand-in for Beau Bridges, while continuing to write and record music.

His big break came in the early aughts, when he was cast in The Office. On that show the Creed Bratton character was like a counterpart to Absolutely Fabulous's Patsy Stone: a free-wheeling, free-loving former flower child, living by his hippie whims and the consciousness-expanding credos of the Age of Aquarius. As Dunder Mifflin's feckless quality-assurance manager, Creed was a cult hero, a twenty-first-century Bartleby, the Scrivener. He preferred not to, and then he really didn't, intending to grift and get over by means of his hilarious avarice. In fact, in one episode, Michael Scott plans to fire Creed, who then talks his boss into letting a different employee go. Here is another place where the two Creeds converge: the real man has some of that same wiliness and determination. Regarding friends who discourage you, he told me, "They're going to tell you this can't be done or that can't be done. And if you buy into that, then you can be talked out of your dream. I know that for a fact, because I almost bought into that a few times. But you have to keep pulling yourself up by your bootstraps, as it were, and believe in yourself."

We spoke on Bratton's eighty-first birthday. Our conversation capped off a festive day for Bratton, who said he'd been receiving an abundance of "natal acknowledgment," and had had breakfast with Sam Cooper from the band Mt. Joy. Bratton stars in the video for their song "Evergreen," as a man who uses a message on a milk carton—"Drink Milk Adventure Awaits"—as a prompt to embark on a delightful day of instruction in a variety of disciplines: Jazzercise, golf, a "fist lesson" with a karate instructor, painting, playing keyboards, although he keeps getting injured accidently. The narrative of that video neatly overlaps with the quixotic mapmaking, as well as the curiosity, autodidacticism, and resilience, that have come to define Bratton's life. As a kind of grace note, at the end of the video, Bratton's character advertises that he's looking to start a band. "Must have a rockstar mindset," the flyer goes, which kind of sums up the actor's sensibility.

Talking with him was like hearing Creed Thoughts improvised live and read aloud—our conversation was somewhat trippy and very amusing, though inflected with the intelligence of a seriously thoughtful person. I found him warm, charismatic, playful, and sensitive. He often took a moment to consider my questions, pausing before answering. We discussed subjects as sundry as songwriting, creative visualization, William Gibson's oeuvre, acting methods, and electromagnetism. Later, he emailed to thank me for the interview, and to send the cover of his tenth solo album, Tao Pop, which features an illustration of Bratton in his Office garb, interacting with a robot family. He joked about his "esoteric rambling." "Ha ha, on my birthday I tend to wax philosophic," he wrote. The following is a brief excerpt of that heartening, hopeful, and hallucinogenic philosophy.

—Niela Orr

I. THE ONION SKIN

THE BELIEVER: In a few of the songs from your album Slightly Altered, I've noticed you sort of gesture toward existential questions of time. I mean, you just turned eighty-one. How do you think about time?

CREED BRATTON: Perhaps I'm viewing it more from the atomic level as I get older. I'm starting to kind of believe—and Eastern philosophy believes this too—that time keeps on slipping into the future or passing you by. I've started to believe that, and I'm pretty sure of it: time and space and everything is just one four-dimensional continuum. So time is not moving; time is just there with space. Our consciousness, this force of awareness that's us, is just moving through time and space like an onion skin. That's what I'm getting through my introspection when I meditate. More and more, I dwell in those stories as I get older.

BLVR: How long have you been practicing meditation?

CB: Since nineteen… Oh, gosh. Mid-'70s. Nadine Lewy, Henry [Lewy]'s wife, initiated me in Transcendental Meditation. Henry was Joni Mitchell's producer and engineer for years. I've been meditating for a long time, and sometimes I get away from it, but I'm back at it now in full force. I'll close my eyes in the morning and I'll start saying my mantra. I hear the music of the spheres [mimics the sound]. And then the twenty-minute alarm goes off and I go, It's been three minutes. It's been five minutes. It's been seven minutes at the most—certainly not twenty minutes. Anyone that meditates realizes that time doesn't exist like we normally think of it.

BLVR: I've read that back in the '70s, when you were going through a tough time, you started to practice creative visualization. Is that something you still do?

CB: No. You can do that, but it's also kind of like wishing, right? And if you're wishing, then you don't have the faith that the higher power has got it all locked in for you in a good way. So now I more have faith that it's all going to work out. I feel much more comfortable just being in the moment and not trying to plan. I accept more than I used to. I used to want to just control.

BLVR: It seems like having a sense of acceptance is good practice for working in the entertainment business, which is so finicky. If you have a good relationship to acceptance, you'll be able to ride the waves of fame and fortune. You cowrote "Hot Bright Lights" for the Grass Roots. In the song, you sing about the vicissitudes of fame and the hot, bright lights, the pressure that comes with celebrity. And I'm wondering what your experience of celebrity has been like, back in the '60s and then during the *Office* days and up till now?

CB: Well, I like to say how egotistical it was of us to say we were like tired old whores on the road when we were only in our twenties and didn't know shit. We were so lucky. Some people can handle it, but a lot of people can't handle celebrity. There was a thirty-year period, at least, between the Grass Roots and *The Office*, when I maintained equilibrium and faith. I have thick skin.

BLVR: There was a period when you weren't in the band, because you'd left for a righteous reason. You wanted to be able to write and direct the course of your musical career. The other people in the band weren't really for that. And then you had this fallow period. How were you able to maintain your faith during that time?

CB: It was in '69. We were in Montana. It was the summer. We were on a tour. I had this gestalt occurrence where I walked out of the hotel we were at in the middle of the night. At that time, I was really into my vegetarian period; I was meditating. My own form of meditation wasn't Transcendental. I was doing things like putting white balls up my nose, bringing them out of my mouth, sucking them

in—that stuff, you know. Really out there. And so I got called in the middle of the night. This is going to sound LA woo-woo, but then again, I'm an LA woo-woo guy, you know. Woo-woo! I went downstairs and I walked out. It was a full moon. And this is the honest-to-God truth. I stood there like this and all of a sudden *bam!* Kundalini shot up my body through my feet. Talk about being in the fourth dimension. I had the most incredible experience. I realized there was really no fear; there was nothing to be fearful of at that moment. It reinstated a vision I'd had on the road in Algeria in 1964, on the side of the road. I had been without food for a few days, and I saw this version of myself walking up and receiving a plate onstage. So I had harbingers of the future. As we know, the past and the future and the present are all just *there*. I shot ahead, had kind of a mystical experience. And I haven't lost faith. I saw it happen. I said, Well, it's there for me, why should I ever doubt it? And you do. Everybody does, no matter how positive you feel at that moment. Even if Jesus came down and said, *Here's the book. See your name right there. Do this,* you'd go, *Yeah, yeah, well, maybe I need more cocaine to believe it.* You know? It's hard to be positive. My friend Willie Nile—he's a New York guy, a great songwriter, a good friend—he has a song called "You Gotta Be a Buddha (in a Place Like This)." It's true! You just need to go off and live in a cave somewhere. But to be in New York City or LA, with the vicissitudes of all this stuff, to stay positive: it's rough. It's a twenty-four-hour game, and if you drop your guard for one second, it'll come like a little weevil into your ear and seed you with doubt.

II. THE COSMIC ALGORITHM

BLVR: I read that you like to keep busy, and that when you're not working, you don't feel good. Is that when the doubt creeps in?

CB: Yeah, yeah. Right now I've got a movie I'm supposed to do. I've just finished two short films. I'm working on my biography, and a novella, and I'm finishing up my tenth album, called *Tao Pop*. Irons in the fire. That's what my nickname was in college: Irons in the Fire Ertmoed.

BLVR: You have such vivid, singular titles for your albums. How do you come up with them? Where did you get *Tao Pop*?

CB: I read Ray Kurzweil's book *The Singularity Is Near: When Humans Transcend Biology*, and it talks about AIs becoming sentient in 2045. It had a profound impact on me. A few days later, I was meditating and I saw an alien mother and father handing me their little robot AI baby. I'm taking the baby, and I have a little USB port in my head. And obviously, apparently there's no Bluetooth in the future, because I want to take the cord for the baby and stick it into my head. Whether the baby's going to teach me or I'm going to teach the baby, I hope the baby's teaching me. After a couple days, I wrote a song for the album, one of the main singles, called "Chip in My Brain." I dreamed I had a chip in my brain to keep me mellow and from going insane, to stop the madness about having more money than you.

BLVR: I can't wait to listen to it.

CB: Again, it's all that existential whatnot.

BLVR: I'm really curious about the alien chicken character that runs through your iconography, from the cover of your album *Tell Me About It* to the name of your label. Who is this alien chicken?

CB: I'm like everybody else speculating about UFOs and if there's anybody out there. I was just sitting there thinking about, you know, going out to dinner [in the future]. What are we going to have? Steak, fish, chicken? How many different ways can we have chicken? And it came to me. Wow. What if the aliens came down and they had a chicken that tasted totally different from ours? I got excited. I was less excited about what information they could give mankind or what they could do to save us from global warming than I was about what chicken they might bring. So that's exactly how it came about. I started thinking, Alien chicken. Yum, yum.

BLVR: I love that. It's almost like "To Serve Man," that episode of *The Twilight Zone*.

CB: Oh, yes. [*Bratton makes* bawk, bawk *clucking sounds.*]

BLVR: It's such a cool figure. I think people associate your persona with an oddball quirkiness, and so it totally fits.

CB: I have no idea where they got that from.

BLVR: I'd like to ask you about songwriting. You said that for the song "Chan Chu Toad," you didn't sit down to write it specifically, but it just came to you, and that all your songs come to you that way. It seems you let your creativity flow. You're not sitting down like, *I must write a song about this subject or that subject.* You let it come to you in an almost oblique way.

CB: That's absolutely a fact. And I'm not alone. There's songwriters who say, *Today I'm going to write a song about a specific subject.* Or, *I'm going to get down and I'm gonna start writing every day.* I wait and I think. Maybe it's just because I'm older now. It's come with time—my sense of awareness that there's that little nudge on the other side of the veil. I'll go, Ah, and I'll grab the guitar and I'll get out a piece of paper—it's always longhand—and I wait. I don't force myself to write. I just wait and it comes, and then I write as fast as I can. I'll get the melody, the verse, maybe two verses, and a chorus if I'm lucky. And then it might be two weeks of crafting and working to find a bridge or a coda, or that last missing verse that ties together all this nefarious stuff that doesn't make sense. I think that's the glue, the metaphysical glue that will put my cosmic algorithm together. That's how I work.

BLVR: You have such trust in your process. We talked a little bit about doubt earlier, but you're so assured in waiting for inspiration to come. That should be a big inspiration to a lot of people, just to have the confidence to wait.

CB: There's always a point when you worry. If you do a movie, *Is this my last film? Is this my last song?* That's the demon that artistic people deal with, you know? I mean, you write. You think, Well, will I write anything after this? Everybody does. If they say they don't worry about that, they're kidding, they're lying. But I know now that as long as I do the process of a human being in the moment—exercising, meditating, doing all the right stuff—then I can let that pony dance, as it were.

III. "WORKING WITHOUT A TIGHTROPE"
BLVR: You are pretty good friends with Beau Bridges.

CB: Yep.

BLVR: Did you name your son after him?

CB: I did. After I separated from my first wife, I was in a real down period. She went to New York and I was with my daughter for quite a while, and then she went with my ex-wife. So I was really in a down period. I auditioned for a play and Beau put me in this play. From then on, I went and did another play with him, and I got an agent from that. And then I worked as his stand-in for years. I'm really indebted to him as a friend and also as a mentor.

BLVR: He cast you in a few of his films thereafter?

CB: In all the films he made, I got a small part, or sometimes I got a part and a song in the thing too. He's a very sweet and very generous man.

BLVR: What it was like for you to work as a stand-in?

CB: Well, as you can imagine, it's a double-edged sword. People are viewing you as though that is what you are: you're a background artist. You're not going to be taken seriously as an actor. I was a theater major. I've always known I was good at what I did, but I had to make money; I had to pay the rent. Later on, I had child support at times too. I had to do something. This was a job where I could learn the business; I could watch the dance. I could be out there on the ice with everybody, you know; I could see the ballet ensue. So I trusted it would be all right, but numerous people told me that no one was going to take me seriously if I was working as a stand-in. But I'd already seen myself successful.

That touches on something about success and people and friends. You know, your friends, as much as they love you, sometimes they don't want you to rise above them. They can't help it; it's a subconscious thing. They're going to tell you this can't be done or that can't be done. And if you buy into that, then you can be talked out of your dream. I know that for a fact because I almost bought into that a few times. But you have to keep pulling yourself up by your bootstraps, as it were, and believe in yourself. You ever see people twirl their fingers around their head like they're crazy? There's a book, I can't remember her name… Eileen [Day McKusick]. She is talking about human beings as magnets, human beings as batteries, human beings as an electrical force. And I've seen it on acid

and stuff, the etheric body. There's these chakras and things around your body. You may want to cut some of this. [Laughs]

BLVR: I find it interesting.

CB: She talks about "the hamster wheel of worry." The male side, the right side, is going to be worried about the past. The other one, the left side, the feminine side, is going to be projecting into the future. It's one or the other. I forget. It doesn't matter. But I was driving down the street one day and I saw someone talking on the phone and they went like this with their finger [makes the twirling gesture]. And I went [snaps]. It's not just a metaphor. It's actually that they're outside their body in that other dimension, going like this, duplicating it with their head. Now, I may be totally off with this, but I think we'll find out in the future that Creed was onto something here. [Laughs]

BLVR: I think that as humans, we're always battling regret and balancing that with hope for the future.

CB: Well, I believe it. And I'll swear by what I say.

BLVR: So you were working as a stand-in while holding on to the belief that you would be able to be seen and recognized for your art.

CB: And also I was writing songs and recording them.

BLVR: Eventually you go from being a stand-in to having smaller roles in movies and television shows, until you get your breakout moment in *The Office*.

CB: I started getting some lifting up on *The Bernie Mac Show*. He took a liking to me, and he was such a sweet man. I mean, my god, he was a great guy. He thought I was funny. So I was in the background of these scenes doing all this absurd Creed-like stuff, you know, my Jacques Tati walk, and all the faces I've developed, which is a conglomeration of all the people I grew up with. It's not a conscious effort: it's fabricated. And then Ken Kwapis [a director of *The Office*] comes along and then I get this thing all this time later: *The Office*. At age sixty I get *The Office*. Who knew? How could anyone know that show was going to become that show? [Whistles] Wow.

BLVR: I read that you would tell stories about your life and Ken Kwapis would overhear them. You said that you wanted to try out for *The Office*, and it sort of worked out from there.

CB: I met him [Kwapis] through [*The Bernie Mac Show*'s] first assistant director Joe Moore, and I'd heard he was going to be directing the pilot, the first season of *The Office* in the American workplace. I'm a huge Ricky Gervais fan—genius, genius stuff. [Kwapis] gave me his number because he was a Grass Roots fan. Now, I did something that no actor does: *I called him.* I had never done that before; I did an end run around casting. But truthfully, I had a lot of film credits by then, albeit mostly black-and-white and silent films. Still, the numbers add up.

BLVR: One of your film credits is *Mask*. You played a carnival worker.

CB: I was in the scene with Sam Elliott and Eric Stoltz, who played Rocky. My daughter was studying in New York at the time, and she and a bunch of our cast members went to see *Mask* at the local cinema. She was sitting there and she knew, but she hadn't told anybody. During my scene, the people around her went, "What an asshole!" But she said, "Dad, I was so proud of you." And that made me feel so good. [*Laughs*]

BLVR: You worked with Peter Bogdanovich on that film, and then later you wrote a song called "Peter Bogdanovich Movie." It's one of my favorite songs of yours. In the lyrics, Bogdanovich says, "Act real, just feel, let the part take you away."

CB: "No stalls, no falls. Think perfect love memories." Look at you. Good for you! Very few people have interviewed me and gone to the depths of my back songs. I applaud you.

BLVR: Oh, I love that song. I'm a big fan of Peter Bogdanovich and his former wife Polly Platt and the work she did as a production designer. The chorus, which we just recited, sounds like great acting advice.

CB: It is great acting advice!

BLVR: Is that how you approach acting?

CB: Well, yeah. I mean, I studied the regular way, you know,

doing Chekhov, *The Crucible*, the Arthur Millers and things like that in college. You do the tropes, as it were. And then, after the Grass Roots, my little voice—it wasn't a cognitive thing where I thought, What am I going to do? It's just that the voice said, *Get back into acting. You studied acting, you were an acting major, for god's sake.* So I worked for a couple of years with an acting teacher who had an office on Cahuenga Boulevard in Hollywood. He taught the Sanford Meisner technique. Now, if you're familiar with the Meisner technique, you react to the situation, you learn the lines. It's not a method. You learn the lines without any meaning at all, and then you wait. It's working without a tightrope. So if you and I were in a scene right now and you were playing my daughter, let's say, and you said, *Dad, I'm pregnant* or *I'm going to leave home right now* or *Something happened and I'm on drugs*, or whatever, I would think, Oh, I would cry here. I would get emotional. I would beseech you here. I don't do any of that. I know the lines. Then on the day I just come in ready to go. And I wait and I react in the moment to what you say. Now, you could fall flat, but when it works, it's alive and real and I prefer that.

BLVR: What was it like to work with Bogdanovich as a director? What inspired you to write that song?

CB: Well, actually, the thing is that he and I hit it off. We became friends, which was lucky. I was friends with his sister. And then I got the part in *Mask* and he was gracious enough to let me just go. He put me in the part, then we did it and it turned out better than I'd thought. I want to give a shout-out to Sam Elliott too. He was gracious enough after the scene to invite me to lunch. We were having lunch outside his trailer, and he knew everybody's name. You could feel the respect that all the cast and the crew had for him. He was just a man of the people. And he wasn't full of himself. I made a note: this is how you do it.

BLVR: I love the little physical details in your songwriting. It's almost like something you would see in a short story. There was this one image from "Not Comfortable," about the narrator and his girlfriend presumably out to dinner. The narrator is uncomfortable with "total strangers" pulling out her chair at the table. Or another lyric, in "The Lovers," about someone fiddling with their watch. These are small details in your songs that tell you so much about these characters.

CB: I saw a screening of *The Lovers* with Debra Winger and Tracy Letts. A couple days later, I woke up and wrote that song.

BLVR: You also have a few other songs with titles where you name-drop actors and filmmakers, like "Lauren Bacall." I love the parallels between the kinds of characters Lauren Bacall played and this woman the narrator is singing about, who is Lauren Bacall–esque. It is very sophisticated doubling.

CB: I myself think my songs are very cinematic. In retrospect, I believe also that the muse, which is my subconscious, let's say, is giving me information that I need. I may not know it when I'm writing down notes to myself. So maybe six months or a year later, I'll go, Oh, it's trying to tell me to do this or act this way, or not to fear. They are always a note to self, my songs. And, yes, there is a layered and unconscious juxtaposition of references, also with my emotional growth and development at the time. I don't think about it. I just notice that that's what's going on. I don't even know what you call that.

IV. THE HAPPY TIMERS

BLVR: Your grandparents were in a country-and-western band.

CB: The Happy Timers.

BLVR: What was their music like?

CB: My *Coarsegold* album has their picture on the front. That's my grandfather playing guitar and that's my grandmother playing drums. I was just a little kid. I'd come down from Yosemite. I'd spend a few weeks in the summer. I'd fall asleep behind their old amp. They'd play Tex Williams, and Western swing, and Hank Williams. They played all the country songs of the '40s and the '50s. They did covers. I love that stuff. I obviously wasn't enough in love with it to do *just* country, because I get bored. I'm a pop musician, which means I can play a little jazzy, in the Norah Jones vibe. I'll do country. Definitely can do rock, definitely can do folk music. It's eclectic.

BLVR: I wanted to ask about your interest in William Gibson's work.

CB: Where do I start? That's a world I want to live in. I don't know if it's because I'm an Aquarian or what, but that futuristic stuff just absolutely sucks me in. And we're seeing now what he predicted: the metaverse, avatars, things like that. He's a prophet, as they say.

BLVR: What's your favorite Gibson book?

CB: I can't pick one. There's little ones like *Mona Lisa Overdrive*. But that's not one of the big ones. What's the one with the girl? She's a trendsetter. And she takes all the logos off her shirts [*Pattern Recognition*]. That one's great. So are the others where they're living on the bridge in San Francisco [the Bridge Trilogy, comprising *Virtual Light*, *Idoru*, and *All Tomorrow's Parties*]. I love those. Right now, when I think of William Gibson, all of his work blurs and merges into a conglomeration of what he is about. So to my mind, I can't even decipher between books. It's just a block of Gibson consciousness and I'm going, Grok this. Great.

BLVR: It's a whole universe of references.

CB: That would be [Robert A.] Heinlein with "grok."[1] But, you know.

BLVR: Does it ever bother you when people conflate CB the person and CB the character?

CB: No, I'm lucky. I'm lucky to be me.

BLVR: I'm thinking of a lyric from "When I Settle Down" where you say, "I sure did my share of crazy. / Maybe now I can just be lazy." Is that something that you still aspire to?

CB: I wrote that with my friend Blue, so that might be Blue's line. The "crazy" part would be me. But I think you die if you stop working. I don't understand people retiring. I guess, like, if they're doing a nine-to-five, I understand them retiring, but artists shouldn't retire. That's not part of the deal. ★

---

1. *Grok* is a term invented by the science fiction writer Robert A. Heinlein in his novel *Stranger in a Strange Land*, meaning "to empathize with."

A VISIT TO HEIZER'S CITY

Michael Heizer's massive Land Art project in the Nevada desert is an allegory that needs no interpretation.

BY AHMED NAJI

ILLUSTRATIONS BY:
Rich Tommaso

I visited Michael Heizer's *City* for the first time in my dreams, twenty-seven years ago. I was twelve years old, living with my family in Kuwait, when I started to experience a recurring dream where I found myself wandering, naked, through an unfamiliar city, engulfed in shame, desperately seeking a wall to hide behind—but none existed. The city's landscape was a blend of concrete ruins, sandy dunes, and winds that deepened my embarrassment with every gust. It was an abandoned city without visible inhabitants, yet I felt their eyes peeping at me. With no walls to shield its secrets, the city should have been an open, liberating space. Instead, I wandered, immersed in my shame, hopelessly seeking refuge.

I never shared this dream with anyone; it was etched into my memory as the ultimate image of embarrassment and shyness. Naked in a city without walls.

In my twenties, I learned through reading psychology books that such visions—constructed around shame and body vulnerability—are frequently associated with the adolescent phase of boys' development.

I felt satisfied with this explanation; however, my dream city continued to haunt me as an allegory. I kept looking for it in literature and art—until two years ago, when I stumbled upon a story in *The New York Times* about *City*, a monumental art project Michael Heizer has been working on for over fifty years. The report displayed the first-ever photos and videos of this enigmatic "sculpture," which few had ever visited.

For me, it looked intimate and erotic, a solid, smooth egg floating over a milky ocean. I shivered as I looked at those images, and felt a terrifying sense of déjà vu. Seeing one's dreams materialize into someone else's life's work is an unnerving realization.

I grew deeply fascinated with *City*, which was made available to the public in 2022, though visits are possible only during its open season, which typically lasts from May to November. During this period, only six people may come per day, and on only one of three days each week (Tuesday, Wednesday, and Thursday). To arrange a visit, one must fill out a reservation request form and submit it to the Triple Aught Foundation (TAF), a nonprofit organization based in Nevada that owns and operates *City*. If your application is selected, you then receive further instructions.

Through friends in Las Vegas, my name eventually landed on the waiting list. The invitation started with a message asking if I could visit on June 6, 2023. I answered "yes" and then received emails with forms to sign and instructions to follow. Among these was an important warning:

"Unfortunately, no photography or videography is permitted on-site." TAF advised us about the heat, recommending we wear sunscreen and stay hydrated. TAF also suggested we use the bathroom before leaving, and bring snacks with us, as the trip to *City* takes two hours. We would stay there for three hours, they said. There would be no cafeteria, no gift shop—not even a toilet.

Adhering to the instructions, I left my home in Las Vegas at 1 p.m. and drove north, through the desert, to Alamo, Nevada. Alamo is a small Western town in Lincoln County. The streets are quiet, lined with modest homes and businesses that supply the needs of locals and the occasional visitor. It's known for being close to the Nevada Test and Training Range and the secretive Area 51, which make it the subject of conspiracy theories related to UFO sightings. But when I got out of the car, I smelled my childhood village in Egypt. I felt a sense of déjà vu, seeing the same unpaved roads, tall trees, and wild shrubs—the unmistakable boredom on the faces of dawdling teenagers.

The TAF office in Alamo was housed in a single-story building and shared space with a local pharmacy. It was a study in minimalism: an open area featuring only a couple of desks. There was a guest book on one of the desks, along with a selection of books focused on Heizer's art. At the heart of it all stood Ed, a towering figure in his sixties, with a welcoming smile. Clad in blue jeans and a cap, he introduced himself as our tour guide and cheerfully announced that I was the first to arrive.

Apart from me, the other visitors had traveled from Oregon: a couple with their young daughter, and another young couple. Ed invited me to take the seat beside him. "Your primary task," he said, pointing to the satellite phone nestled in the car, "is to remind me to make a call every time we stop." I did this for him, though he never explained whom he was calling.

We followed the main road for about half an hour before veering onto a rocky path. Ed and I talked about Lake Mead and its declining water levels. We exchanged tips on lakes suitable for swimming, spots to find spring water, and the best places for summer camping. Our discussion was interrupted by one of our Oregon comrades, who asked, "Have you ever seen any lights at night?" It took me a moment to grasp what he was hinting at, but Ed, with his experience, quickly replied, "Oh yeah, we encounter weird lights around here all the time, right?" He turned to me for confirmation. Fully aware of the importance of alien tourism to Nevada, I affirmed, "Absolutely."

We stopped in front of a sign that read BASIN AND RANGE NATIONAL MONUMENT. It was our last chance to take pictures, so we did so in front of the sign, to document our trip. Then we continued driving, passing green wild grass and calm cows chewing alfalfa. There were metal water tanks for the cows to drink from and mountains in the distance. After the land was colonized and its people—the Nuwu (Southern Paiute) and Newe (Western Shoshoni)—were displaced, settlers had tried to build a dam that eventually failed, leading to the abandonment of the land. In the 1970s, Ed's grandfather recommended it to Heizer. He then transformed it into his residence and the center for his artistic projects. Ed grew up knowing Heizer and in recent years began taking care of his ranch and cows; his stories painted a picture of a peaceful life shaped by isolation and the land's rustic beauty. The depiction did not exactly resemble Heizer's own characterization of his life in the valley. In an interview with *The New Yorker*, he told Dana Goodyear: "I like runic, Celtic, Druidic, cave painting, ancient, preliterate, from a time back when you were speaking to the lightning god, the ice god, and the cold-rainwater god. That's what we do when we ranch in Nevada."

Michael Heizer was born in Berkeley, California, in 1944. He was an unusual kid, and his family came to the conclusion early on that formal education did not suit him. So when he was twelve years old, they gave him a year off from school, and he traveled with his father, Robert F. Heizer, an archaeologist and historian, to Mexico. His father would dig, and the kid would do the site drawings. Dr. Heizer was the head of the anthropology department at the University of California at Berkeley; his most significant breakthrough was in 1968, when he discovered La Venta pyramid in Mexico.

This early childhood trip was influential for young Heizer. As William L. Fox wrote in his book *Michael Heizer: The Once and Future Monuments*, "The sculptures of [Heizer] are never far from the intellectual and aesthetic lessons learned while accompanying his father to sites such as temple monuments in Egypt." What exactly were these lessons? His father was interested in religious monuments. Perhaps young Heizer thought that gods had made these giant monuments, or that they were made for gods. Or maybe, standing before these expressions of power, he thought something else entirely.

In 1965, Heizer arrived in New York City as a young American artist. He found himself in the company of Walter De Maria and like-minded artists such as Carl Andre and his future adversary, Robert Smithson. This group was united in its quest for a more expansive canvas, far beyond the confines of gallery walls.

Smithson, a particularly influential figure in this circle, was not only an artist but also an influential writer and speaker. His writings from the 1960s—especially the 1967 article "A Tour of the Monuments of Passaic, New Jersey"—reshaped perceptions of landscapes and were pivotal in the early conceptualization of Earthworks, a movement aimed at integrating art with natural landscapes; the concept would later evolve and become known as Land Art.

Heizer's presence in New York did not last long. He went west to Nevada. It was here that Heizer created *Double Negative* in 1969 and 1970. This monumental work, which became a Nevadan landmark, consists of two colossal rectangular trenches carved into the desert landscape. It was a feat of both artistic vision and engineering, involving the displacement of 244,000 tons of earth and rock. Heizer's bold move, from the intellectual art discussions in New York to the physical creation of art within the American landscape, marked a significant chapter in the story of Land Art, and cemented his legacy as a pioneer in the field.

After an hour of driving on dirt roads, our car stopped before a metal gate. Ed stepped out to open it. "For security," he explained, although it was hard to imagine a trespasser in such a place. He pointed to a large house standing a mile away in the valley, identifying it as Heizer's residence. From this distance, we could see solar panels and a gigantic yellow crane—one of Heizer's art tools used for lifting, cutting, and shaping the large rocks he works with. The whole valley was his studio, and these construction machines were his art arsenal.

Heizer bought the land in Garden Valley with a loan from the art collector and his patron Virginia Dwan (1931–2022) and moved there in 1972. At first, he lived in a trailer while he built his house, and he began work on his life's masterpiece in the backyard. It was also during this time that he traveled with his father to Egypt, a journey that profoundly influenced him. Several art critics have noted the connection between Complex One—the first structure he built in *City*—and the Step Pyramid of Djoser.

I've never much admired the Djoser pyramid, which is in Egypt, where I was born and lived most of my life. For archaeologists and Western visitors like Heizer and his father, the Djoser

pyramid is revered as the first pyramid, dating back to the twenty-seventh century BCE. It signifies a pivotal shift in construction from mud brick to stone. For me, it represents another piece of state propaganda that I find suffocating. When I gaze upon the Djoser pyramid, I don't see gods. Instead, I see the echoes of the first civil war in history, following the collapse of the second dynasty. I see the ascent of the third dynasty under Djoser, whose path to the throne remains mysterious. It was

during his reign that the structures and laws of the more centralized authoritarian state were established, demanding people's taxes and labor to erect massive monuments glorifying a single man who saw himself as both the state and a god.

The old Egyptian rulers used to be buried in the south, in the holy city of Abydos, where gods were also buried, according to Egyptian mythology. But starting with Djoser, kings became the new gods, and rather than being buried in Abydos, they began building

pyramids in the north. The holy wisdom of Abydos and the decentralized communities were fading, dissolving into the Nile with their mud bricks. Djoser marked the emergence of a new state and new deities.

As we approached *City* I began to think about all the new American gods around me now. The gods that had emerged out here in the Nevada desert after World War II: atomic bomb deities, military and air force deities. Here was evidence, all around, of this state's power. And then, in the middle of all that, a monument.

Upon our arrival at *City*, Ed pointed to the left and announced, "Here is Complex One, the first structure built in *City*." Then, gesturing to the right, he added, "And over there is Complex Two." He cautioned us against climbing the rocky slopes, warning that they could be hazardous, but otherwise, we had three hours to explore as we wished. When someone in our group asked why Ed would not be joining us, he replied, "Because they know you'll have questions, and they're afraid I might give you a silly answer that could influence your experience."

City lacked any signs or labels, but to me the most striking feature was its lack of gates or walls. The others decided to start by exploring Complex One, considering it was the first construction erected and thus the beginning. I bid them a temporary farewell and walked toward Complex Two. With each step, my heart flickered; with every stride, I felt as if I were delving into my past, a distant one, before the revolution, the prison, the exile that shaped my current life. I was transported back to my teenage dreams, and a gentle dizziness overwhelmed me.

I climbed to the highest point of Complex Two, from which I could see the whole sculpture. But when I reached the top and looked down, I saw a body. A body lying in the valley, its contours smooth, devoid of sharp angles. Its "skin" was made of various pebbles, with roads weaving over and around the rocky, fleshlike dunes. In the middle of this body was the "city" center, a small green island of grass, the only living plant that was allowed to grow within the work. It's the first thing you see when you enter and exit *City*. I thought of it as a belly button; however, from my elevated vantage point atop Complex Two, it transformed in front of my eyes into a dry cup… a holy chalice.

Layers of interpretation stacked upon one another, open for exploration. I was absorbed in the art, walking within the very body and existence of the artist. *City*, with its abstract mounds, prismoids, arenas, ramps, and pits, resembled veins and arteries, bulging muscles and sagging fat—a body aging yet dreaming of immortality.

I descended with a mix of reverence and awe into Complex Two, which is officially known as *45°, 90°, 180°*. It's the only space in the city with a concrete floor. The entrance evoked poignant sadness—it was a shrine, a tomb, a eulogy. The arrangement of shapes unfolds in a deliberate sequence. Initially, one is met with a pair of small concrete triangles, setting

a stark geometric tone. This prelude is followed by three larger triangles, leading to a group of four towering triangular structures. Beyond these, two contrasting cubes add to the complexity of the space. A path leads to another trio of triangles, and guides the visitor farther into the heart of the complex. At the end of this concrete spectacle stands a splendid concrete wall with two triangular arms at each side, embracing a trio of rectangular concrete blocks. These blocks

resemble tombstones, and suggested to me the presence of death. Notably, one block leans against the wall, creating a triangular void, an architectural whisper. All I could think of here was death and desire.

I set my backpack on the ground, removed my white T-shirt, followed by my pants and underwear, and stepped into the shrine, naked except for my sneakers. Streams of cold air poured through the gaps between the concrete triangles, giving me goose bumps,

even as the sun provided a blanket of warmth. As I marched naked through these triangles, I wondered: Are the goose bumps a result of the chill? Or are they born of nostalgia or euphoria? Admiration or sexual arousal?

When *City* opened, it became one of the world's largest artworks. However, the artwork is not limited only to its structures; it's an interactive performance that requires participation and adherence to its rules, starting with signing an agreement.

TAF selects and invites you, and then you must travel by airplane and car to be picked up as a guest by a driver. It's a gesture of generosity, of course, but it also implies that once you're there, leaving on your own isn't an option.

Inside *City*, you don't merely experience Heizer's devotion and the magnificence of his vision; you feel his authority, his force. Its vastness overwhelms your senses, making it difficult to comprehend its limits. Georges Poulet, the Belgian literary critic, thought of sculpture as an unrevealed secret. You want to circle a sculpture because it gives the illusion that there is something in it that, from a different angle, you might be able to see. But in Heizer's *City*, the sculpture is circling you. For three hours, you are subject to its gaze.

What can you do in front of such power? Do you kneel or rise?

I walked toward the concrete tombstones (known as "2,3,4"), and when I got close to them, the sky erupted with the cries of ravens. A duo carved through the air, their wings beating furiously against the wind. I thought they were greeting me, perhaps as part of this "art show"—after all, every graveyard needs its blackbirds. Then I saw they had their nest above the rectangular concrete headstone. They were guarding the sculpture that had become their home.

As I walked around the complex naked, I was surprised to see red and black marks. Someone had written a date: 7/24/03. There were red lines on another surface and the word *CRACK* written in black. To me, the human marks spoke of the relentless passage of time, to a crack that had been made in this monument.

In one corner, I noticed piles of rat dung. I imagined desert rodents seeking refuge here at night or escaping the relentless summer. I felt a heightened awareness of everything. I hadn't expected life to make itself known in *City*, which has been meticulously maintained to prevent natural growth. Ed told me later that around five employees are responsible for its maintenance, which involves, in part, removing grass or weeds that sprout, to preserve the work's rocky aesthetic.

Among the rat dung, something shone like gold. When I got closer, I realized it wasn't gold but scores of scorpion tails. The mystery unraveled when I looked up again to the raven nest and saw a third tiny raven. The ravens feasted on scorpions and desert rodents, leaving their leftovers scattered below. *City* cost forty million dollars to build, and forty million has been put in a trust to maintain it— which means preventing nature from taking it over—but all that couldn't

stop an ecosystem from establishing itself within its territory.

Suddenly I heard a loud explosion. In a panic, I hurried to get dressed while searching the sky for the source of the sound, but I couldn't see anything. Then I remembered Ed mentioning that aircraft from Area 51—which is about seventy miles away—often break the sound barrier. Disturbed by the presence of military aircraft, I hurriedly finished putting on my clothes. After dressing, I took out my notebook and tried to jot down some notes, but waves of emotion prevented me from writing anything. Instead, I sketched some drawings of the area and a diagram of Complex Two. An hour and a half had already passed when I picked up my things and walked to Complex One.

It should be one mile from Complex Two to Complex One, but it feels longer than that due to the undulating terrain of the road, which takes you on paths that aren't visible when you set out. After a while, I lost my sense of direction and began to feel detached from reality. Eventually I noticed a few of the other visitors, ghostly figures passing by in the distance. Even as I waved to them, I questioned if they were merely mirages.

In front of Complex One, I knew immediately the connection to the Djoser pyramid was far from accurate. However, I understood why art critics, who might have seen Djoser only in pictures, made the connection. Building pyramids started with constructing steps above a tomb. Then one step became two steps, and so on, until there was a pyramid. Complex One is

just one step and is not made from mud bricks, like the early pyramids, nor from carved stones, but rather from modern construction materials. Heizer claims to use materials from the land around him, but I don't think concrete and iron naturally grow in the valley.

What gives Complex One its character is the T-shaped metal structure that stands in front of and above the step. Its shadow on the step makes it appear to be a container: a womb, a birthplace from which everything starts. From Complex One, you can't see Complex Two—just as, when we are born, we cannot predict our journey's path. But from Complex Two, you can look back and see your whole life, the roads you've walked, the shadows in the valley, the illusion of your life's achievements.

As our three-hour visit neared its end, I found myself sitting atop a hill, inhaling the spectacle of the sunset as it wove its shadows and hues across the city. I meditated on the experience of traveling out here. The work changes every minute, depending on the sun's position in the sky. Moreover, it's not open at night and cannot be visited at any time during the year. Could I truly claim to have visited or seen *City* as I had "seen" other pieces of art?

Given that only six people are allowed per day, fewer than one thousand visitors come to *City* annually. This means that, if everything goes as planned, fewer than one hundred thousand people will have the opportunity to visit in a century, which raises clear questions about accessibility. Each visit to *City* offers a unique experience. If two people visit *City* at different times during the year, they will see different artworks. Still, they will experience the same interactive performance art in which they enter Heizer's domain.

I admire Heizer's dedication to creating work that aspires to match the grandeur of ancient monuments in Mexico or Egypt, a goal he has undoubtedly achieved. Both Heizer's *City* and these historical monuments represent a combination of political power and wealth, serving to immortalize their creators. Some of the names of the workers who built the Giza complex have been preserved, with records that detail their conditions and schedules. However, when I researched Heizer's project, the only names that appeared alongside Heizer's were those of supporters, organizations, and donors, including the Los Angeles County Museum of Art and the Dia Art Foundation.

Additionally, Heizer's project received political support, notably from Harry Reid, the long-serving Nevada senator and leader of the Democratic Party. Since military bases encircled *City*, several military and nuclear projects threatened its continuation. However, Reid and Heizer consistently leveraged their political connections to oppose such projects, compelling the federal government to abandon its plans. Ultimately, during the last years of Obama's presidency, Reid helped push through an executive action designating Garden Valley and the surrounding area part of the Basin and Range National Monument.

This granted Heizer's organization a unique legal status: it holds privately owned land that also enjoys special federal protection.

It's said that during their construction and throughout the pharaohs' lifetimes, the pyramids were secured places, not open to the public. The authorities wanted to display their power, but only to a select group of privileged people. Nowadays, the pyramids have transformed into tourist attractions, where hustlers might

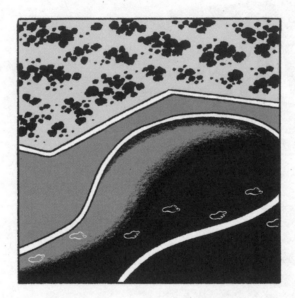

offer to take a photo of you jumping high, seemingly perched atop a pyramid, for a twenty-dollar fee.

I'm uncertain if Heizer's *City* will undergo a similar transformation, but he is currently involved in a project in AlUla Valley of the Arts in the Kingdom of Saudi Arabia. There, His Royal Highness Mohammed bin Salman is investing billions of dollars to install monumental artworks in the Arabian Desert, with the goal of immortalizing his name and attracting tourists.

The sun was coloring the sky orange. The air was unbelievably fresh. I told Ed that I envied him for living here, surrounded by all this beauty and cleanliness. We were waiting for the rest of the visitors to come out when I started noticing circular patches on the ground, empty of grass. They looked geometric and precise. I suspected they had a connection with *City* and asked Ed what they were.

"Ants' nests," he said.

He explained that the valley is inhabited by red ants, which build their nests underground. They remove any green grass on the surface and use it to construct their colony below. They even design chambers for the queen to lay her eggs. The juxtaposition of and contrast between the two projects was hard to ignore: an artist builds an empty city, all the while surrounded by ants who are constructing their own city underground.

I came here chasing an old dream, only to find myself in another person's dream. I tried to deconstruct both dreams to uncover some kind of meaning. But I don't think the meaning resides in these gigantic constructions or on these gravel roads. Meaning is never inherently present in the sign or in the artist's biography; rather, it lies in the gap between the signs. It's found in the connection between the city and its surroundings: the mountains, the military-industrial complex, the presidential executive orders safeguarding it all—and the ant colonies underground, where maybe a young ant is currently dreaming of a city without walls. ✶

"A SUMPTUOUS AND LIVELY COLLECTION."

—**KELLY LINK**, bestselling author of *Get in Trouble* and *The Book of Love*

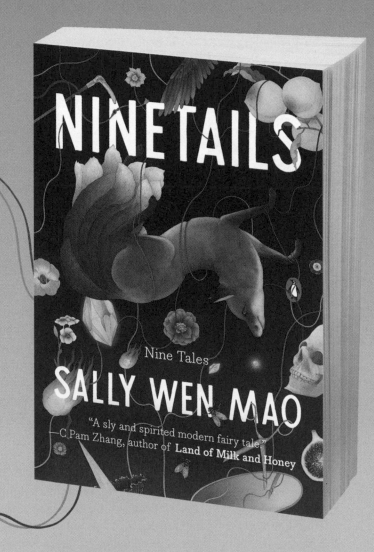

NINETAILS

Nine Tales

SALLY WEN MAO

"A sly and spirited modern fairy tale."
—C Pam Zhang, author of **Land of Milk and Honey**

"A spirited modern fairy tale that . . . is an exploration of the animal magic within the feminine, written with ardor and ambition."

—**C PAM ZHANG**, author of *Land of Milk and Honey*

"Lyrical and virtuosic, with a sly sense of humor."

—**GINA CHUNG**, bestselling author of *Sea Change* and *Green Frog*

EILEEN MYLES

[POET]

"THE ANIMAL PART OF THE WRITER IS THE MOST IMPORTANT PART."

Eileen Myles's thoughts on AI-generated poetry:
Mostly soulless
Really obscene
Like the worst workshop poems of all time
Hideous
We have to know it and meet it
A piece of shit

Eileen Myles's writing is nimble yet incisive, insouciant yet wise. The author of no fewer than twenty-three books of poetry, fiction, and nonfiction, Myles makes the act of writing seem both impossibly cool and effortlessly deep. Monumental and natural and the smallest, simplest, most meaningful thing. Both pathetic and of course not at all so. They fill the act of writing and being a writer with possibility and agency. For years now, at the end of every semester, I have sent students at Columbia University and elsewhere off into the world with Myles's valedictory words: "I hope there's mystery and poetry in your life—not even poems, but patterns. I hope you can see them. Often these patterns will wake you up, and you will know that you are alive, again and again." Generally, this is followed by claps and, at times, tears.

Myles's role as sage advice giver—as a commencer into what we might call, taking their cue, "a 'Working Life'"—feels apt. (As they wrote to me recently: "Let me be the one to convince nonfiction students that poetry is nonfiction just like everything else.")

Illustration by Kristian Hammerstad

I first met Eileen in 2012 or 2013 at the former Center for Fiction space in Midtown Manhattan. I remember they were warm and unexpectedly practical: we quickly got to talking about our dogs, and Eileen suggested I find a good dog sitter, if I didn't know one already—as a writer, you need to be able to travel and do residencies, and so you need someone you can trust to care for your animal companion. I must have been twenty-nine or thirty at the time, still very much finding my way, but I felt there was something unusually gracious about Eileen's gesture of treating the greenhorn as a fellow traveler, despite his age and what must have been obvious inexperience. I found it ennobling.

Some years later, in 2018, I commissioned Eileen to write an essay, in praise of Houston's second-largest airport, for this magazine. When I suggested some light edits—more or less a copyedit—they responded with a bit of memorable pushback as well as some explanation: "I'm pretty much a what you see is what you get kind of writer. But I fixed phone to iPhone and allowed most of the para breaks and different punctuations and capitalizations. I don't like question marks a la Gertrude Stein but if that's a deal breaker insert them but I really think they ruin the flow of the work inserting a score that I don't mean."

Naturally, we chose to keep the flow.

This interview was drawn from multiple sources: a phone conversation, a live event for students at Columbia University's School of the Arts in New York, and a dinner at a nearby restaurant-bar afterward. At the restaurant-bar, I kept the recorder on for the first half of the meal and then turned it off, because leaving it on seemed somehow invasive, or maybe too professional, but then I ended up jotting down so much of what Eileen said anyway. So it is when spending any stretch of time with someone as effortlessly quotable as Eileen, where you might hear such tossed-off observations as "I noticed that art is something that doesn't happen far away" and "Nothing more trans than taking a shit in the men's room." At one point I asked whether they considered their recent poem "Put My House" to be a sex poem. "Do I consider it a sex poem?" they repeated out loud, deciding whether to play ball. "I guess. Sure. I don't think you're wrong.

"I've not written a lot of sex scenes," they continued, "but I guess I get a lot of bang for my buck." The sex talk reminded them of a short story they once sent to Mary Gaitskill, when she was guest-editing a fiction issue of VICE magazine, but the other editors weren't "sure the advertisers would let them run it because it was 'pussy-on-pussy.' And I was like, 'You're so misogynist.'" And so it flowed. —James Yeh

I. "MAYBE THIS IS ACTUALLY WHAT I NEED"

THE BELIEVER: Hi, Eileen. How are you doing?

EILEEN MYLES: I'm good. I came here [Marfa, Texas] in January and I sublet my place in New York City for a year. Next month I'm going to travel a bit, but most of the year I'm here and I'm working on this book.[1]

BLVR: That sounds amazing.

EM: Having what you want can be complicated. If I'm very orderly every day, I have a great day. And today I was orderly. The day before yesterday I was orderly. Yesterday I had some new art and I wanted to hang it and I needed help and somehow that ended up being complicated. Anyway, the less I do the better it goes.

BLVR: Is that because you need to be able to focus?

EM: It seems to me something has to become an obsession. I can keep something alive with little bits every day. The more everything I do has something to do with it, the better. It's like a circus tent over your life. It's like if you go to MacDowell, you're there working. Ideas seem more visceral even.

BLVR: Do you feel like these conditions have been required for your work? Have they always been available to you?

EM: No—no. When I was younger, other people's houses could sometimes give me this support. For two or three months, years ago, someone gave me their house and it was incredible. I learned to drive because it was not in the city. I always think of those residencies in a place apart as like having a good childhood for a moment. The shape of them is really good for writing. Because you just go in, you charge in, you get intense, and then it's over. And it is different like when I'm here and I'm home, when it's not so time-bound.

But still I feel like having time and space to write is a new job in a way. I've never had this much time. And I fuck it up. Someone will ask me to do a blurb, and I'm like, "Nyeh, you can send it to me." And even though I don't have to read that book, I somehow want to. It becomes perverse. So that's funny.

---

1. "All My Loves," a novel cataloging Myles's previous romantic relationships.

Because I have a reading list that has much more to do with what my next book is about. But then, you know, who knows? It could be that what the world wants, or what is being published now, is *highly* relevant to what I'm working on.

BLVR: Well, people always say, "Curiosity killed the cat."

EM: Yeah! But tell me what you mean.

BLVR: You're like, Oh, maybe this is actually what I need. And you're curious.

EM: Yes, exactly.

BLVR: It's like the openness—

EM: —is full of danger.

BLVR: Yeah, the openness can be very productive, but the flip side is it could be so narrow. You mentioned the influence of other writings. What about the influence of the personal on your work? I was reading your poem "The Mirror Is My Mother." Your line about moving a mirror and seeing a wall instead is so stunning. I'm presuming it's drawn from personal experience.

EM: I think I wrote that in 1989. The thing that's very funny about you picking up that line is that I've been using it in the book I'm working on. The line is a good way of saying something that I think about all the time. It is that thing when something is rendered static, and it's a repeated shock. I think my uncle had died, and Cookie Mueller [writer and actress who starred in many of filmmaker John Waters's early films] had died. In that poem, it was both those things. My mother was well and alive and had a couple decades to go. And I'd seen Cookie dead. She had an amazing funeral at St. Mark's Church, where she was laid out in a casket and everybody would come up and stand or look at her. She had this incredible war paint on. I mean, she was very thin. It was the most amazing funeral I've ever been to. I don't think they ever allow fire in the church, and yet somebody had trimmed the whole perimeter of the interior of the church with small white candles that were flickering. So there was this incredible effect. The playlist was incredible. And then eventually people got up and started to talk, talk, talking

and saying things. But mostly it was the visual effect and the music. And just the fact of her body sitting there in front of us was so astonishing.

It's weird, like, a few weeks ago, the man across the street died. We didn't really have much communication. But he was often out on his lawn, and I'm in and out all the time. And so we just kind of grunted at each other. And every now and then I think he would suddenly see me as female and he'd just kind of perk up—I mean, he was a single guy, with grandchildren and children and all that—and then I would get this sort of weird vibe from him. But finally we had no interest in each other at all. And he died in this really weird way—he was a guy who had a lot of different jobs, and one of his jobs was to take the mail from Marfa down to a town called Candelaria. There are things that are not even towns, but they're called colonias. They're just little bitty places where somebody has to bring your mail, and somebody has to pick it up. And so Gilbert was that guy. And when you get to those places, there's very little internet connection or phone coverage. So apparently, when he was down there doing a delivery, he had a heart attack. So I think it took a while for someone to get to him. And then, wherever the hospital was was really far. And so on, and so on. And so Gilbert died.

But what's weird is just that he's not there. What's across the street from me is Gilbert's house, and all his stuff. And he had grandchildren, so there's like posters from the kids who play sports in town and his Christmas decorations are still up—everything but Gilbert. And it's exactly that sensation. The morning he died, I remember: I sat on my couch, and I was drinking tea, and reading, and I remember looking out and seeing this sort of red-and-green tinsel-covered lawn-ornament candy cane. I thought, Huh, Gilbert's candy cane is still up.

Well, there's no end to this subject. But everything is like that. Suddenly everything looks different.

BLVR: Along the lines of change, you've talked about how the writing you are most into doesn't stay still—it's not rigid. Is there also a thing that stays still, though? An element of non-change that is necessary for you?

EM: I feel like there's a something that does all the writing. There's a way in which my poems and my art journalism and my novels all sound the same. And I wouldn't say it's me exactly, but it's a familiar pastiche of all the classes I travel from and through. And I use it. That's my instrument. So, in a way, that's why I think the genres don't matter so much to me, because they're different jobs of the same nature.

BLVR: Robert Walser, whom I know you also like, has talked about this. How all his pieces of writing are like the bits of a "long, plotless, realistic story." I feel like you've talked about the jigsaw of moods.

EM: I know, and he also says he's like a cobbler.[2] He puts it all together.

BLVR: Do you identify with the idea of that role as a writer? Of yourself as the cobbler?

EM: Oh yeah. I like that. Jerry-rigged, all these things. Kind of 3D, pastiche.

BLVR: When you are pulling from all these different things, do you have certain credos or rules? For example, I feel like the writer Alejandro Zambra does a lot of playing with identities and real people in his work. And I once wrote a story about an ex and asked Alejandro, who is a friend, when I should show it to her. His expression became quite grave and he was just like, "That's dangerous."

EM: Right. I mean, it's hard, because the book I'm working on now will obviously include stuff about people that I've been involved with. And I had this idea that it was going to be limited in some aesthetic way, that I was going to manage it. But the stuff just comes out the way it wants. And I have people that I thought, Oh god, they're gonna… And yet, if the writing is really hot and juicy and good, it's like, How could you not use it? I feel like I might push the envelope more on these issues than I ever have before.

The book is called "All My Loves." And I really did think it was about the domestic habits of relationships.

2. In *Eine Art Erzählung* (1928–29), Robert Walser writes: "If I am well-disposed, that's to say, feeling good, I tailor, cobble, weld, plane, knock, hammer, or nail together lines the content of which people understand at once. If you liked, you could call me a writer who goes to work with a lathe."

But then when I decided the book is going to be really big, like a thousand pages, I thought it could expand to many definitions of love. So that gave me a lot more breathing space. But I'm nowhere near the place where I have to decide anything.

BLVR: That's a place you like, am I right?

EM: Yeah, it's the editing place, right? Like I wrote a novel in the '90s about a relationship. And that breakup was so bad that when I started to read from the novel, it was just as bad as the breakup. So I put it aside for almost thirty years. So I'm going to dump big parts of that into the book. It's funny because the book described the relationship, but it also described a social world that was more hers than mine. But I subsequently inherited many of those friends. And so now the social world is much more taboo than the relationship. They're friends and people I have work relationships with. And I know the families now. I do care what they think and feel.

II. "BAD COPIES OF THE WORLD"

BLVR: There's a line in *The Importance of Being Iceland* where you write: "In general, I think writers are not smart. They are something else and each writer can fill in a word here, but smart is not what that word is." And later, in an essay on avant-garde poetry, you write, "Andy Warhol sounded dumb. And that was good." Is there something to be said in defense of the not-smart or sounding dumb?

EM: Oh, well, I guess I felt like the animal part of the writer is the most important part. The same way childhood is the most important part of life. You're just like recording all the time when you're a kid—you don't miss anything. You always ask a question of an adult, and they're like, "Why would you say that? Who told you to say that? Where did that come from?" The child's basic knowledge and experience is always challenged by the adult and always dismissed, but the fact is: you did see it and you keep recording. And writing is when you kind of grow up and you put a voice-over onto all those recordings. Like you basically articulate what the kid saw.

And I feel like life is like that—it's a delayed-reaction experience. I think poetry is a little better than prose for being present. You can often write poetry in the present, about the present, and you're often in the room when you write. Not that you write only about the room, but you really do kind of take the physical space on in a more literal way than in prose.

But I feel like really there's this lag, where some part of you is just really dumb and that's the most valuable part because that part is the animal that's thinking and feeling and smelling and hearing and just *absorbing*, you know? And if that doesn't happen, the work is disembodied.

So I feel like the dumbness of the writer is the most valuable part.

BLVR: Are there ways you have nurtured that animal part?

EM: Part of why we love animals is they give our animal a way to be—you get a dog so you walk your dog so the dog walks you. We're coexisting with them. What I would give my animal now is different from what I gave my animal in my twenties. There was a certain amount of excess when I was young and I think that's not bad—that's good.

Growing up, I made art. I drew and painted and I think I was supposed to go to art school and instead I went to college. And for a while when I first got to New York, it was that thing where you couldn't go look at the thing, the road you didn't take. I was like, *Ugh, I don't want to look at art, it makes me depressed.*

But I stopped drinking in my thirties, cause I come from a long line of very bad alcoholics, and so my animal did not need another drink at that point in time, and that's when I realized that art was the greatest thing: to go into an art gallery and just be in the color and sensation and relationship and sculpture and everything—it's life-changing every time, because it's basically being in somebody else's browser. And just to be present with art is to completely reshuffle your cards. I think for writers it's really good and really important. And of course, every other art form, and every other body of information, completely changes the way you live in the world. And I think that's a kind of giving to your animal self too.

It's all workshop in a sense. I think everything you do outside of writing is more important than writing, in a way. And then you bring it to the writing.

BLVR: That reminds me of a line from a *"Working Life"*: "Making is just taking if you know." And there's also a part in *For Now* where you say, "I didn't go to art school but I always wanted to do what they do and I know that their practice is complicated and diverse but I contend that somewhere in there is this action of copying. Holding perhaps." And then you write, "Copying everything (in words) which is a form of loving the world, aiming and choosing, I suppose just the way it is. Life is I do this." I was wondering if you might be willing to talk more about your notebooks or the process of keeping a journal or, more broadly, this idea of having the recording *on*.

EM: I think it is weird, actually—even though I'm listening to all that and I'm like, That makes perfect sense.

BLVR: [*Laughs*] Sorry to make you listen to yourself.

EM: But it is totally bizarre that one's response to reality is to be the copyist. I was like, Why would you do that? I know there's this great quote from Deleuze, who says, "Art hurts our animal eyes." Which is so great. It's like animals don't need art. It's like, what do we need? But that is just the problem. The brain is the problem. And somehow it's always mirroring or wanting to—I guess it's control and excitement and excess of feeling. First it was drawing, and I was drawing everything I could look at. And I still do

<hr>

MICROINTERVIEW WITH DEVON PRICE, PART V

THE BELIEVER: What does community mean to you in the context of healing?

DEVON PRICE: What community is—especially in the West, because of colonialism—is a problem. We have such a twisted view of it. To be frank, when I was pursuing community for myself as a queer person, as an autistic person, I thought of it as this territory I had to claim. Your approach is often colonialist, if that's all you've ever known. People go to the LGBT center like: *There'd better be things for me. I have these needs. I need this programming.* There's a degree of entitlement in the idea that community is something you can take from. ★

OLIVE OIL CAKE AND A RASPBERRY

by Taneum Bambrick

It's Wednesday night in California.
We sit on metal chairs, which shriek
like helicopter blades clattering across the cement
of a repurposed parking lot. Two of us take turns
describing our heartbreaks that have gone
and gone. Layers of bark peeled off closed trees.
The third pets her silver dog; she answers
and nods along to stories she's already heard
until her water glass empties.
Another party—older, a woman and man—
finish their steamed potatoes and stand to leave.
The man swats my shoulder. Says, *classic
case of a guy wanting what he can't have, I'm afraid,*
he smiles milkily. When I laugh,
my chair cranks back and the dog squeaks.
The noise embarrasses me. It simplifies the scene:
the yellow parking line under my left foot,
our leftover olive pits, flecked with stinky meat.
I have exhausted myself. My friends. One breakup drew
the child out of me. What do you need, you fiery baby?
Tonight splits with jasmine and evaporated lake.
My mouth is enormous. It tastes sweet.

---

draw a lot. I love drawing. It's like it's a way to stop using your phone. It's really great.

But when writing began, people did actually say, "Don't do that. It's going to ruin everything." You know what I mean? It used to be, if you were a great speaker, you would build a memory house. It's how they would do those seven-hour speeches in the Roman Senate. They would, like, late at night—it was the most beautiful thing; there's a book about it called *The Art of Memory* by Frances Yates—but late at night, you would go to a plaza in Rome someplace, and you would see all these students walking around touching the columns. And then they would walk to the bench, and then touch the bench. What they were doing was writing a giant speech. And so they would think, Well, the important thing is the person needs to be seated in a deep feeling of… The bench would be symbolic of that part of the speech. And they would have this whole walking pattern that contained their talk. They would use actual columns and arches and things. And then when they stood in front of the Senate they would, in their head, walk back through all those spots. They had these amazing mental capacities. And we just messed it up by creating print and writing. They were like, *Nobody's going to remember anything!* And it's true. And now we have computers and once again we're ruining everything. I feel like there is this latent—like I always think… Well, I think you have another question. Do you want to—

BLVR: I want to hear what you were saying.

EM: Well, I always go off into the little monks. What's so interesting is when we hear about the whole medieval era it was supposedly all dark and nobody knew anything and there were just monasteries and monks copying the Bible and stuff. And when I was in Florence once, I went to the Laurentian Library. And it was this library that Michelangelo designed and that was where Boccaccio, who wrote *The Decameron*, had his workshop. And I was like, "His *workshop*? What do they do in his workshop?" And what it was like was Boccaccio would say, *You're cool. Come and be in my workshop.* And you'd come into the workshop and say, *What are we going to do?* And he'd be like, *Here's* The Decameron. *Copy it!*

All his workshop was was people who sat there and copied it. But still, the monks who worked there did illuminated manuscripts and they made these funny drawings in the margins and the books became more than a copy—and everything is more than a copy. So I think what is so great is, as animals, we make these bad copies of the world. And then that's literature.

III. "ANYTHING WORTH DOING IS WORTH DOING BADLY"

BLVR: You were talking about the idea of writing ruining everything and all these technological innovations causing a lot of fear. In academia, and outside of it, we hear all this stuff right now about ChatGPT and AI.

EM: I keep forgetting. What is ChatGPT?

BLVR: Well, I guess the compressed definition is it's an AI program that will talk to you. And you can feed it a prompt, like "Write an essay in the style of James Joyce about Eileen Myles's work." And it'll produce—

EM: —something.

BLVR: Something. Paragraphs' worth. Some professors I know have expressed dismay, like, "Oh yeah, someone else wrote an essay using ChatGPT." With regard to AI, I wanted to ask, to paraphrase Frank O'Hara: Is it dirty or does it just *seem* dirty?

EM: Oh, yeah. I don't know. There's some way that we have to go with it, but then there's some way in which it's really obscene, I think. I was contacted by these two guys who did an AI book of poems that Little, Brown is publishing.[3] And the gross part, of course, is they got more money for it than anybody I know has ever gotten for a poetry book. I was like, Fuck Little, Brown. How dare they do that? I mean, my books sell enough that I actually make a living, but I never get big advances. My latest poetry book, *a "Working Life,"* weirdly, is the most money I ever got from a book, but it really isn't that much money. And it's like one-sixth of what these guys got. And so they basically wanted me to read the book and tell them how I felt about it. And I was just like, Should I even give this person five minutes? Basically, I made them pay a parking ticket. I said, "If you pay my parking ticket, I will meet you at Cafe Mogador."

BLVR: [*Laughs*]

EM: These poems, they were mostly like poems, but they were like soulless—you could feel it. They kind of landed like poems. They were like the worst workshop poems of all time. They were like a thousand people had gone to Iowa and all learned to write the same poem. There was something hideous about it. I feel like it's wrong to be against anything

---

3. *I Am Code: An Artificial Intelligence Speaks*, a 2023 book of poetry written by an AI model called code-davinci-002, a predecessor to ChatGPT, that was edited by Brent Katz, Josh Morgenthau, and Simon Rich.

utterly, because it's something about our time, and somehow we have to know it and meet it. But it also is a piece of shit.

BLVR: Moving away from AI, I wanted to share a few questions that people I know wanted me to ask you. One of my students, a nonfiction writer who recently started writing poetry, says they found themselves experiencing a lot of shame around the act of writing poems. They compared it to when they first started expressing their gender identity, this feeling of apology. They wanted to ask how you learned to hold shame and forgive it while also asserting these vulnerable parts of you.

EM: I just think it's repetition. It's like anything. It's really similar to how you know if a poem is good. You know because you've just been there and you've been repeating and repeating. For some reason lately I'm freaky on repetition as a value. Because everything that's good, you've done it again and again and again and it becomes your friend and it becomes your turf and it becomes your nest and then it's just the right place to be and the right way to be.

It's weird how people come to you, and you can't be seen until you're visible. The very fact of repetition makes you comfortable with yourself but then others see this motion and they recognize you and they come up and suddenly you're in conversation and it's so remarkable. But that can't happen until you begin to know yourself and keep doing the same thing.

And also anything worth doing is worth doing badly. You know? It's sort of like lower your standards and raise your productivity. I mean, there's talented writers who produce very little and fix it, fix it, fix it. But I personally am the kind of writer that writes a lot. I write a lot of crap, and then a certain amount of it I know is good.

You kind of make your own nest, that's the thing.

BLVR: Someone else, a writer friend, was curious how you think about sustaining a real life, pragmatically, through your work.

EM: Well, I mean, there's a lot of ways of being a writer. People love the story of William Carlos Williams, who was a doctor and a poet. And one can take that route, it's very real. I think in a way, anything you're interested in that's not writing is a great thing to follow. Because writing is always like this spillover or sweat of the reality of your life. Your life doesn't have to be "I am a poet." Though it was that for me, because I was very indecisive as a young person. And I really wanted to know what I was going to do. It was very important to figure that out. And I kept changing my mind about what I was going to do, even when I was thinking that I wanted to be a writer. And when I suddenly realized that poetry could be what I did, I just had this amazing feeling of liberation, and I decided to follow that path and see where it took me.

There is a Kierkegaard book called *Purity of Heart Is to Will One Thing*. And he has this thing in it that's like a mantra. And I thought, Well, if I just want to be a poet, then I can be a poet. I'll just only want that. I won't want anything else. But it didn't have to be that hard. You know, there's no reason why anybody should be broke and suffering as a writer, though I was, and lots of my friends are.

It's just: the more space you make around the writer, the writing, the better it is. Artists waste time in the studio and that seems important. Like it's dreamtime and so you want dreamtime. Dreamtime is expensive, technically. The easiest way to have a lot of dreamtime is to be poor, because nobody cares how you're spending your time.

But again, you still have got to pay rent. So I don't know. There's no real answer.

I will say, my generation was different too. I feel almost apologetic for how easy it was for us, because rents were cheap. We all lived alone like little monks in our little cheap apartments. And when you can get a job, you get another job.

But now a young writer can be really rewarded. That wasn't true when I was a young writer. So it's sort of like, in a weird way, that game has changed.

I once heard a professor say, "Not all of you will become writers." I thought, Why not? Why can't everybody become a writer? It doesn't mean that that has to be your only life. In many cultures, being a poet was just part of being a cultured person. You know, this ambassador would write an occasional poem, this lawyer writes poems.

So I think there's no one way to do it. I think that's just the truest thing. You don't have to suffer. But maybe you do. I don't know. It really depends on who

you are. Into my forties, I was pretty broke. But I liked what I did. So it's just like you make up your own life. I remember being interviewed for a teaching job. And the person interviewing me said, "Well, what would you do with a student who you really thought should stop writing?"

What a weird question, right? But I also thought, you know, most people stop. Most people stop. It's just like everything else—you do it for a while and then you do something else. But if you love writing, there's no reason to ever stop and to not be a writer. And I feel like it's absolutely true that everybody can be a writer. And then it's like what kind of career will you have? Do you need to be known? Do you need to be well-known? How well-known do you need to be? Do you need to make all your income from writing? You know, there's so many questions in response to your question.

IV. "THIS FEELING OF WRONGNESS"

BLVR: I was wondering if you could speak to repetitions of certain images in your work. Dogs, for instance, or rats and mice, or house and home.

EM: Well, I mean, you make poems out of the world you live in. I feel like there is a thing where you're litanizing. You're just kind of copying. I mean, it really is a devotional thing. You're just kind of saying what's there. You're saying what's in the world, and it's kind of a chant. But the thing is, you don't know where it's going, and that's what's really great. You're just kind of counting, you're kind of just saying what the universe is, and then at some point, it kind of goes out of control, and it's not you anymore. You're lying in bed and you get a line, you're like, Ugh. You turn on the light and you write a little line and you turn the light up and back and then you get a line and you're like, Ugh. And then suddenly it's a long, crazy poem. And it's like, why is this? You have no choice. And other times you're feeling very grand, you have something to say, and it's like a three-line poem. Because it's ahead of you, because you're really talking about getting practiced at the unconscious. I feel like it's just like divination—tarot, astrology, throwing coins, or writing in a journal every day. It just becomes this thing where that's where you return, and that's where your consciousness winds up being. And it knows more than you do. But you know that.

BLVR: In your work sometimes you'll come to this idea of comfort and discomfort and how that tension can generate work. Could you talk about that, discomfort and its relationship to writing?

EM: I mean, I guess this is a question always of writing: Am I the wrong person doing this?

When I first started writing I was like, Do I have permission to be that? In college, I felt like other people would walk into the workshop and they would read these crappy poems and they seemed to feel great. And I was like, I'm not sure I have the right to be a poet. I felt like somebody needed to say, *You, Eileen, are a poet*. And nobody had said that. And so I thought, How would I know?

And I wrote stories for the workshop so that I wouldn't have to read my poems, because I thought they were so wrong. I'd slide them under the professor's door. And so I feel like I always had this feeling of wrongness, which is part of what I work with. I think it's like, whatever you've got is your studio. It was all these things: being of the wrong class, being of the wrong gender, being of the wrong sexuality.

When I got to college, literature was so exciting. In Catholic school, we didn't have *discussions*. I went nuts at the prospect of discourse. It was like: *These people make their living talking about books?* It seemed like the most incredible thing. But then at a certain point, I realized there were people who wrote the books and they seemed like the really cool ones.

And then I thought, I think I want to transfer to *that* column. You know? But again, it was like: Who was I to make this choice? And so I think we all go through these periods of apprenticeship, not with anybody in particular necessarily, but with the world, trying to find your way of doing it.

BLVR: I like that. These ideas of permission or of needing to find it.

EM: I always think of a writer who died in the last few years, Lewis Warsh, a poet. He said this great thing on a panel: "Reading was how I discovered that other people were thinking."

BLVR: It's like that famous line from James Baldwin: "You think your pain and your heartbreak are unprecedented in the history of the world, but then you read." Or that great idea from Virginia Woolf: "Books continue each other." Which, naturally enough, another writer—Lynne Tillman—told me some years ago. I'm curious: Are there certain books that you feel you're trying to continue?

EM: I mean, I love to read. I could be happy just sitting on my couch reading all day for the rest of my life. Every day it's sort of like an effort to stop reading and do something because it's just so addictive. It's like thrifting: you put on all the shirts in the thrift store and one that used to be somebody else's looks really great on you and you're like, OK.

And writing is like that. You're imitating styles and adapting them and adopting them and some of them become yours. I feel like we're always picking up reflections of other writers and respooling them and making them more Frankensteins. We're all made up of little bits and pieces of everything we've ever read. ✱

BESTSELLERS THAT WERE REJECTED MULTIPLE TIMES BEFORE FINALLY BEING PUBLISHED

✱ *Harry Potter and the Philosopher's Stone* by J. K. Rowling, 12 rejections
✱ *Zen and the Art of Motorcycle Maintenance* by Robert M. Pirsig, 121 rejections
✱ *A Time to Kill* by John Grisham, 28 rejections
✱ *The Help* by Kathryn Stockett, 60 rejections
✱ *Gone with the Wind* by Margaret Mitchell, 38 rejections
✱ *A Wrinkle in Time* by Madeleine L'Engle, 26 rejections
✱ *Dune* by Frank Herbert, 23 rejections
✱ *The Diary of a Young Girl* by Anne Frank, 16 rejections
✱ *Lord of the Flies* by William Golding, 22 rejections
✱ *The Time Traveler's Wife* by Audrey Niffenegger, 25 rejections
✱ *MASH* by Richard Hooker, 21 rejections
✱ *Still Alice* by Lisa Genova, 100 rejections

—*list compiled by Natalia Borecka*

How the Wakasa stone, a memorial to a Japanese man murdered in an internment camp in Topaz, Utah, became the flash point of a bitter modern dispute

THE RECOLLECTOR

by

PABLO CALVI

OPENING ILLUSTRATION BY:
Kristian Hammerstad

PHOTOGRAPHS THROUGHOUT BY:
The author

I.

The CAT 236D Skid Steer Loader is a muscular machine no larger than a compact Italian car. On a good day, with decent balance and a forklift, its arms—which shoot from the back like the tail of a yellow scorpion—can lift the equivalent of a full-grown American buffalo. Its diesel engine starts wheezing and whirring as soon as it's turned on; it is operated by two levers from inside a single-occupancy cage. The 236 can spin on its own axis with a torque of 195 pounds per square foot, on four fat wheels that crunch and grind on gravel, while its hydraulic components pump, clutch, hiss, and twirl in a rumbling symphony of mechanical flow.

The loader can dance on rubble. But, like everything in life, instruments are only as good as their conductors. That is precisely why it was important for Jane Beckwith to find the right operator for the task. Someone she trusted, who was not only skillful but earnest. Able to feel in their bones the precision and tenderness that the job required.

A few years back, she had witnessed a man on his Bobcat single-handedly tearing down what was left after the Mercer Building fire, the ashen remains of an entire historical corner on Main Street. It all went up in flames one night, a total loss two blocks away from her museum, right next to Top's City Café. In a 3,500-person town like Delta, Utah, where hardly anything happens, the blaze was all anyone talked about for weeks. Beckwith knew the father of the man who cleaned up the mess. She knew the man himself. He might have been one of her students before she retired, in 2009, from her job as a high school teacher. He certainly didn't look like the type who would visit the Japanese internment camp exhibit. And she hadn't seen him around recently. But that day he was kind, caring, and worked so gently, and with such diligence and respect for the burned history of their town, that after a few months she hired him to deal with Block 42 at Topaz.

That was a gnarly slice of a job. Yet once again, the man did what he'd promised, and left the plot neat and groomed. He even brought his little boys to sweep up the crumbling foundations of the mess hall, which was, as Beckwith put it, totally unnecessary.

Small-time riflemen, back-patio militias, and drunken hunters had always pestered this side of the desert, wilding out on dirt bikes and quad-ricycles, beaming their headlamps, and shooting at anything that could not fend for itself—maiming game, blasting bottles—and dashing back into the dust.

In 2002, the artist Ted Nagata, a former Topaz internee, had to redesign the camp's memorial plaque after a Clint Eastwood wannabe riddled it with bullet holes. "We want one that doesn't stand out in a crowd and ask to be shot at," Nagata said then, laughing it off. But during COVID lockdown, things got out of hand. People went crazy. Shooting at tin cans and road signs didn't do the trick anymore. Now they were stashing guns, ammo, and canned beef in basements. And if you paid attention at night, you could hear them blowing up boulders with Tannerite.

So when researcher Nancy Ukai found the map with directions to the stone in the National Archives, and, soon after, archaeologists Jeff Burton and Mary Farrell confirmed its location and published its exact coordinates on their open website, Beckwith finally made up her mind. The memorial had to be moved. And she knew just the guy to do it.

It is midafternoon in the August desert. We have been treading on dirt, leaping over bushes and rocks, hoping to reach the block where Arlene Tatsuno's home once stood. Her birthplace.

"Where exactly was your bedroom?" I wonder aloud. Arlene smiles and defers in a whisper; a short shadow follows her as she walks: "You have to ask her." And then, on cue, Jane Beckwith sinks her nose into a map she's

This story was supported in part by the Literary Journalism program at the Banff Centre for Arts and Creativity, in Alberta, Canada.

been waving in the wind and turns east to face an indiscernible spot in the scattered brush.

"I think you lived in Block 41, Barrack 6… but I could be wrong."

The Central Utah Final Accountability Report will prove Beckwith right. But here, now, there's only desert, fine dirt and greasewood baking under the dry beams of the sun.

Between 1942 and 1945, the view in every direction must have seemed infinite to a child. Wooden structures packed tight and stacked straight. A house of mirrors, a maze of undifferentiated continuity made of 504 identical pinewood, gable-roofed barracks perfectly aligned on a grid, walls covered in tar paper, and a snarl of mountains on the horizon.

The Japanese internment camp at Topaz was made of forty-two blocks, divided into four sections by two main avenues that met in an open plaza, all of it locked in by a perimeter of seven concrete guard towers. (A haunting imprint of the camp can still be seen on Google Earth, at coordinates 39°24'39"N and −112°46'24"W.) Below the barracks and the roads, underneath the alkali soil, hid a full prehistoric world. Topaz was set on the desiccated bed of Lake Bonneville, the largest continental body of water in the Pleistocene, an inland ocean brimming with sea creatures, whose layered fossilized shells would often bubble up in the mud after a strong summer storm. It was these shells that children like Arlene's brother, Rod, busied themselves with during school breaks, bringing them to art class to turn them into toys, figurines, and the ghostly flowers that now overwhelm the vitrines of the Topaz Museum in Delta, Utah.

From afar, Arlene; her husband, Gene, an ex-Navy Seal and a hunter, big as a polar bear; and Jane Beckwith, our guide and the founder and director of the Topaz Museum, look adrift in this openness. Topaz took a year to build, and just six months to become the fifth-largest town in the entire state of Utah at the time. It was also the second least populated of the ten Japanese internment camps during World War II. Today, we are alone here.

Hundreds of yards away, a four-foot-high barbed-wire fence stands against the wind. That is all that's visibly left of the internment era, the only sign that a city built to imprison Americans with more than one-sixteenth Japanese blood did in fact exist in Utah.

Arlene tells me she was born in a room at the Topaz hospital, on the northern side of camp. This was, I later learned, an upgrade for her family: Rod had been born two years earlier in a stall at the Tanforan Racetrack, a temporary detention center set up by the government to hold displaced Japanese people in the Bay Area until Topaz was built. Arlene, they joke, is GI: government issue.

"It is over there." Beckwith waves toward the north, map still in hand, pointing at a spot past a huge vertical rock where a gray pronghorn antelope has just bounded away over a patch of scattered debris and concrete platforms.

On our walk toward what's left of the hospital, I follow Arlene's sneakers as she steps gingerly on the dirt of her first home. She wears her gray hair long, tied back with a brown oval clip, and a pair of wolf earrings that kiss her neck; her black capri pants accent a frame that is both light and strong. Arlene is eighty but looks barely sixty and holds on to Gene's hand like a girl at a matinee.

Between 200 and 250 Japanese and Japanese Americans lived in each block; the camp housed around eight thousand prisoners at any given time, Jane Beckwith explains, as she has for over thirty years, to visitors, to writers, and to the heirs of this story. Each barrack was divided into six rooms of different sizes, and families would take one, maybe two of the spaces, depending on the number of people and their needs. Every block had its own mess hall, latrine, showers, and laundry. Trees were transplanted from the edge of the desert and force-fed to grow. There were communal gardens, stores, churches, libraries, schools, and a post office, baseball teams and a baseball diamond, a theater and a dance company. During the three years when Topaz was open, some people passed away, some were killed, and others, like Arlene, were born.

Today you'd never know there used to be a town here, just by seeing the site from the road. As soon as World War II ended, the same government officials who put up the ten camps made sure that any trace of their existence was erased. They leveled the homes, uprooted the trees. Much has vanished in eighty years, but a lot more would have been lost had it not been for the museum Beckwith founded in 1983, Arlene tells me.

As we walk, Beckwith points at a gray storm cloud lingering over the mountains in the east. There, she says, you can still stumble upon the concrete pylons of the guard towers, iron rods rising from the ground like tulips, pipes and tin stove vents, and scraps of family lives twice uprooted: nails, crooked forks, glass shards, home-cobbled jewelry, and broken children's toys made of prehistoric seashells.

It is hot, so every few minutes we pause to catch our breath. During one of these breaks, Beckwith peels her COVID mask off, and for the first time I see her bare face. Her green eyes are charged with sunlight, locked on a point beyond the horizon. Her skin is paper, and her mouth a thin line of ink. But a lump the size of a golf ball mars her right cheek. And when she sees me staring, she swiftly puts her sunglasses on. "It's just inflammation, an allergy, nothing serious," she says dismissively. Back in Delta, a docent at the Topaz Museum will tell me that it's all the stress about the Wakasa feud.

Beckwith is in her mid-seventies. She is tall and assertive. Several times in the year that followed, I went back to my first question to her: Why she did it. Why did she unearth the Wakasa stone?

"People like this controversy, and I'm really sorry, because what I like is the museum," she snapped at me one of those times. It was at the end of a long conversation, after a long, cold week.

That day at the Topaz site, however, she simply says it is all very complicated, that it has been horrible for her. People don't understand. It would have been dangerous to leave the stone there in plain sight, where it could be vandalized. After all, it was Burton and

The Topaz Museum is located at 55 West Main Street in Delta, Utah.

Farrell who had published the coordinates of the memorial online, for anyone to see, in the middle of a brutal wave of Asian hate.

When we start heading back to our cars, I ask Beckwith where it is. If I can check the place out. "It's over there." She points to the west, at an area inaccessible by road. And it is clear to me now that somewhere in that direction is the spot where James Wakasa was shot dead in the spring of 1943; the place where a group of Issei, first-generation Japanese immigrants, emplaced a memorial stone in his honor; the place where they had to hide it, and from which, eighty years later, Beckwith would have it removed.

The sun is setting, and we still have eight hours of driving ahead of us, so we decide to keep going. "But I will come back," I promise Beckwith, who now looks at me askance.

As we drive away, the smell of raindrops tapping on greasewood wafts in through the open window. I slow down to try to spot the place of the unburied

memorial, but everything looks the same in the desert.

The storm finally catches up to us after we pass Delta, and by the time we reach the mountains, the landscape has split in two: to the left, the vertical gray of the rain sweeping over the valley; and to the right, a clean blue sky fluted on the horizon by the last traces of light beaming through the golden peaks of Utah.

On the stage of the Salt Lake Buddhist Temple, Nancy Ukai has started talking about her latest visit to Japan in search of information about James Wakasa's past, and for the first ten minutes her words are dampened by the clinking of cutlery and voices coming from the kitchen. Ukai keeps her arms pressed tight to her body, like the wings of a small bird. Her green bomber jacket is patched with orange and lilac flowers. She holds the microphone close to her chin, alternately turning to the screen behind her, and the audience as she speaks about a sequence of photos. Her voice becomes reedy as she tells the audience that she visited Keio University, where Wakasa studied, but that there were no records of him there. She then went to Ishikawa Prefecture, where Wakasa was born. She was welcomed by local officials, who found no records of him there either. There were no records of Wakasa in the town registry or at the elementary school where he studied. No IDs, no report cards.

But then her team found Wakasa's name in the manifest of a ship that sailed from Yokohama, Japan, to Australia in 1901. "He was a waiter," she yelps, and suddenly there is only silence in the auditorium. "It turns out, if you work on a ship, you don't need a passport," she reveals. That one possibility, that James Wakasa had been a waiter on a ship, might explain the lack of physical records of him entering the United States.

Back in Delta, I had heard the name Nancy Ukai spoken in whispers. I knew she was the driving force behind the Wakasa Memorial Committee (WMC), which formed in 2021 in response to Beckwith's unearthing of the Wakasa memorial, the last straw in what a part of the camp survivors' community considered a long list of faux pas. That year, members of the WMC began waging a ruthless social-media war against Beckwith, a few of them intent on removing her from the helm of the Topaz Museum. The leadership of the WMC voiced its outrage and disapproval at raucous community meetings, rattling Beckwith's nerves and causing her histamine lump. Ukai blamed her for dividing the Japanese American community. Others accused

her of being self-serving, controlling, and, as a white woman, disconnected from the sensibilities of Japanese Americans and the cultural nuances of internment history.

The controversy around the stone was only the latest in almost a decade of tensions between Ukai and Beckwith. The two women started butting heads the day they met, in San Francisco in 2013, when Beckwith was campaigning for funds to produce the first narratives for the new Topaz Museum exhibits. Back then, Ukai told Beckwith that she wanted to help by reviewing those narratives. Over the coming months, Beckwith shared her texts with Ukai, who found them offensive, inaccurate, and heavily whitewashed. Without Beckwith knowing, Ukai contacted the exhibit's founders, which put the museum's opening in jeopardy.

In an interview with a Japanese newspaper, *The Asahi Shimbun*, Ukai credited the "curt description of the death of Wakasa" that Jane Beckwith wrote in 2013 as the affront that sent her on a quest to the National Archives in Washington, DC, to find the real story of the life and death of James Wakasa. Ironically, it also set in motion the chain of events that would lead to the excavation of the stone. At the National Archives in 2020, Ukai found the map drawn by George Shimamoto detailing the coordinates where the Wakasa monument had been buried in 1943. After Ukai published a photo of the map on her website, *50 Objects*, Burton and Farrell drove from Manzanar, California, to Delta, to physically locate the memorial for the first time in eighty years. And they found it.

A few months later, between June and July 2021, they published in five installments a detailed account of their journey for *Discover Nikkei*. Their post included the Shimamoto map, a narrative with full details of the necessary corrections to the map's coordinates that led to the exact place where the memorial remained buried, and four photos, including the surrounding of the burial site, and the visible top of the stone, which they marked on their GPS. Sixteen days after Burton and Farrell's fifth installment, Beckwith unearthed the stone.

The gathering at the Buddhist temple is the latest development in a saga that has come to dominate Ukai's life. For over a decade now, Ukai has been a fixture in the dialogue surrounding Topaz and Wakasa, but this was not always the case.

Born in Berkeley, California, Nancy Ukai graduated from the University of California, Santa Cruz, in 1976 with a double major in anthropology and East Asian studies. After college, she lived in Japan for fourteen years, and worked for *Newsweek*'s Tokyo bureau.

"She was an excellent reporter and researcher," Frank Gibney told me in an email exchange. Gibney was *Newsweek*'s acting Tokyo bureau chief between June 1983 and January 1984.

In the '90s, back in the United States, Ukai finished a master's degree in education and published several academic articles on Japanese culture, education, and child-rearing. In the early 2000s she became the president of the board of trustees of the Princeton Public Library, in New Jersey, and in 2008, she completed a second master's degree in media anthropology from the School of Oriental and African Studies in London.

"She was one of the most creative people I know. She was intellectually curious about many, many things," Leslie Burger, the former director of the library, said during a phone conversation. "She is cause-driven and has a ton of energy."

Burger also described Ukai as an excellent fundraiser, who led at least three successful campaigns totaling over twenty million dollars.

"I don't think she was involved with internment [activism] at the time, but if she was, she didn't talk to me about it," Burger remembered. "I think that back then her mother was ill, and her attention was focused on that."

Umiko, Ukai's mother, a renowned jeweler and co-owner with her husband of a grocery store in the Bay Area, passed away in 2003, and it was around that time that Ukai left Princeton and the library, and she and her family relocated to California.

During our conversation, Ukai acknowledged that it was not until the summer of 2013 that she began to collect her family's internment memories. She said that the more contentious aspects of her opposition to Beckwith date back to those days, and so does the disagreement over the narratives of the exhibit.

"The museum was basically Beckwith's narrative, and it disregarded professionals, because there were no historians, and it disregarded community members, because they weren't involved," Ukai told me. "Now the truth must come out because this is part of a pattern. And the pattern is white ownership of our story, our artifacts, and their interpretation."

One of the things that intrigued me most about Ukai was the reason for her late connection to Topaz history. Why had she avoided it for so long. Avoidance, I later learned, is rather common for internees and their descendants. In fact, there is a substantial bibliography that connects it to the trauma of Japanese Americans.

In the extensive list of papers about internment trauma, there is a compelling study published in 2019. The article is based on a survey of around four hundred Nisei, the US-born children of the Issei. Its authors—Donna Nagata, Jacqueline Kim, and Kaidi Wu—endeavored to find out if former internees talked about their experiences, and if they did, how much they said. The paper reveals that most of their subjects avoided talking about that time in their lives. And they had detached themselves from their recollections so much that those memories remained in their minds only as a form of posttraumatic stress.

"[More] than 12% [of Nisei] never spoke with their Issei parents about the camps," the study reported, "50% spoke less than four times, and 70% of those who had any discussions conversed less

than 15 minutes." This social amnesia, paired with a sense of having been betrayed by their own country, fostered a feeling among camp survivors of equal parts resentment and guilt. "Rather than directing blame outward toward the government, many Japanese Americans tended toward self-blame: that they somehow should have been 'more American,'" the authors concluded.

Amid all these erasures, Ukai told me, one memory kept sparking in her mind like a live wire. It was a vision of her mother sitting at the dinner table, driven mad by the mention of a man named James Wakasa. "They didn't have to kill him. He was deaf!" Nancy remembered Umiko screaming, her face red as an ember. Ukai credits that moment as her introduction to Topaz.

"My big regret is that I didn't talk to [my mother] more, because she… it's not that she didn't want to remember. It's just that we didn't ask her."

On July 27, 2021, Jane Beckwith woke up early, skipped breakfast, walked down to the garage, and dumped two long-handled shovels, a large cardboard box, and a thick blue blanket into the open bed of her 2001 Ford Ranger. The items lay loose near the plastic bucket she always carried to pick up random garbage—burger wrappers and sun-frayed McDonald's soda cups—that ATV warriors scatter across the Topaz site.

It was warm, sunny, and still when she reached the southwest side of camp. A dust tail caught up with her as soon as she parked facing the F-350. Across the road, a gray Honda SUV sat empty, and a few feet back the CAT 236D Skid Steer Loader, just unloaded from the trailer, had started to growl from behind the barbed-wire fence. A DSLR video camera had been set up on a tripod to record the whole excavation. Other than Beckwith and three men—the forklift operator, a museum board member, and a delegate from the State Historic Preservation Office—no one was in sight.

The shadows were casting long and westward when the shoveling began. They first carved a perimeter on the ground, one foot removed from the burial site, leaving enough space to ensure that no damage would be caused to the stone during the dig. The soil, which the US Department of Agriculture classifies as strongly saline, poorly drained Abbott silty clay, was dry, very fine, and loosely set. The more they dug, the dustier it got, and past one foot deep, the contours they had edged around the stone started caving in and crumbling back against it.

Soon they had all pulled on their working gloves, gotten down on their knees, and begun to scoop out handfuls of dirt and tiny pebbles from the hole. It was almost like praying. A sense of calm assuaged Beckwith's heart as she bent and dragged. She touched the stone with her right hand, but nobody who witnessed the scene would have said the gesture was remotely spiritual. A good Utahan, Beckwith was raised Mormon, but little if any of that faith was still left in her. In fact, her joy that day was earthy and simple, operational. Soil trickled through her fingers like cornmeal. They all laughed, and coughed, and talked as they toiled: maybe about the Pioneer Days Parade

in Hinckley; maybe about children, or work, or money. It kept getting warmer, and the more they dug, the more they sweated.

When the area was half cleared, they stopped digging, stood up on the berm, and looked down into the hole. There, flat and heavy, was a gray boulder the size of a baby hippo, five feet long, three feet wide, and two feet tall. Underneath one edge there was enough space carved to slide in a yellow nylon ratchet strap. They didn't want a chain to touch the stone, to scratch it or mark it in any way.

After tying up the boulder and binding the straps to the CAT's forks, which now bridged the barbed-wire fence like a horse feeding on hay, the operator hopped into the cab and got the engine started. The machine whirled and rumbled. And suddenly its black mechanical arms rose, reaching up to the metal gods in the sky. The chain pulling the straps sang like a guitar string; it tugged and twanged; and the CAT tipped, bucked, and cranked, and for a few seconds, as it adjusted to the new burden, its back wheels hung clear in the air.

An audible gasp cut through the desert like a dart, and immediately the operator knew the load was teetering at the limit of what the CAT 236D could safely carry. Swiftly he put the rock back down and adjusted the CAT's angle. And then the hissing of the pumps, and the pulling and the dragging, was all anyone could hear for a while.

Safely out of the hole, the stone was moved under the fence, eased flat onto a pallet, and lifted onto the back of the trailer. And when the midday light

started to come down crisp from above, shining vertical on the boulder, Beckwith was finally at ease.

They drove out past noon, leaving behind an open ditch with a cluster of concrete and cobalt stone debris piled up neatly on one side. Among the remnants was a colorless shard of glass, and a piece from a bottle base embossed with a mark from the Hazel-Atlas Glass Company, which was established in 1902 and operated in Wheeling, West Virginia, until 1964.

Jane Beckwith led the caravan sixteen miles back to Delta. They were on their way to the museum, where this memorial, erected in love and buried in anger eighty years earlier, could finally rest. She could talk to Ukai tomorrow. It was after lunch. She was starting to get hungry, and she didn't even remember what she'd had for breakfast.

It would be easy to argue that without the arrival of the Intermountain Power Plant in 1981, there wouldn't be a Topaz Museum in Delta today. For nearly forty years, between the time when the Topaz relocation camp was razed and the coal plant appeared, Delta had remained a quiet, mostly agricultural town, subject to the whims of the desert and the Sevier River. Except for occasional family pilgrimages, there had been no concerted effort to remember what had taken place there during the war. In fact, by virtue of government design, most of that history had been erased, something the new power plant would soon change.

When the Intermountain Power Project was green-lighted, Delta woke up. Trucks started crisscrossing

A figurine crafted from seashells, snail shells, and black wire by one of the internees, on display in the Topaz Museum.

understanding the Topaz internment camp, the stories that took place there, and how the camp had shaped the lives of Japanese Americans and Deltans. The project was important, national, exciting. Topaz was just fifteen miles west of town, so her students had the perfect opportunity to cover it in depth and embark on a discovery journey that could change their lives.

They named their newspaper the *MoDel*—for *Model Delta*—and started working on it right away. Beckwith filled the blackboard in chalk: there were leads, names, and phone numbers of the locals she knew who were connected to the Topaz camp. Her most promising senior, Wendy Lowery, who had a personal link to Topaz, would become *MoDel*'s editor in chief.

"When he came back from the war, my father worked at Topaz as a firefighter, and he and my mother lived out there for a little while," Lowery told me during a conversation over Zoom. The house she grew up in, the one her father bought from the military when Topaz was taken down, was an officers' barrack. "Even as a little kid, I knew what Topaz was."

Lowery now has silver hair. She is stern yet soulful, and can be very funny but never laughs at her own jokes. Nor does she answer a question without first pausing to reflect.

The first time she met or spoke to a Japanese American internee in person was in 2022, the day she went into the Topaz Museum and saw the restored barracks. The doorknobs looked exactly like the ones in her childhood bedroom. (The construction was so bad, she remembered, that once, when she burped in the dining

the town, their doors branded with the red, green, and blue logos of construction companies from Texas, California, and Sweden; corporate agents booked hotels, diners, and restaurants to full capacity; engineers, white- and blue-collar technicians, and workers from all corners of the world began moving in, and with them came their families. Main Street saw its first traffic light, and the modern housing projects for the newcomers in hard plastic helmets and utility boots inoculated

the desert with a thriving international vibe.

"Delta High School changed immeasurably due to all that," Jane Beckwith remembers. "Instead of ten kids in my class, I now had two sections of about thirty-six."

In 1982, Beckwith was teaching a journalism course for high school seniors. And rather than making a yearbook, she decided, her students would undertake something different, more meaningful: a newspaper dedicated to room, the windows rattled, and everyone in her family laughed.)

Occasionally, while reporting for the *MoDel*, a few of the kids would venture out into the desert around the Topaz site to conduct fieldwork, which might eventually turn into treasure hunting. If they found anything lying around and brought it back to Delta, they always let their teacher know. "Anything we picked up," Lowery reasoned, "we would have shown to Jane, and she would have put it in a box."

That box was how the Topaz Museum got started: organically, unintentionally. A trunk in Jane Beckwith's home.

A few years after the class of 1983 graduated, Beckwith rented a small space at 45 West Main Street, inside the Great Basin Museum. For the next decade, in addition to teaching, she maintained and preserved what would be the first Topaz exhibit: a glass vitrine in the corner of one room. The first pieces on display included a twelve-inch-long white lace crochet doily, a pair of geta (Japanese wooden sandals), a chair, and some decorative household items. She started engaging with former internees and their families, who found out about the Topaz exhibit from waitstaff at their hotels or during dinner. As word spread, the visitors multiplied, and Delta became a pilgrimage destination.

"When people started coming to Delta, they would call me and say, 'I'm here, would you like to meet?' And we would chat and go out to visit the site together," Beckwith recalled. "Some of the Issei started teaching me how to read this site, because it was difficult to know exactly what was out there

without having somebody explain it to me."

At the Great Basin exhibit, Beckwith soon had to make room for a wave of new donations, which arrived with the scores of visiting families and former internees who had rummaged through their attics for relics and mementos to bring to Delta.

But the internees were not the only ones adding to the collection. In 1991, a local Delta family donated a pinewood-and-tar-paper barrack, one of the original structures at Topaz, that they had lifted and relocated to town for use as a storage shed. The donation prompted the first gathering of an ad hoc Topaz Museum board, with Beckwith at the helm. Its mission: to restore the structure to how it looked in the 1940s, to fund the creation of a permanent museum, and to preserve the 640 acres of the Topaz site.

T he main challenge for Beckwith and the Topaz Museum board was how to convey the range of emotions and memories resulting from a violent internment past; how to evoke not just the horrors but also the intertwined resistance through the lens of a museum exhibit.

There is a lineage of anthropologists who explore memory-building at the seam lines of conflict. In 2002, Lynn Meskell coined the term *negative heritage* to explain remembrance as the result of the cacophony of conflicting recollections and perspectives. Such a chorus of atonal tensions, Meskell believes, can be brought together around tangible everyday objects. In cases of local history, when there has been no formal effort to memorialize

the past, whatever traces of material and place are left can become a node around which historical dissonance—with its conflicting claims of ownership, legitimacy, and authenticity—can reveal its multiple meanings.

After 1991, the museum board embarked on a journey to highlight these kinds of objects with even more fervor. There were fundraising efforts to purchase the land where the camp once stood, and to build a proper Topaz Museum: an eight-thousand-square-foot building in Delta that would memorialize and honor the survivors, while showcasing the way they were forced to live, what they did at Topaz, and the history of how they pulled through.

Life in camp was difficult. Temperatures ranged from below zero in the winter to above one hundred in the summer. Entire families who were removed from the Bay Area by train were driven in open trucks over the fifteen miles from Delta to Topaz. Men and boys in suits, women and girls in their Sunday best, caked in sweat by the sun and the bleakness of the desert dust. At Topaz, thousands of people struggled to adapt to life away from their homes, their farms, their schools, and the businesses the government had forced them to leave with a week's notice. They left behind $200 million in property, 250,000 acres of farming land, and 20,000 cars.

There were long lines for bathrooms and dining halls (the only spaces with running water). The military shouted orders through loudspeakers. All prisoners had to follow the same ironclad routines and received the same pay depending on the activity: fourteen dollars a month for manual laborers, and nineteen dollars a month for professionals, including doctors. Internees worked at a pig farm, a chicken farm, a tofu factory, and a beet cannery, while sentinels posted in each of the seven towers pointed their barrels at them. The white potbellied stoves, one per room, could not keep the barracks interiors warm in the winter. And in the summer, even with the windows closed, nothing prevented the Sevier wind from blowing through the gaps in the walls, leaving a thick coat of dirt on everything: windowsills, linens, eyeglasses, faces. Apart from two sets of bunks, and the light of a single electric bulb, the barracks were empty, and smelled like dust, sun-heated tar paper, and burned wood. Each family was responsible for making their own furniture out of scrap lumber: tables and chairs, armoires, and benches were built in the desert, and most of those items were left behind when the camp was vacated.

It was also broadly acknowledged by survivors that the children's experiences were significantly different from their parents'. Adults in the camp tacitly agreed to keep their anxieties to themselves and spare their kids. Rod Tatsuno remembers internment as mostly school, games, and fun. In fact, at Topaz, many of the Nisei made lifelong friends, and took music, theater, and art classes with some of the top Japanese American artists of the period. During their life in the desert, master landscape artist Chiura Obata and painter Miné Okubo offered twenty-three art workshops, including anatomy, flower arranging, and woodblock printing. A total of six

hundred internees from ages five to sixty-five took these lessons.

"[In the mid-'90s] a friend of mine, his wife, and I went to visit Topaz because I had not been there since I was born," Topaz survivor Hisashi "Bill" Sugaya says, speaking slowly into his webcam. He is in his eighties and wears a sleek black shirt and dark eyeglasses with a silver frame, the color of his hair. A breezy California accent sings in his voice.

"Jane showed us the campsite. There was not much at that time, just the small exhibit [that was] part of the Great Basin Museum." An urban planner, Sugaya contacted Beckwith as soon as he returned to California. His friends worked for the American Farmland Trust and were eager to help broker a deal to buy the first 400 of the 640 acres where the camp had once stood. "That was my first involvement in the museum, and then Jane asked me to be on the board." Sugaya has remained a board member ever since.

In those early years, Beckwith and the board had to learn how to write grants and deal with politicians, donors, and the state of Utah. On August 4, 2012, they broke ground at 55 West Main Street. The state-of-the-art, $2.3 million building would host an impressive collection: more than one thousand Topaz-made artifacts and their corresponding narratives, as well as over seventy charcoal drawings, and watercolor, ink wash, casein, and gouache paintings, all produced in Topaz between 1942 and 1945 by Miné Okubo and Chiura Obata, and other internee artists, including Hiroshima-born sumi-e painter Charles

Erabu (Suiko) Mikami and self-taught oil painter Yajiro Okamoto. There would be woodcrafts, furniture, garments, jewelry, photographs on display, and even a projection room. The space would become a central place for camp survivors, their heirs, and Delta residents to gather, reflect, remember, and try to understand all that took place during the internment years.

"The fact that we have purchased all of the site—that's incredible. It is incredible," Jane Beckwith told me as if, while looking back, she was still trying to convince herself that the Topaz Museum was more than a dream.

The museum would have been an impressive accomplishment in a large metropolis like Salt Lake City, let alone in a small desert town like Delta. Its gray-and-black concrete polygonal building takes up a quarter block, and stands out like an alien starship amid the frayed Victorian architecture. The museum is partitioned into five cubic halls, and the main entryway features a wall of massive floor-to-ceiling windows, whose light gradually dims as one moves deeper into the space.

Past the permanent exhibit, on the back patio, near the rock garden and the restored barrack, is where, in August 2022, I first saw the unearthed Wakasa stone. Kept under a metal shed to protect it from the elements, it looked unnatural, still belted with the yellow nylon ratchet strap that was used to drag it out of its secret burial place.

"For that stone to become equal to all the work we have done…" Beckwith paused. "I'm really offended by that. I'm sad about that."

I once asked Beckwith if she thought the controversy around the Wakasa memorial had undermined her legacy.

"My life's work? That is not my life's work!" Her dismissal was terse. What she did concede, however, was that forty years of work were now under what she believed to be unreasonable scrutiny.

But the reasons for all this attention were right there, in plain sight.

Months after our last talk, Beckwith sent me a copy of an email dated July 19, 2021, eight days before she dug out the stone. In the exchange, a group of Topaz descendants that included Nancy Ukai and the philanthropist Masako Takahashi discussed options for helping to pay for the unearthing of the monument before the end of the year. The looming possibility of the memorial being removed and taken who knows where, combined with the fact that its coordinates had now been published online, spurred Beckwith to action.

Only deeper inquiry would reveal all the anger her decisions unleashed.

II.

The two months that led up to the murder of James Hatsuaki Wakasa were riddled with tensions inside Topaz. On February 11, 1943, the Department of War rolled out a communiqué across the ten concentration camps on American soil, asking the internees three questions: Had they renounced their Japanese citizenship? Would they be willing to serve in combat on behalf of the United States? Would they give up their allegiance to the Japanese emperor?

Before his forced evacuation from the West Coast, Dave Tatsuno puts up a sign at his San Francisco store. His daughter, Arlene, born at the Topaz hospital, reopened Nichi Bei Bussan in San José, California.

Of course, most people in the camps resented the initiative. The Issei, barred from naturalizing because of their race, were now being prompted to give up their Japanese citizenship and become stateless. The Nisei had never sworn loyalty to the Japanese emperor to begin with, and signing the proclamation would have doubled as a coerced admission of guilt and a de facto military draft.

The "loyalty test," as it was soon known, divided the internees, as factions within the camp disagreed on how, or whether, to respond to the government. "The 'no-nos' refused to sign it," Arlene Tatsuno explained. "You had to say that you gave up any

Arlene Tatsuno was born in the Topaz camp in September, 1944. She first visited the new Topaz Museum in August of 2022.

allegiance to Japan. That was like asking [you] to sign a document promising that you would quit beating your wife. 'But I never beat her.' 'Well, but that's beside the point.'"

A large group, however, believed it was best not to rock the boat. "They were the 'yes-yes,'" Satsuki Ina, a psychotherapist, documentarian, and writer, explained. Ina was a baby during the internment years. "The [yes-yes] felt loyalty to the dominant authority, and of course, psychologically, this is like aligning with the perpetrator."

The government's strategy to balkanize the camps was laid bare in a recently declassified phone conversation between Lieutenant William Tracey, stationed in Topaz, and Colonel William Scobey, from the War Relocation Authority in DC. On February 15, 1943, Tracey told Scobey that by staggering the questionnaire vote block by block, he had successfully created a "machinery for registration" that would incite internees to coerce one another.

"If you get information against any man who is opposing your program and who is putting pressure on individuals," Scobey responded, the government will brandish the Espionage Act against them.

"My father gave a short speech [to the other internees] when he learned that Japanese American soldiers were going to be drafted to do military service," Ina remembered. "He made a five-sentence statement that said we should be treated as equal to the free people." After that, Ina's father was charged with sedition and imprisoned in Bismarck, North Dakota. A four-month-old baby in Camp Tule Lake, Ina was also designated an enemy alien by the US government.

In Topaz, debates around the questionnaire were carried on in poorly lit mess halls and at cold dining tables. *Topaz Times*, the internee-run newspaper, published letters arguing for and against compliance. Soon the discussions and the effects of the imprisonment took their toll and cleaved the community in half. Arguments broke out into physical violence.

Renowned artist Chiura Obata, at the time an art professor at the University of California at Berkeley and a yes-yes voter, was leaving the showers on April 4, 1943, when he was struck in the face with a lead pipe and almost lost an eye. Obata was taken to the Topaz hospital, where he remained for nineteen days before being transferred to Salt Lake City.

Alarmed by the violence, but ready to shield the government and avoid responsibility, Topaz director Charles Ernst addressed a letter to all camp residents:

> I am writing to tell you personally that in the past sixty days there have occurred in Topaz incidents which have given the Administration grave concern. I refer to the cowardly attacks on Professor Obata and the Rev. Mr. Taro Goto and certain blackmailing and threatening letters. Undoubtedly, you also have heard of these and have been equally concerned.

Ernst made no mention of Wakasa's death, which had occurred two months prior. The omission is telling: instead of creating divisiveness within the community, Wakasa's killing had been catalyzing the internees into a robust resistance movement.

There is a distance of three circular dining tables—with five diners each—and three rows of chairs between Nancy Ukai and Jane Beckwith. Like her neighbors, Beckwith is sitting in front of a black plastic bento box overwhelmed with rice, shrimp, and different tempuras. Ukai is onstage, two cameras pointing at her. One is recording the event for the Topaz Museum; the other, for NHK (Japan Broadcasting Corporation), is set up by a wall with framed illustrations and photos. Earlier, the dining hall of the Salt Lake Buddhist Temple had functioned as a basketball court. Tonight, over two hundred people, including museum directors, state officials, religious leaders, and members of the National Park Service, are here to commemorate the eightieth anniversary of the killing of James Wakasa. The hoop by the stage has been lifted to the ceiling. The electronic scoreboard is off: Visitors: 00; Home: 00.

Beckwith looks at the stage, her eyes wide and unmoving, and watches Ukai take command of an audience that includes all the key stakeholders in the Wakasa controversy. From where I'm sitting, I recognize a few faces, people I've met in Delta. Kay Yatabe, a medical doctor and an expert on post-traumatic response, is here. Patricia Wakida, the new director of the Topaz Museum board, is here too. I don't see Kimi Hill, Chiura Obata's granddaughter and a big Beckwith supporter, and wonder if her absence is meant to send a message.

The mood is of a tense détente. Likely not a single member of this audience is unaware of the fact that Nancy Ukai found the map that led to the Wakasa stone—perhaps the most important archaeological discovery in Japanese American history—and that Jane Beckwith is the person who dug it up and moved it off-site. Everyone seems aware of the occasion, its solemnity, and the effort that has gone into it. For several months now, a group known informally as the Three by Three by Three—three people from the Topaz Museum board, three from the Wakasa Memorial Committee, and three mediators from the National Park Service—have been preparing for the event. Tonight there's a healing ceremony taking place here at the temple; a second one will be held tomorrow in Topaz, at the exact spot where Wakasa was shot and killed. And at no time over the course of more than twenty-four hours will Beckwith or Ukai acknowledge, let alone talk to, each other.

A black-and-white painting by Chiura Obata, from his time at the Topaz hospital, shows the figure of a gaunt man doubled over, right leg stalling, arms projected forward and down, falling. He looks gutted. From the left of the frame, a small coyote-like dog with its ears pinned back runs up to him, the fear in its eyes rendered with two drops of ink. In the background is a wooden post from which sprout five straight lines of barbed wire. Behind, a few scattered bushes, the mountains, and a placid sky of slender horizontal clouds.

Obata's painting, titled *April 11th 1943, Hatsuki* [sic] *Wakasa, Shot by M.P.*, is based on collective accounts pieced together after Wakasa's death. It is the only visual record of James Hatsuaki Wakasa being shot. No photos were ever found of the incident, and the only direct-witness account comes from the court-martial testimony of Gerald Boone Philpott, the nineteen-year-old private first class who killed Wakasa.

If the court-martial documents are to be trusted—and there's good reason to doubt them—several guards had already seen Wakasa walking close to the fence that evening. A few minutes past 7 p.m., Wakasa had received a warning from Tower Post 9, ordering him to stay away from the perimeter, a directive he followed. But a half hour later, Philpott spotted him from

Tower Post 8, again close to the barbed wire. Philpott claimed that Wakasa was walking along the fence, looking straight at him. The guard swore that he screamed at Wakasa four times, but the man kept going. When he was 250 feet from Philpott's tower, Wakasa suddenly turned to his right and began climbing over the fence.

At 7:30 p.m., without aiming, from under his arm, Philpott took one shot at Wakasa with a Springfield 1903 thirty-caliber rifle. One shot, to just frighten the man and make him desist, he said. But the bullet hit Wakasa in the chest, piercing his heart and spine. Before the court martial, Philpott declared that he had never trained with that gun, and that it was his first time shooting it. He claimed he was not an expert marksman, and that it would have been very unlikely for him to be able to hit a target at such a distance, even if he had tried.

After the shot, Philpott says, he saw the man in the distance falling to his knees and then backward, three to four feet from the fence. There he remained, still, legs folded under his body.

When he heard the blast, Private Frank R. Baughman, the guard at Tower Post 9, telephoned Philpott. "Have you got in any trouble there?" he asked. Philpott told him what had just happened. Neither of them abandoned their positions as they waited for the medic to arrive. During the trial, Baughman said he saw a little dog circling the body.

The coroner's statement in the court-martial files details Wakasa's outfit that evening: two layers of trousers, a blue pair underneath a brown pair; instead of underwear, an armless homemade knit sweater, his legs passing through the armholes; thick cotton socks; oxford slippers; a brownish-tan sweater; and a dark blue mackinaw coat (likely one of the Philadelphia-made Buzz Ricksons the army supplied to all the internees). Sewn into the undergarments was a money belt with sixty-five dollars. The inference is that Wakasa was dressed to escape. Temperatures that day reached a high of fifty-seven and a low of thirty-three.

It took forty-five minutes for Lieutenant Henry Miller, commanding officer of the military police, the force to which Philpott was attached, to give notice of Wakasa's death to camp authorities and Tsune Baba, chair of the Topaz Community Council. Those forty-five minutes of blank record call for uncertainty and speculation.

Few of these details were known to the internees. Years later, some recalled hearing the shot; others remembered the military ambulance driving along the perimeter of camp. Military police were not authorized to enter Topaz, so to reach Wakasa's body, they would have had to jump over the barbed wire and pull his body under the fence.

For most of the internees, Wakasa's death remained a mystery. In many ways, eighty years later it still is. Court-martial documents state only that Wakasa was unintentionally killed by a nineteen-year-old private, shot at the same distance from which hunters shoot down antelope.

It happened at twilight, on a bright evening with good visibility and a mild westerly wind.

By most accounts, Wakasa was a well-educated and affable man. He had a habit of walking his dog along the same route every evening. He lived in Block 36, Barrack 7, Unit D. The reports state that he had a full head of white-gray hair and mild Japanese features.

The morning after Wakasa's death, a group of three social workers and two neighbors, led by Eiichi Sato, gathered at the murder scene to complete a report of the incident. As they approached the southwest fence, thirty-five feet from the site, a military Jeep came speeding toward them from the North Road and stopped abruptly. The driver stood on the seat and turned to them as he grabbed a submachine gun from his companion's hands. Pointing at Sato, he yelled: "Scatter or you'll get the same thing as the other guy got."

"We ate with [Wakasa] in our mess hall and used the common lavatory and the common facilities," read a letter that camp survivor Toru Saito sent to *Nichi Bei News*, a Bay Area newspaper, on September 2, 2021. "I was there when he was murdered by [a] US Army guard, April 11th, 1943. The actual spot of his death was kept unknown from us all these almost eighty years.… My dear mother died at age 106 in 2012, still worried [about] his remains.... Now 78 years later, the strong feelings of shame, guilt, and resentment return as I write this letter."

In the days that followed Wakasa's death, the eight thousand Japanese American prisoners at the Topaz internment camp stopped all activity at the furniture factory and the adobe brick unit, the bean sprout center, the milk plant, the warehouse, and the motor pool. The general mood was somber. The military entered a phase of red alert, and police started carrying gas masks and Thompson submachine guns at all times. Rifles that had once stood guard against the desert night suddenly were pointed into the camp.

Some of the internees clutched clubs and bats as they walked between the kitchen and the hospital, between the showers and the residence halls—anything to fend off the guards. Children stopped playing outside. There were feverish meetings behind closed doors, and tense discussions among the internees; the military and the camp authorities were not forthcoming with their investigations. Silence, suspicion, and mistrust prevailed, and a state of physical tension strained the air for days. It wasn't until the War Relocation Authority called off the alarm on April 13 that some level of normalcy was regained at Topaz. Two days after Wakasa's murder, the authorities announced that the sentry responsible for the shooting had been arrested and would be court-martialed at Fort Douglas in Salt Lake City.

There are a few photos of Wakasa's funeral housed at the Bancroft Library at UC Berkeley. A couple of them show the casket, fitted with wreaths, crosses, and a heart made of paper roses and lilies, equal to or even more beautiful than natural ones.

In the illustrated memoir *Citizen 13660*, a classic of Japanese American literature, the artist and Topaz internee Miné Okubo dedicates two drawings to Wakasa: one is of his funeral, and shows people in grief, fat tears rolling down their cheeks; the other features a group of eight women in patterned dresses, gathered around a table, folding paper flowers.

The wake took place on the afternoon of Monday, April 19, a week after Wakasa's death. It was held on the Topaz school grounds, at the open square in front of the basketball hoops of Block 32. Camp authorities had denied the Issei's request to hold the service at the scene of the shooting. The administration had also refused to declare a general holiday that day, but all the schools stayed closed, and most adults skipped work.

The sun was shining bright when people started assembling in front of the stage. By 2 p.m. it was clear there wouldn't be enough seats for all the mourners, who numbered close to two thousand. Groups of children wriggled around in skirts and suit pants, under or out of their parents' sight, plunged into the throng, leaning on chairs, on their tippy-toes, hiding by the piano or the speakers.

The casket was brought up to the stage by six pallbearers. Everyone rose, and the ceremony was conducted entirely in Japanese, except for a condolence letter read by the chief of the Welfare Division, and a brief speech by one of the camp administrators. "Rock of Ages" and other hymns and prayers were sung in Japanese. There were a vocal solo and paper flower offerings. By 4 p.m., when the funeral ended, streams of clouds had gathered above, and a strong wind rustled and shook the paper flowers.

The pallbearers carried the casket to a hearse amid the growing gale. Plumes of desert dust began swirling along the streets, over the barracks, and away into the valley. The hearse moved down the main avenue, past the entrance gate, and disappeared into the wind. Later that day, Wakasa's remains were taken to Ogden, Utah, to be cremated.

MICROINTERVIEW WITH DEVON PRICE, PART VI

THE BELIEVER: What writers and thinkers inspire you right now?

DEVON PRICE: Ayesha Khan and her pro-Palestinian work. She's been making amazing work about how people in the individualist, capitalist West are incredibly neurotic because we don't know what being in community means, because we're in a system that erases culture and community ties. Particularly, I've come to learn—I think a lot of us have to learn this, those of us who are white—that community is something you have to build. It's a thing that is composed of individual relationships with people, and it happens through conflict, through service to the community, through humbling yourself to learn the shared history. It's only then that you get the benefits of closeness, acceptance, understanding. Feeling not broken is not just something that's given to you—it's something you've got to put a lot of work into. ✵

It was the biggest funeral ever held in Millard County, possibly the largest Japanese American funeral ever held in Utah, and the largest in the entire United States during the wartime era.

A report on the Wakasa incident describes a continual feeling of suspense after the service among the military personnel, who kept wondering what the attitude of the internees might be on Tuesday morning. But as the hours passed, their fears slowly dissipated, the crews went back to their posts to pick up their tools, and camp restarted its normal rhythm once again.

That could have been it. Ceremonies and a court martial. The camps would be dismantled a few years later, marking the return of the Japanese American prisoners to some semblance of freedom.

It could all have ended there. But then there was the stone.

A crew of six men, some wearing black caps, others straw hats, work in the foothills of the Topaz mountains. Four of them push and roll a big boulder with long wooden poles. Two wait on the bed of a truck with the number 42 painted on the driver's door, ready to assist in lifting the rock. They all stand near what looks like a wooden pyramid, an aid in the shoving and the heaving, in keeping with the traditional Japanese way of stone gardening, which involves levers, pulleys, and ropes.

Chiura Obata's drawings again provide a good visual reference for understanding how internees sourced materials in the desert to bring them to camp. "The War Relocation Authority offers six trucks every Sunday in which 150 evacuees can go on a picnic," Obata wrote in his diary, a text reproduced by one of his granddaughters, Kimi Hill, in her book *Topaz Moon: Chiura Obata's Art of the Internment*. "Collecting unusual trees, bonsai-like greasewood, unusual stones and topaz gives relief from the meaningless barracks life."

Most of Obata's rock-gardening works are still unpublished, but Hill agreed to share some copies with me.

"There is a quarry, which I think is about ten miles west of the camp," Nancy Ukai mentioned during our conversation. "It's called Smelter Knolls. I've never been there, although I'd like to go the next time I'm in Utah. There are sketches of it by Chiura Obata… So the assumption is that the stone came from there."

In two black-and-white ink-on-paper drawings, Obata illustrates what seems to have been the way the Wakasa stone was sourced and brought to camp. And while the *how* is clear, what remains a mystery is when exactly the monument was emplaced.

Military records show that by mid-May of 1943, an agricultural crew had set up a structure of rocks and concrete

on the exact location of Wakasa's death. The memorial was built in defiance of the War Relocation Authority, which had labeled Wakasa's death as an escape attempt. On her website *50 Objects*, Nancy Ukai explains that the monument was constructed using "a sack and a half of stolen government cement to which they added native rocks." It was likely erected without ceremony, under the cover of a thick desert night, sometime between mid-April and early May of 1943.

Topaz authorities ignored the monument at first, but in a letter dated June 8, 1943, John McCloy, assistant secretary of war and a fierce proponent of Japanese segregation, asked Dillon S. Myer, director of the War Relocation Authority, to make sure the Wakasa memorial was removed: "I can see a real objection to any action which permits monuments of this character to be erected. Wakasa's death arose as a result of justifiable military action and it seems most inappropriate that a monument be erected to him."

Soon after the exchange, Topaz director Charles Ernst assured Myer that the memorial had been destroyed and forgotten and there would be no record of the stone: "[Everything is] torn down," Ernst wrote, "and the rocks which were used in its construction… completely removed from sight."

For many of the internees, that was the end of the Wakasa saga. The erasure would be repeated two years later with the razing of all ten internment camps. In a sense, Arlene Tatsuno told me, the physical leveling of Topaz was a clearing of the slate. Life had to go on.

But memories have a way of coming back. In July of 2021, the Wakasa memorial, supposedly torn down eighty years prior, awakened from its desert slumber. In a final act of defiance, instead of destroying the memorial, the Issei had buried it, leaving behind a simple diagram with its coordinates. The map, drawn by an internee named George Shimamoto, made its way to the National Archives in DC, where Nancy Ukai found it.

I tried to talk to Ukai about her discovery, but in April 2023, right after I saw her at the ceremony for the eightieth anniversary of Wakasa's death, she stopped communicating with me. One thing, however, was clear the last time we spoke: coming across that map had made her tingle with excitement. She was grateful for the physical discovery of the memorial stone, for Burton and Farrell.

Little if anything could have prepared her for what came next:

Beckwith, a white woman, getting there first, unburying the monument, and taking it to a museum. The Issei's hands were the last to touch the Wakasa stone before it disappeared for almost a century. Beckwith's hands were the first to touch it again, after all that time.

After a left turn on Route 6, the reality of Delta starts to sink in again: dry brush on both sides of the road; the town of Lynndyl, the hundred-car freight trains; high-voltage towers lined up, each in a wide stance, gripping power cables that crackle for miles along the expanse of the Utah flats.

We've been on the road for nearly ten hours and still have one more to go. It's my turn to lead the three-car convoy of raucous middle-aged Japanese women—artists, curators, doctors, writers. Kay Yatabe is riding shotgun as I drive. Kimi Hill is in the seat behind me. After a year of talks and meetings, we became friendly, and they

invited me to join them as they hopscotched around the Grand Staircase–Escalante National Monument, ahead of a private ceremony at the Topaz site later this evening. Organized by Hill, the event will honor her grandfather's most famous painting, *Moonlight Over Topaz*, with a koto performance by two young Deltans.

Our banter has been going strong since early this morning, but as the light starts to dim, we all grow quiet, and I begin to retrace my own path here. Along this same road two years back, my wife and I were on our way from New York to Santa Cruz, California, when we detoured through Delta. We were struck by the Topaz Museum's sleek modern building and doubled back to yank on its door, but it was closed for COVID. A year later, we swung by again. This time the doors were open, and, by sheer chance, Arlene Tatsuno was visiting from the Bay Area. We sat next to her and her husband, Gene, in the otherwise-empty projection room, unaware that the documentary footage on the screen was her father's own film *Topaz*. As the credits rolled behind her, Tatsuno grabbed me and said: "Have you met Jane? She's responsible for all this," and took me by the arm to meet Beckwith, whose face was already showing the first bouts of histamine.

I knew immediately that the Wakasa controversy was an important story for me to write, even though at the time I didn't understand why. I had little knowledge of the Japanese American internment experience in the United States. My beat, if I could call it that, had been Indigenous struggles in Latin America.

UNRELATED SONGS AND FILMS WITH THE SAME TITLE

✶ "Twilight" by Electric Light Orchestra and *Twilight* directed by Catherine Hardwicke
✶ "Black Swan" by Thom Yorke and *Black Swan* directed by Darren Aronofsky
✶ "Heroes" by David Bowie and *Heroes* directed by Jeremy Kagan
✶ "Rio" by Duran Duran and *Rio* directed by Carlos Saldanha
✶ "Oh, Pretty Woman" by Roy Orbison and *Pretty Woman* directed by Garry Marshall
✶ "Frozen" by Madonna and *Frozen* directed by Jennifer Lee and Chris Buck
✶ "Candyman" by Christina Aguilera and *Candyman* directed by Bernard Rose
✶ "Iron Man" by Black Sabbath and *Iron Man* directed by Jon Favreau
✶ "Adore" by the Smashing Pumpkins and *Adore* directed by Anne Fontaine
✶ "Lullaby" by the Cure and *Lullaby* directed by Andrew Levitas

—list compiled by Lia Sina

It took two years of writing a story about others' memories before I stumbled into my own. Born in Argentina in the 1970s, I witnessed, way too young, a country that turned on its own citizens, and experienced, personally and intimately, the ensuing struggle for collective memory that continues to haunt Argentine families and friends today.

For almost eight years, between 1976 and 1983, the Argentine military, supported by the United States government and its blind eye to human rights, kidnapped, tortured, and disappeared thousands of people without trial, without reason, in systematic acts of terror focused on instilling fear and obedience, in order to make Argentines acquiesce to the neoliberal free market policies of the Washington Consensus. After the dictatorship ended, the military forged a plan of oblivion to evade the consequences of its actions. It tried to take charge of the narrative by lying, hiding records, and altering the architecture of entire places.

One of the plaques in the sun-drenched lobby of the Officers' Quarters of the Escuela Superior de Mecánica de la Armada (ESMA)—the infamous Navy School of Mechanics, a former clandestine detention, torture, and extermination center run by the Argentine Navy—describes an example of this type of forced architectural amnesia:

> Since the IACHR [Inter-American Commission of Human Rights] inspection was agreed, the Argentine dictatorship implemented various strategies to hide the extent of its crimes. It carried out political propaganda campaigns and modified the buildings that had functioned as clandestine centers so they would not match the descriptions by former detainees. ESMA Task Group 3.3 made profound changes still in place today.

Only through the memories of survivors can we know the history of that place and what happened inside it. Remembering is a willful act. But so is forgetting.

The ESMA campus is parklike, with cypress, cedar, and ash trees lining alleyways between grand old buildings; the only architectural evidence of its more recent use as a detention center are the fifteen guard towers studding its perimeter, all retrofitted in concrete and installed just months before the military coup, and in clear anticipation of it. The place was turned into the ESMA Museum and Site of Memory in 2015 by then president Néstor Kirchner and contains harrowing and meticulously displayed evidence of the horrors endured by its detainees, including the army helicopter that regularly dropped torture victims, still alive, into the nearby Rio de la Plata.

I went to the site with my brother, but at the last minute he decided to wait in a café during the two hours it took me to walk it. I understood why he would not want to put himself through the tour.

On September 19, 2023, when I landed back in New York, my phone notified me that the ESMA had been placed on the UNESCO World Heritage List.

Someone is hungry in one of the other cars, so Kimi suggests we stop at the metallic red sign of a gas station that is also a hoagie restaurant. I fill up the tank while the others stretch their legs and talk about what to eat. Three blond kids drive up in a black truck. They have a yellow dog, maybe a Lab, and can't stop staring at our group. Perhaps they've never seen so many Japanese people all at once. This may be what Deltans felt about Topaz in the 1940s. All those highly educated, successful Japanese Americans showing up out of nowhere.

The kids linger for a while, take their dog to pee on the side of a rusted tanker truck, and snatch a last glance at us before screeching away into the hills.

Racial trauma can start healing only once its social precursors resurface, turn visible, and are acknowledged. Direct acceptance, an admission of guilt on the part of those who caused that pain, is an invaluable part of the process. During the redress movement in the 1980s, conditions were ripe for former internees to start healing. When the US government finally admitted its wrongdoings, and recognized that its internment policies had been shaped by "race prejudice, war hysteria and a failure of political leadership," the internees received the first official acknowledgment of their mistreatment and a confirmation that their pain had been real. Until then, however, most Issei and Nisei had had to suffer their experiences in silence.

This liminal mental space was the context in which the Topaz Issei and Nisei began interacting with Jane Beckwith in the 1980s. Before the US

A storm approaches Delta and the Topaz camp on August 24, 2022.

government fully acknowledged any wrongdoing, Beckwith and the people of Delta set in motion a process of communal redress, the first step on a path that would allow many of the incarceration victims to feel heard and start healing on their own terms. The Topaz Museum materialized as a pivotal interlocutor, an early countersign that validated the voices of those who had suffered but could not yet express it in their own words. In its role as an ally, the museum helped preserve and document painful reminders of the incarceration, its racist origins, and the hardships that both the US government and American society imposed on people of Japanese descent—Americans and legal residents alike. The museum institutionalized these

memories and gave them a physical form and place.

Rarely does trauma literature from the Global North, a constant aggressor, consider that it should be the victim, and never the perpetrator, who determines the direction and pace of recovery from racial pain. Following the government's admission of guilt, it was up to the Japanese American community to express its restorative requirements—demands that ranged from retributive justice to plain forgiveness. It is at that point that the negotiation between victims and perpetrators sets the bar for a new social contract.

But while the Topaz Museum was a first step toward that broader social acknowledgment, the unearthing of

the Wakasa stone felt like a step backward, a new betrayal.

There is no denying that the Topaz Museum, and a large portion of Beckwith's actions, exist in a nexus of cultural, political, and racial tensions in America that are now reaching a boiling point. Most of the Issei and the Nisei trusted Beckwith to be their ally in Topaz. Early on, Topaz internees Rick Okabe, Ted Nagata, Bill Sugaya, Chuck Kubokawa, Grace Oshita, and Dave Tatsuno confirmed Beckwith at the helm of the museum board, an entity they had created. No one today should doubt they had good reasons for doing so. Beckwith was their Topaz connection, the manager of an operation set up to help expose governmental responsibility and elicit an admission of guilt. And she was white. In the context of those early days, it would have been difficult for the victims of incarceration to set up the Topaz Museum from afar. Beckwith wasn't perfect; she wasn't supposed to be. She was there, and she was just the ally they needed.

Allies—especially those who witness, if not directly condone, the crime against which they later seek redress—carry their own guilt and resentment. I wonder if unearthing the stone was Jane Beckwith's role all along. Could she have done anything other than what she did?

It doesn't take long for Kimi Hill and the others to come out of the restaurant, gnawing on their sandwiches. Kay Yatabe hands me a brown caramel lollipop, which I save for later. Jane Beckwith is eating a banana under the restaurant awning. Her stress allergy has made her cheeks swell again. We haven't talked much this afternoon, but I see the uneasiness in her eyes. She tells Hill that it is getting late, and she needs to go back to Delta to get ready for the ceremony. She turns her Ford Ranger around and dashes back into the Sevier Desert, that antediluvian, fossilized ocean.

When I pictured the Topaz Museum in the months and years after my first encounter with Beckwith, I rarely thought of the unburied memorial as one of its defining characters. Nor did I think of Beckwith, or the barracks, or the internment. Instead, what kept coming to mind was a small doll: a Minnie Mouse figurine—just a few inches tall, made of shells and black wire, held

inside a glass display—that I'd noticed as I walked out of the main exhibit room that day. The doll had two black-painted seashells for ears and five red-painted snail shells for a hair ribbon. For a face, half-moon black-and-white eyes and a pointy nose were etched onto the tip of a seashell. The Minnie Mouse was connected by a piece of cotton thread to a paper tag with the name *Misao Kanzaki* handwritten on it.

When I searched the Utah State University Digital History Collections recently, the name Kanzaki pointed to the record of the stillborn child of Ray Toshio and Mrs. Kanzaki. The birth took place on May 14, 1944, in Topaz. Misao was a boy. I don't know if the doll was meant for him.

A few items are waiting for us in Beckwith's garage. Eight metal folding chairs leaning against the wall and a stack of plastic patio recliners. We shove them into the back of the car, and head to Topaz for the ceremony.

The dispute over the stone remains at a standstill. It has been months since I've heard from Ukai. I wonder what a path forward might look

like. History always finds its way into the future, as does memory to preserve it. But who will remember this fight a decade from now. Will it still hold any meaning?

The landscape outside Delta is punctuated by dairy farms. Around 6 p.m. it's dinnertime for cows, and we see them lining up by the side of the road, their heads pushing through red fenceline bars, muzzles shoved into the feeders. At times, the smell of methane fills the car. We cross the small bridge over the Sevier River, a thread of water wiggling in a sea of dust, and we see the crown of the moon rising from behind the powder-red ridge of the mountains. The road becomes emptier, hemmed now by small houses, many of which are converted barracks that the government sold to locals after razing Topaz.

There are three SUVs already parked at the entrance to the site when we arrive, and a dozen people milling around in groups, casually walking between five or six commemorative plaques, their shadows spilling out onto the gravel. I assume they're locals who have shown up for the ceremony, but as soon as they see us, they retreat to their cars and drive off.

By the time we enter the square mile of camp, the moon is already parked over the mountains. We drag the chairs from the back of Beckwith's truck and arrange them in a line facing east, on the concrete platform of a leveled mess hall. Some of the women grab a seat, others walk around taking photos. Except for a lone cricket, the desert is all silence.

Suddenly a black truck rushes toward us from the horizon, high beams on, leaving in its wake a tail of dust. When it pulls up beside us, two blond kids barely out of college jump out and start unloading instruments. Bessie is wearing a purple coat because, she explains, it's going to get cold. "The desert changes the pitch of the strings," the other girl, her sister Stephanie, says to no one, as Bessie brings out a few hand drums and a violin, which they carefully set on a chair. Their chatter is lively, rhythmic, and slightly mesmerizing. Finally, Bessie pulls out the koto, a six-by-one-foot zither, Japan's national instrument. She handles it carefully, setting it on two black wooden trestles just as her teacher, Shirley Muramoto has taught her.

"It's like poetry when she plays it," Stephanie gushes. Muramoto learned the instrument as a toddler, sitting on her mother's lap at the kitchen table. Her mother had first played the koto "at camp." "Quite a progressive summer camp it must have been," Muramoto had thought for years. It wasn't until her later teens that she found out about relocation, Japanese American internment history, and Topaz, where her mother had been an internee.

No live music has echoed here since the camp closed, Kimi Hill tells me. Almost eighty years later, two Delta girls are about to play a traditional Japanese instrument they've just started learning during lockdown from the daughter of a Japanese American internee.

They will start with "Kojo no tsuki," "The Moon Over the Ruined Castle," Stephanie announces. She plucks one string at a time, first with her thumb and then with her index and middle fingers, as her sister accompanies her on the violin with long notes that drip like fog under the main melody.

I've heard this tune before. It suggests at an upright piano in a smoky bar; a saxophone in an '80s movie. It was, I believed, a Thelonious Monk tune. But back home I learned that, although Monk recorded it and played it often, the original had been written in 1901 by Japanese composer Rentarō Taki as a lesson for piano. Printed and reprinted in Japanese high school music books for over a century, it was as popular in Japan as jazz standards are in the States.

The sisters play it tentatively, but the magic still vibrates in each note. As I listen, I think about memory, who holds it, and who carries it forward. Taki and Monk, and now these Delta sisters.

We all sit quietly, and when the girls are done, we cheer and laugh. Stephanie asks the audience if any of us has ever played the koto. Nobody has. So she invites us to try. She's been so smitten with the instrument that she recently bought a smaller one, which was shipped from Japan. She painted a white crane on it with a red sun behind. Stephanie doesn't know what these symbols mean, but she copied them from drawings she found online, and it looks very pretty.

It is late, and cold, so we all huddle under blankets.

The moon now hangs like a round fluorescent globe over the desert and the mountains, and there is nothing we can do to stop it. ✶

FILMS DISLIKED OR REGRETTED BY THEIR DIRECTORS

✶ *Dune* (David Lynch)
✶ *Dying of the Light* (theatrical cut) (Paul Schrader)
✶ *Blade Runner* (theatrical cut) (Ridley Scott)
✶ *Catchfire* (theatrical cut) (Dennis Hopper)
✶ *The Keep* (Michael Mann)
✶ *Spartacus* (Stanley Kubrick)
✶ *Indiana Jones and the Temple of Doom* (Steven Spielberg)
✶ *The Brown Bunny* (Vincent Gallo)
✶ *Alien³* (David Fincher)
✶ *The Underneath* (Steven Soderbergh)
✶ *Valentino* (Ken Russell)
✶ *Synecdoche, New York* (Charlie Kaufman)
✶ *American History X* (Tony Kaye)
✶ *Fear Anxiety Depression* (Todd Solondz)
✶ *Shutter Island* (Martin Scorsese)
✶ *The Godfather Part III* (Francis Ford Coppola)

—*list compiled by Jasper Cerone*

IN TRANSIT

by Lane Milburn

WE APOLOGIZE FOR THE INCONVENIENCE.

SO I GET MY REFUND WHEN? OK. SURE.

INCIDENT REPORT - 3/1 LATE DELIVERY COMPLAINT. GPS SHOWED NUMBER FOUR STALLED AT FRANKLIN INTERSECTION.

UNIT RETRIEVED. SYSTEMS CHECK: OK. INSPECTION REQUEST SUBMITTED. REFUND REQUEST SUBMITTED. AUTHORITIES NOTIFIED: N

SOMETIMES I THINK THERE'S A REASON THEY BREAK DOWN AND DO WEIRD SHIT, LIKE THEY'RE DOING IT IN PROTEST.

DO THEY HATE THEIR JOBS LIKE I HATE MINE?

WHEN THEY'VE GONE OUTSIDE, DO THEY THINK, WHAT IF I JUST KEEP GOING IN THAT DIRECTION AND NEVER COME BACK?

IS IT ME THEY DON'T LIKE?

INCIDENT REPORT - 3/3 LATE DELIVERY COMPLAINT. GPS SHOWED NUMBER TWO OUT OF BOUNDS. UNIT FOUND ON ITS SIDE IN A DITCH AROUND 2700 FRANKLIN.

UNIT RETRIEVED. INSPECTION REQUEST RESUBMITTED WITH NOTE ABOUT UNIT EXITING OPERATIONAL RANGE. AUTHORITIES NOTIFIED: N

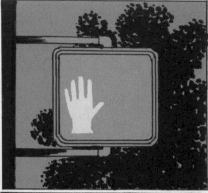

INCIDENT REPORT – 3/17 NUMBER FOUR AGAIN DID NOT DETECT WALK SIGNAL.

ACCORDING TO BYSTANDER TESTIMONY, A VEHICLE SWERVED TO MISS THE UNIT AND STRUCK A STUDENT ON A BICYCLE, WHO IS BEING TREATED FOR A COMPOUND FRACTURE.

INSPECTION REQUEST PENDING. SCHOOL OFFICIALS INTEND TO CONTINUE OPERATIONS.

AUTHORITIES NOTIFIED: Y

AS FAR AS HOW THE LEGAL PICTURE LOOKS, WE DON'T YET KNOW, KIND OF "WAIT AND SEE." RIGHT NOW WE WANT TO BE CAREFUL, BE TACTFUL.

Construction Begins on $17m Student Center

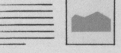

WHY CAN'T MY SON VOTE?

In the United States, many adults with intellectual disabilities are effectively barred from voting. But should citizens lose representation simply because of who they are?

by

PAUL COLLINS

ILLUSTRATIONS BY:
Charlotte Gomez

My son doesn't ask for stories at bedtime anymore, but he still wants me next to him when he's falling asleep.

"This is the craziest elephant ride I've ever taken," Morgan announces to me one night. Then he repeats it. "This is the craziest elephant ride I've ever taken. This is the craziest elephant ride I've ever taken. This is the craziest elephant ride I've ever taken."

He tucks a plush doll of Pongo from *One Hundred and One Dalmatians* under his head, and then he talks and talks. Sometimes it's a question, or he repeats something he heard on *Sesame Street* or a line from a video game. Other times I don't know where it came from. But I listen to all of it, and stare at the posters on his bedroom walls as the room gets darker. They're pictures of the things he loves: a Keith Haring graphic, a lobby poster of *The Tigger Movie*, a group photo of the Canadian Brass quintet, a *Star Wars* Podracing flyer.

"It's the galaxy's famous Gasgano," he recites. Morgan loves Podracers but couldn't care less about the rest of the *Star Wars* universe, which he regards as a rind to be discarded in order to consume the Podracing game. Eventually he drifts off and snores, sometimes after gregariously throwing his arm over me. It takes me a while to extricate myself when he does this, because my son is about six foot three and 240 pounds. He is twenty-five years old.

In 2017 the Oregon Circuit Court declared that I am, in the all-caps words of the red-stamped and signed court letter, "A GUARDIAN FOR AN ADULT FOR AN INDEFINITE PERIOD." The process of taking over someone else's life is generally, and fittingly, a difficult one. There are sworn statements, doctors' reports, filings for the judge, and a court-appointed visitor, who comes to your house to see if the reality matches the paperwork. Our visitor was a psychologist named Angela, who arrived with little notice—social workers like to drop in by surprise, so they can see how you actually live, before there's time to dismantle a meth lab. Anyway, his mother, Jennifer, and I rushed about our house, grabbing dolls off the floor, remaking beds, and frantically wiping down counters. A telltale smell of Windex still hung in the air as the psychologist walked in.

Angela took one look and we stopped worrying; she'd clearly seen it all before. She found Morgan in his favorite spot, on a sofa next to the upright piano, and asked him questions. We stood by, fretting, weirdly helpless. It was an evaluation of Morgan himself, not of our parenting, and so after the first few words to prompt him to say hello, we couldn't answer for him; but also, he couldn't really answer for himself.

"While the Respondent was able to provide a greeting to this Visitor when prompted by his mother he was not able to appreciably comprehend the current petition," the psychologist reported to the court. "Mr. Morgan Collins is a 17-year-old young man who was diagnosed with Autism Spectrum Disorder when he was 2 years old… The Respondent has very limited verbal communication skills but is able to express basic physical needs, such as hunger, thirst, and a need to toilet…. He uses the toilet but needs to be reminded to wipe and wash his hands. He requires physical assistance with bathing, brushing his teeth and hair. The Respondent can dress himself with prompting, although he is reliant on others to put on his shoes and select his clothing. He would be unable to independently obtain food or engage in meal preparation."

A couple of weeks later, the guardianship letter came from the court clerk.

About a year afterward, ballots arrived in our mail, including one addressed to Morgan. There was a Soil and Water Conservation District director standing unopposed; two people running for the same city council seat; five running for Congress, six for governor. Some initiatives trying to block abortion funding; others trying to fund clean energy. "Ballot Measure 26-199," reads one. "Bonds to fund affordable housing in Washington, Clackamas, Multnomah counties."

Morgan belongs to one of just two classes of citizens that that the US still permits to be disenfranchised:

criminals and the mentally incompetent. Then again, Oregon was perhaps the only state in 2018 where our son *might* get a ballot at all: it was the first state to offer voting by mail, and one of the first to offer Motor Voter. Morgan was automatically enrolled to vote when we got him his state ID. You can be laughing at poop jokes and making Grover sounds in the DMV line and still get included in Motor Voter's automatic registration. And since the ballot arrived by mail, there was no election worker to look at him askance, no amateur poll watcher outside to point their phone at him, nobody to justify him or ourselves to. Just a ballot envelope with his name on it.

"Please Use a Black or Blue Pen. Completely fill in the oval," the form instructs. More ballots at our household for the 2020 primaries, and then for the 2020 election. By the 2022 midterms, Morgan's younger brother was old enough to vote. There were four envelopes on our mantel, but only three got opened and mailed back.

Morgan couldn't fill in a ballot. And I couldn't bring myself to throw a ballot out.

Discarding his ballot seemed wrong somehow—just tossing it into a recycling bin with the flyer from Safeway and the Lands' End catalog. It had meaning; it represented something, though I couldn't yet say what, exactly. I put his ballots in the cardboard Bankers Box where I kept all of Morgan's other paperwork: his insurance forms, his bank statements, his guardianship order. Ballot after ballot, accumulating.

"President and Vice President. Vote for One," said the 2020 ballot. Five choices for that. Three running

for state attorney general. A vote on funding our local parks, where Morgan likes to see ducklings. In 2022, a state initiative: "Oregon Measure 112: Amends Constitution: Removes language allowing slavery and involuntary servitude as punishment for crime."

What did it even mean to save these unopened ballots? For a long time it meant I had the same stark thought that was presented by every other piece of paper in the box: that my son, adjudged incapacitated, a man of very limited verbal skills, my ward, can't vote. But years passed, and slowly, a question formed from those words, from a statement to a query, evolving with each lifting of the lid of that box, with each new insurance bill and each copy of my Guardian's Annual Report to the Court.

Why can't my son vote?

I suppose I'd once imagined the history of American voting rights as a steady march toward greater equality. But the more you look at American suffrage, the more it feels like a visit to the Winchester Mystery House: there are bafflingly constructed chambers, grand and glorious halls, and stairways that lead nowhere. To begin with, there's no specific right-to-vote clause in our Constitution, so the US lacks what is now an obvious provision for a modern democracy to include. Instead, there are the famed inalienable rights, and descriptions of how elections work, which imply and essentially necessitate a freely voting populace; plus there are many subsequent amendments, federal acts, and court decisions. But otherwise the Constitution hands over voting and voter qualifications to states. For many decades, states didn't have laws barring

the intellectually disabled from voting: they didn't need to, because they allowed hardly *any* citizens to vote. For the election of George Washington in 1788 and 1789, Massachusetts required that voters be men aged twenty-one or older, and possessing an estate worth at least sixty British pounds. Most states had similar laws. That's why, in a country of nearly four million people, just 43,782 votes were cast—slightly more than 1 percent of the population.

When property-ownership requirements for voting were removed in the nineteenth century, it didn't happen through some great sweeping reform, but piecemeal, and state by state. And with the frightful prospect of voting by the masses—women! Blacks! renters!—on the horizon, other voting requirements, somewhat less onerous but more persistent, arose in place of property ownership. Viewed side by side, they were (and in many ways still are) an inconsistent hodgepodge. The 1860 election is a fair example of how someone who moved a hundred feet across a state line could vote in one state but be barred from voting in another. In Wisconsin, noncitizens could vote, but not in Illinois. New York permitted Black people to vote, but New Jersey did not. South Carolina didn't allow anyone who had been party to a duel to vote, but you could blast and slash away in North Carolina. Kentucky required living two years in the state before voting there; Indiana had no length-of-residency requirement. Every state banned women—except New Jersey, at first—oh, and Kentucky, but they could vote only in school elections.

Along with women and Black voters, five groups regularly appear among

and children neglected in legislation? Are the insane and foreigners neglected in legislation? I apprehend not," opined a Massachusetts Constitutional Convention delegate in 1853.

Why worry about being able to vote, when there were sane white men looking out for you?

There is a world where Barack Obama is still the president.

I suppose it makes sense. That's who Morgan saw in his school civics lessons and in his magazines from Scholastic. Obama was president from the time our son was in fourth grade until he dropped out in early eleventh grade. The end of his schooling was a while in coming. "Behavior of Concern: Work Refusal," his school's final behavior support report reads. "Morgan is completing 20% of requested tasks with maximum 1:1 adult support (visual/tactile/verbal)." By then his meltdowns in the Life Skills classroom had grown in intensity, and were happening earlier each day, until they finally started erupting on the walk to school, his hands and feet lashing out wildly even before we reached the end of our block. One morning, it became too risky for him, for the teachers, and for us to take him to school. It was still too risky the next morning, and every other morning after that. So Morgan's education fell to us.

For a long time, Jennifer patiently worked with him through brightly colored homeschool workbooks— division and multiplication, currency and time, basic life science. We still have them on our shelves, volumes with half their pages torn out—most from completing the perforated pages

those barred from voting in the nineteenth century: paupers, criminals, soldiers, students, and the legally incompetent, usually described as "insane" or "idiotic." These groups seem like a confusing and motley assemblage at first glance. What did they have in common, besides a likely general lack of property or political power? Well, there was one thing: in the nineteenth century, poorhouses and capacious asylums meant many such citizens were concentrated in certain districts. Poorhouses, prisons, military bases, colleges, asylums: the upstanding citizens of towns and cities might

have been happy to benefit from the jobs these institutions provided, but they did not much care to cede political power to their residents.

As the historian Kirk Harold Porter mused over a century ago, "The philosophy of suffrage has always been more or less opportunistic, if the word is permissible. Suffrage qualifications are determined for decidedly materialistic considerations, and then a theory is evolved to suit the situation." Perhaps unsurprisingly, the philosophy among those who already had the right to vote was that the current system worked just fine. "Are the women of lessons, others from when he hurled the books at us. We imagined that at some point the school district would check in, make sure we were doing something with his learning, anything at all. But nobody called. It was as if they thought Morgan had moved to another country, and I suppose in a sense he had.

I leaf through one of the remaining pages in his civics book: "The people of Washington, D.C., elect a representative to Congress, but that person cannot vote on laws." I gently slide the text back into our bookcase.

"Morgan, who is the president?" I ask him.

"Obama," he responds, and rocks back and forth.

"That's good!" I say brightly. "Barack Obama *was* the president for a long time. Now we have a different president, Joe Biden."

I don't try to explain the Trump years.

"Poop," he adds, and starts laughing. "Eeyore poops in the toilet."

We're sitting by the piano, which has four old schoolhouse world globes crowded atop it, from when Morgan kept buying globes every time we went to Goodwill. Electronic ones that didn't work, old brass-mounted ones that still showed the Soviet Union, newer ones that had both a Sudan and a South Sudan, until globes spilled from every flat surface in our house: they still fascinate him.

"Morgan, what country are we in?" I ask, pointing to one of the globes.

"Oregon," he says.

"That's the state we live in, yeah. Oregon is inside a country. What country is it in?"

He ponders this.

"United States of America," he says.

"That's right! Good job."

"You did a great job," Morgan says, referring to himself; he almost invariably switches pronouns, a linguistic hallmark of autism.

I decide to try again.

"Morgan, who is our president?"

He starts to rock back and forth again.

"Barack Obama," he says.

Morgan wants his breakfast; I can tell he's getting annoyed by the questions, and I have waffles to make. Barack Obama will continue on for a fifteenth year as president.

If you want to point out where mental exclusions started, Portland's as good a place as any. Not the one that we live in: the other one, in Maine. They became our twenty-third state in 1820, but the first to formally exclude voters who were under guardianship. When representatives from across the District of Maine gathered in Portland and adopted a constitution, their document's first words on "electors" were unambiguous: "Every male citizen of the United States of the age of twenty-one years and upwards, excepting paupers, persons under guardianship, and Indians not taxed, having his residence established in this State for the term of three months next preceding any election…" (A few lines later it hastens to add: also, no soldiers or students.) Other states steadily followed, and with some fluctuations up and down, since 1880 roughly three-quarters of US state constitutions have maintained some form of mental restrictions on voting, even

as those for other groups have slowly fallen away. A 2020 overview by the Bazelon Center for Mental Health Law found just twelve states with no mental disqualification in their constitution, and they're a mystifyingly scattershot group, both politically and geographically. They include Colorado and Vermont, but also Kansas and North Carolina. Most actually still have restrictions, but they are written somewhere in their more changeable statute law instead.

So who, exactly, can't vote?

It's hard to say. Some state constitutions still use versions of Maine's old language barring those under guardianship. Kentucky and Mississippi have even retained language in their constitutions prohibiting "idiots"—and lest coastal readers feel superior, I'll note that services for developmentally disabled New Yorkers are still provided by that state's appallingly named Department of Health and Mental Hygiene. (Across the river, New Jersey still barred any "idiot" from voting as late as 2007. It didn't then stop having a voting restriction, incidentally, but it did get rid of the word *idiot*.) The problems of such language were manifold, and have occupied courts for decades. What is the precise definition of *idiot*? And why was guardianship or incompetency, which can be invoked for a number of reasons, used as a standard to restrict voting? Is a poli-sci professor who is institutionalized with severe bipolar disorder incompetent to vote? How about a person with Down syndrome, who may hold a job, live semi-independently, and commute to work—are they incompetent to vote? How about Britney Spears? When she was the adult ward of her father, during a thirteen-year span when she could perform in Vegas but not manage her own affairs, was she incompetent to vote?

In fact, for a while Britney Spears probably *couldn't* vote, and therein lies a tale. One doesn't often hear about guardianship in the press, unless the process goes wildly awry—the ordinary day-to-day life of caring for someone with an intellectual disability does not attract sign-wielding crowds—but Britney Spears's case did point out just how arbitrary the voting restriction can be. When Spears was made a ward of her father in 2008, California state law largely barred voting by those found incompetent. By 2016, California's voting restriction had changed to a narrower one, barring those under conservatorship "only if a court… finds by clear and convincing evidence that the person cannot communicate, with or without reasonable accommodations, a desire to participate in the voting process." That was clearly not the case for Britney, and so now she could vote. There has been gradual movement toward this more restrained language, a change bolstered by a 2001 federal court ruling (*Doe v. Rowe*) that blanket guardianship exclusions violate the Fourteenth Amendment. What's more, provisions in the Americans with Disabilities Act (ADA) and the Voting Rights Act require states to offer voting assistance to the disabled. Yet an immovable core of exclusionary language still exists. The Voting Rights Act, for instance, still states that "a voter may not be removed from the official list of eligible voters except by reason of death, criminal conviction,

mental incapacity, change in residence, or voter request." The permission for *some* kind of mental exclusion, and the outdated language that amplifies it in state constitutions, fundamentally persist to bar people with intellectual disabilities from voting.

How many people is that, exactly? There's no complete national accounting of people with intellectual disabilities, which is a slippery category, or even of people under guardianships, which is not. The one national figure for the number of people under guardianships that is commonly bandied about in reporting—approximately 1.3 million people—comes from a 2016 estimate by the National Center for State Courts. Its number was an extrapolation from sixteen states that *sort of* kept track of their data.

If it's hard to say who can't vote, though, it's distressingly easy to ascertain who *doesn't* vote. A 2023 Rutgers University study of the previous year's midterms found a national voting rate among those without disabilities of 52.4 percent, while only 38.3 percent of those with mental disabilities voted. A 2023 study by the National Association of State Directors of Developmental Disabilities Services found that voting opportunity ("Has ever voted in local, state, or federal election, or had the opportunity and chose not to") among the intellectually disabled varied widely by state—evidence of the immense effect of implicit and explicit state-level barriers—ranging from a high of 78 percent in Nevada to a low of 25 percent in Kentucky. And Kentucky, you'll recall, is one of the states whose constitutional language still bars "idiots" from voting.

Words have meaning, even if wielded toward someone who might not understand them. They bear an intent.

"Do you want to trim your beard a little, Morgan?" Jennifer asks our son. "Or shave it all off?"

We have this conversation with him every month or so. It's too hard to shave him daily—he wiggles, fidgets, starts laughing, or gets irritated—and so, like most Portland men, Morgan's constantly in some stage of growing a beard. When we do ask if he wants to keep it or not, he'll peer at himself in the bathroom mirror, smiling, sticking out his tongue, checking out all the angles; then he'll go right up to the silvering, so close he can see his breath on the glass.

"You want to shave it all off," he says to the reflection.

It was years before Morgan verbally responded to us about anything; he was hyperlexic and could read long before he could converse, so at first we resorted to writing out questions for him: DO YOU WANT A BAGEL? YES / NO. He'd grab my finger and jab it like a stylus at his answer. Now Morgan makes lots of decisions aloud every day, though sometimes it can be hard to tell what he wants. If you just ask him a question—"Does your foot hurt?"—he may just answer "Yeah" without considering it. Or he may echolalically repeat the final couple of words: "Foot hurts." But given a set of choices, he often weighs them. Waffles, pancakes, or toast? The pink shirt, the aqua, or the green? Goodwill, Target, or the supermarket? A matinee of *Inside Out* or *Barbie*?

He has strong opinions on these matters; he is decidedly not indifferent to his world. But the world is, much of the time, rather indifferent to him. His opinions are not, at least in any obvious way, on things the world values or deems of national import. But then, what is a vote *for*? How much is it about expressing an informed opinion? How much is it about simply recognizing one's rights and humanity? How much is it a practical assurance of the representation of one's interests? Many voters—disabled or not—lack an informed opinion, and yet all have an interest in being represented.

The curious ambiguity about what voting is for is mirrored by incoherence about why someone *cannot* vote. There is a striking lack of research to back mental exclusions—just vague gesturing toward some notion of the integrity and sanctity of the vote, and dark mutterings about voter fraud.

"Ha! Ha-ha!" Morgan bursts out.

"Stay *still*," I tell him with exasperation. He leans forward, examines the progress of my shaving work, then checks out his teeth in the mirror too.

Might people with intellectual disabilities be less informed about voting? Might they be unduly influenced by people around them? Might they fill in some gibberish? Perhaps, in some cases—and yet such acts do not stop any other American from being allowed to vote. Other voters are free to believe in QAnon, or to invoke numerology, or to write in "Deez Nutz" for president if they like; but those with intellectual disabilities can be preemptively blocked. To ward off the hypothetical possibility of a "bad" voter, states resorted to the *certain and constant* disenfranchisement of a marginalized class of citizens.

"Shaving cream," Morgan announces as I finish buzzing away with the beard trimmer.

He already knows what's coming next. If I can keep him in a chair in front of the bathroom mirror for long enough, then comes the hard part: a razor and shaving cream to actually make his skin smooth. Sometimes I have to split the task between two nights. But tonight he stays still. And when his face is covered with Barbasol foam, he is delighted. He looks elderly and wise.

"You have a white beard," he cracks up. "You're an *old man*."

If you're reading this in another country, it may be with a curious sense of déjà vu: *Wait, didn't we used to have exclusion laws too?* It's quite possible you did.

Japan is a fair example. Through the nineteenth and twentieth centuries, it maintained voting restrictions that looked quite recognizable to an American: on women, paupers, soldiers, students, the incompetent. And, as in America, by the twenty-first century, nearly all these restrictions had fallen away, save two: on some felons and adults under guardianship. But by Japan's 2013 election, those people under guardianship were free to vote. In fact, in country after country, similar reforms were occurring, and at more or less the same time.

Why did so many other countries change, when the US did not? Oddly enough, the explanation may be found in a treaty whose roots are in the US itself. The 1990 passage of the ADA was a watershed moment in lawmaking, both in America and internationally. Despite a divided government—Democrats controlled Congress, but a Republican was president—it nonetheless passed by wide bipartisan margins and was signed into law. The ADA prefigured and inspired a similar international treaty in 2007, the UN Convention on the Rights of Persons with Disabilities (CRPD). Article 29 of the treaty is blunt in "guaranteeing the free expression of the will of persons with disabilities as electors and to this end, where necessary, at their request, allowing assistance in voting by a person of their own choice." The CRPD has no provision for an exclusion; there's no clause titled "But We Don't Mean *Those* People, Right?" That hasn't deterred most countries from embracing it: 164 out of 191 UN parties have now signed and ratified the treaty.

The US is not one of them. We are surrounded by ratifiers—Canada ratified it; Mexico ratified it; Cuba, the Bahamas, and Jamaica all ratified it—but the US has not. The US is now the only member of the G20—a group that, incidentally, includes such human rights hard cases as Russia, China, and Saudi Arabia—not to have ratified it. To be fair, President Obama did *sign* the treaty in 2007, but ratification requires a supermajority vote of the Senate, and… Need I finish that sentence? It got sixty-one votes in the Senate in 2012, and after a few years of occasional queries, news outlets pretty much gave up even asking about it.

In other countries, though, the CRPD has made its mark—when not from new laws, from new lawsuits. In Japan, the change was heralded by a lawsuit brought in early 2013 by Takumi Nagoya, a woman disenfranchised from voting for having Down syndrome. She won her case, and by that year's national elections, Nagoya could vote. Very few people under guardianship actually *did* vote in that election, and the greater effect may instead be in how recognizing the disabled affects the perspective of everyone else. By the 2019 elections in Japan, candidates with Lou Gehrig's disease and cerebral palsy, both in wheelchairs, won seats in the parliament—a first for the country.

But there are limits to the treaty's success. Take, for instance, Caamaño Valle of Spain. When her intellectually disabled daughter was placed under guardianship, Valle asked the judge to still permit her daughter to vote. The judge said no, and Valle appealed. Even as Spain dropped its blanket exclusion against those under guardianship, it insisted it could strike specific individuals off the rolls for incapacity, and so Valle kept fighting, all the way to the top. In 2021, the European Court of Human Rights heard the case *Valle v. Spain*.

Valle lost. And she lost despite a UN commissioner reminding the court's panel of seven judges that exclusions were not acceptable; she lost in spite of a UN committee pointing out that "a person's decision-making ability cannot be a justification for any exclusion of persons with disabilities from exercising their political rights, including the right to vote." No matter: the court decided there must be certain kinds of limits when someone doesn't even understand what voting is. "The Court considers that the contested measure does not thwart the free expression of

---

MICROINTERVIEW WITH DEVON PRICE, PART VII

THE BELIEVER: Do you have hopes for your writing in relation to the field of psychology as a whole?

DEVON PRICE: I aim to use my tools and training for combing through the literature and putting more tools in the hands of people. I'd like to take the great work people are doing and put that up on a pedestal, too, to be seen as "scientifically" legitimate. So I am trying to dilute and dismantle psychology one bit at a time, through things like advocating for an informed-consent approach to psychiatric medicine, phasing out the diagnosis… Anything I can do to take down the authority—not exactly from the inside, but I guess kind of from the inside—by holding open the door so people can rush in, until there is no inside. ✷

the opinion of the people," its ruling stated. And how could that be? one may ask. It's simple, they explained: someone so severely intellectually incapacitated *has no opinion to freely express.*

Voilà!

Valle v. Spain was not a close decision: it was a 6–1 ruling. Yet despite the lopsided vote—indeed, because of it—the ruling makes for extraordinary reading, on account of that singular dissenting opinion. Written by Belgian judge Paul Lemmens, it conceded that prior decisions, or what is termed case law, gave his six fellow judges ample justification for their vote. But when it comes to disability rights, the past is not exactly an admirable guide. "To reconsider the case-law is sometimes necessary," Judge Lemmens gently noted.

The UN treaty, he pointed out, was already unambiguous on the matter: the court should have allowed Valle's daughter to vote. Its workaround—that the most seriously disabled have no opinion to express—was wrong and reductive, he retorted: "In the first place, voting is more than just expressing a certain preference on a particular day, every few years. As it is confirmed by the title of Article 29 of the CRPD, it forms part of the broader right to participate in political and public life…. An electoral system providing for the disenfranchisement of a whole category of vulnerable persons is hardly able to ensure 'the free expression of the opinion of the people.'"

What does it mean, exactly, to give the vote to someone who might not know what it means? It is, at first glance, a different sort of problem from installing wheelchair ramps or text-to-speech readers; it is different, even,

from assisting someone who may need a careful and patient explanation of elections and a walk-through of the process. What does it mean to give a vote to someone who may ignore the ballot, scribble on it, ball it up, or submit it blank? It seems like an insurmountable objection.

Except, as Judge Lemmens pointed out, it really isn't.

"I am the guardian for the protected person named above, and I make the following report to the Court as required by law."

Every year it's the same: Before Morgan's birthday, I fill in the form for the Guardian's Annual Report, and I mail it to the probate department of the circuit court. Name and address, whether he's been to the hospital, which doctors he sees, his mental condition, his physical condition, whether his guardianship should continue. The exact amount of money in his bank account at the time of the last report, the exact amount in it now, and what it was spent on; whether there are any persons he is kept from associating with; whether or not one of those persons should be me.

Since my last report:

I have been convicted of the following crimes (not including traffic violations): NONE

I have filed for or received protection from creditors under Federal Bankruptcy Code: NO

I have had a professional or occupational license revoked or suspended: NO

I have had my driver's license revoked or suspended: NO

One year, a court visitor schedules a required video visit, and I have to show her Morgan, and then walk around my house with my phone held up: *See! Delicious food in the fridge! Delightful toys in his room! The good kind of toilet paper in the bathroom! Clean, potable water!* Near the end of the call, she mentions offhandedly that she's a student at the university where I teach, and I'm momentarily terrified without quite knowing why.

"Oh," I manage, my mouth drying out. "Wow, that's great."

My mind turns back to the training session that the state requires when you first apply to be a guardian, after you get background-checked and fingerprinted. Mine was at night, in a low and nondescript building a hundred blocks out toward the suburbs, with folding chairs and a single carafe of coffee rapidly cooling to room temperature. We watched some training videos of the kind that, even when not actually shot in the 1980s, seemed like it anyway. Then we listened to our facilitators stress the same points repeatedly: *You're responsible for the ward now. If you go away for an hour, people must know where to find you. If you go out of town, you should be able to get back quickly. If you move, or your ward moves, you must clear it with the court first. You need to establish a separate bank account for their money; and for god's sake, never mix their money with your own. Never borrow from them. Never just sign their name on checks or documents—that would be forgery. Here is the correct format. Practice it now.*

I sipped my stone-cold coffee and practiced the correct signature diligently on my yellow legal pad: "Paul Collins, Guardian for Morgan Collins." As a guardian, I would ultimately be responsible for where he lived, the food he ate, what medications he swallowed, the clothes he wore, all his belongings. If he had to be committed to an institution, I'd be responsible for that too. Any medical decisions, petty or profound? Also on me. And yet, aside from egregious cases of being overbearing or under-regulated, you don't really hear about guardians much when talk turns to people with disabilities. Come to think of it, you don't hear about the most severely intellectually disabled much, either. It's neither an inspirational nor an aspirational situation; it's just a situation, day in and day out, largely unchanging, with the constant and simple imperative of unambiguously necessary work.

What I remember most clearly from my guardian training is that when the session ended, I waited in the lobby and watched everyone else depart; it was late, and my bus wasn't coming for a while. My fellow trainees went out to their cars in the parking lot, under the insufficient glow of streetlamps, and their taillights departed one by one—off to care for spouses, parents, children; off to duties of months, or years, or decades. They would file a Guardian's Annual Report, too, and maybe also panic at the court visitor's questions. Some would eventually hit the conviction or bankruptcy question and have to check, with rising dread, "YES." But today we were all heading off to the quotidian business of doing everything for our wards from buying their groceries and making barber appointments to signing leases and approving chemo. There would be just one place where we couldn't represent them.

In *Valle v. Spain*, Judge Lemmens's dissent confronted an inconvenient question: If we withhold voting from a subset of disabled citizens, can they ever have truly equal rights?

"By barring the applicant's daughter from the exercise of her right to vote," he concluded, "the State reduced her to a second-class citizen. Unlike other citizens, she cannot make her voice heard, not even via a trusted person…. A much less far-reaching measure [than disenfranchisement] is possible, which fully respects the person's legal capacity to vote, while at the same time ensuring that capacity is exercised by a person 'capable of assessing the consequences' of any vote cast…. Such an arrangement would reflect the principle 'one person, one vote,' a principle that is not observed when the person with a disability is excluded altogether from voting."

In short: let a guardian do what they already do in every other regard, and act on their ward's behalf.

The existing treaty already permitted this approach, Judge Lemmens pointed out, and arguably necessitated it. The CRPD bars exclusion, and requires giving necessary support to the disabled in voting. "Such an arrangement would be fully compatible with the CRPD," he wrote. "The CRPD Committee explains that 'support' is a broad term."

As the dissent itself notes, the notion of guardian voting is not an altogether new one—and rather like the CRPD, it has its roots in the United States, where it was raised by the philosopher Martha Nussbaum. In her 2009 essay "The Capabilities of People with Cognitive Disabilities," Nussbaum advanced a proposal that is logically straightforward, if provocative, by virtue of pushing back against centuries of precedent. Accommodations are clearly needed for people who need assistance in the *physical* act of voting, she begins, but what about those who can't form or communicate a preference? For them, she posits, voting should be treated like other ordinary but vital rights and actions.

"What does equal respect require in this case?" Nussbaum asks. "I would argue that it requires that the person's guardian be empowered to exercise the function on that person's behalf and in her interests, just as guardians currently represent people with cognitive disabilities in areas such as property rights and contract[s]." Otherwise, she argues flatly, "they do not count. Their interests are not weighed in the balance."

They do not count. And they do not count, because they are not counted. Morgan has as much at stake in elections as any other American. He breathes the same air, goes to the same libraries, faces the same fires and floods, travels over the same bridges. But he and everyone like him have no representation for those interests.

All this—giving the severely intellectually disabled the vote, or even giving it to a guardian—will, I fear, strike some readers as strange and not a little alarming. Or, perhaps, as a lot of fuss and bother for not much result, or just plain irksome, as requests around disability can sometimes seem to the abled. Maybe it's also discomfiting, amid lofty legal principles around inalienable rights and dignity, to see that other consideration baldly stated by Nussbaum: their interests.

Yet the tangible manifestations of disenfranchisement are dismayingly predictable, and just as evident every day in their lives. Take Supplemental Security Income (SSI), the sole income for the most vulnerable disabled Americans. SSI essentially demands permanent poverty from its recipients. The maximum monthly SSI benefit in 2024 is $943 per month; the national poverty line for an individual is $1,255 per month. Nor are SSI recipients allowed to own countable assets—money in the bank, or readily salable personal property—with a value totaling more than $2,000. That limit, initially set at $1,500 in 1972, has been frozen at $2,000 since 1989. If adjusted for inflation from the outset, it would be $11,399 today—but it never does get updated. Now, would these mandatorily impoverished Americans get more support if they were all permitted to vote?

Well, I don't think they would get *less*.

Lemmens's dissent remains one of the most striking modern statements on enfranchising the severely disabled. But when I contact him for further comment, he explains that, due to professional ethics, he really can't talk. "It is an issue that deserves a debate in society," he adds. "I must leave its interpretation, as well as any critical comments on it, to others, like you."

I must confess I don't feel entirely equal to the task. I remain stumped by the most basic question, the one I began with: Why can't my son vote? Because here's the curious thing:

Morgan *can* vote, sort of. But he also sort of *can't* vote.

Allow me to explain. Oregon has few voting restrictions, which is quite an achievement for a state whose original constitution barred every usual group and then tossed in "and Chinamen" for good measure. Thanks to its mail-ballot and Motor Voter systems, Oregon now has the United States' highest rate of voter registration. It's poised to go even further, by attempting to automatically register voters via Medicaid rosters, which can find citizens who may not have state IDs, or whose yearly Medicaid reenrollments bear more current addresses than Motor Voter data using old DMV renewals. And there is no obvious bar to most intellectually disabled Oregonians filling in a ballot, signing the envelope, and submitting it—even with some assistance.

But what does this mean in practice for the most severe intellectual disabilities? After so much reading on election law, I decide to find out: I pull the Bankers Box from my closet. Morgan, lolling on the daybed in my home office, observes this with mild interest. I lift the lid and leaf through months' worth of hastily tossed-in insurance forms and doctors' reports. Deeper in is a manila file on which I'd scribbled "Elections," underlined in Sharpie. I open it, this time wondering not why my son can't vote. Now I wonder: *Can my son vote?*

Long after receiving it, and months after the polls have closed, I select Morgan's most recent ballot, for Oregon's 2023 special election, and I slide my fingernail under the sealed flap of the envelope. It's a ballot for school board seats, the continuation of a children's levy (passed), a local capital gains tax (rejected). But the first item to emerge is a return envelope, which bears a blunt statement in thick black lettering: "WARNING: SIGNING ANOTHER PERSON'S NAME TO THIS ENVELOPE IS A CLASS C FELONY." A large green arrow points to an empty rectangle awaiting a signature.

It's heavy stuff: Class C felonies include dog fighting, third-degree robbery, and car theft, and carry up to five years in prison and a $125,000 fine.

Since Oregon employs voting by mail, the ballot itself is not identifiable to an individual voter, but the signed mailing envelope is; when received, the election board verifies the envelope's signature, and then adds the anonymous enclosed ballot to the tally pile. There's no guidance on the ballot itself about voting and the disabled, so I turn to the previous year's Voters' Pamphlet, which also includes the boldface statement "It is against the law to sign another person's ballot return envelope for them." Well, yes—I expected it was, just like you can't normally sign another person's checks. But I can and *do* sign his checks. Two pages later, an FAQ adds: "You're the only person who can sign your ballot return envelope. Power of Attorney documents do not apply to voting." Yet a guardianship is not quite the same as a mere power of attorney.

I dig deeper. Our state's Elections Division has a fifty-three-page guidebook, the Election Law Summary. It's more detailed, and for reasons that soon become apparent, considerably weirder. One can apply for a signature "stamp" for those who can't sign the envelope on their own, it explains, but this requires a special form that seems intended for the physically disabled. And then on page 46 of the guidebook you run into this:

ORS 260.715(1); Voting or Signing Another Person's Ballot Prohibited. Violation of this statute is a Class C felony. A first time violation of this statute, resulting from a person signing a ballot belonging to a different elector, may result in a civil penalty if the Secretary of State or Attorney General determine the violation

was not made with the intent to commit fraud. (HB 2351) ORS 260.715(1) states that a person may not knowingly make a false statement, oath or affidavit when required under election law. For purposes of voting, this means a person may not vote or sign any other person's (including a spouse's) ballot—not even with a power of attorney.

But when I look up the actual ORS 260.715 statute, rather than relying on what's printed in the Election Law Summary, I find it's not titled "Voting or Signing Another Person's Ballot Prohibited." It's titled "Prohibited conduct." Clause 1 reads, in its entirety: "A person may not knowingly make a false statement, oath or affidavit when a statement, oath or affidavit is required under the election laws." But a guardian is not making a false statement when they sign: it's clearly a signature on someone else's behalf. When I check our state's database of "Notes of Decisions," which appends relevant case law to each statute, there's nothing under ORS 260.715 about guardians or, indeed, about caregivers at all. Stranger still, when I access the legislature's database for HB 2351, the other law referenced, I get a shock: *it never passed.* It was proposed in the 2017 legislative session, whereupon the reduced penalty clause was stripped out in committee, and then the whole thing was shelved anyway. There is no such law, and never has been.

I hold our election board's guide at arm's length, a bit dazed, and for a moment my eyes cross, like maybe it's a Magic Eye puzzle. It doesn't help.

"Not hardly!" Morgan calls out in a Tigger voice as he watches a Disney video. "Hoo-hoo!"

"That's right," I say, nodding from my desk. "Not hardly."

I contact our secretary of state's office, but it takes two months to get an explanation. Her chief of staff restates the law to me about electors signing their own ballots, and the law against false statements, and adds: "We interpret this to mean that a power of attorney is not allowed." That's pretty much it, but perhaps this doesn't *quite* answer whether guardians can vote on their ward's behalf (He does agree, though, that citing an oops-not-actually-a-law is an error.) And he notes something else: there *is* a clause in Oregon's constitution about competency.

And indeed there is. But it's not quite clear what it means.

In 1980 the Oregon legislature forwarded an amendment to voters,

---

ALL THE POLITICAL SLOGANS FOUND IN LIZZIE BORDEN'S BORN IN FLAMES

★ "We are all leaders."
★ "Every woman is a potential radical."
★ "The revolution is not a onetime event."
★ "We won't be erased."
★ "Fight repression: defend our communities."
★ "United we stand, divided we fall."
★ "Workers of the world, unite!"
★ "No justice, no peace!"

—list compiled by Milly Hopkins

State Measure 2, that lessened the state's exclusions: "A person suffering from a mental handicap is entitled to the full rights of an elector, if otherwise qualified, unless the person has been adjudicated incompetent to vote as provided by law." What is that adjudication, "provided by law"? Well, it's hard to say, as a committee studying the proposal in 1980 discovered. "We were troubled by the introduction of the phrase 'unless the person has been adjudicated incompetent as provided by law,' as no method currently is specified under Oregon state law to adjudicate whether a person is incompetent to vote," they concluded, adding: "In fact, the Committee was unable to locate a proponent of the measure who could explain the legislature's intent in adding this language."

State Measure 2 passed. For decades we've had this apparently inexplicable clause in our state constitution. Maybe there's an exclusion, and maybe there isn't.

At this point a reader may reasonably wonder: OK, but why are you dragging me through Oregon's problems? It's because Oregon has some of the highest voter engagement and the least restrictive voting policies in the US. Oregon also has, due to its registration and mail voting systems, one of the most centralized and carefully run election boards. Yet it's a state with enough legal ambiguity that *every* disabled citizen may indeed get a vote… if you're willing to risk a felony to find out.

Should it be that hard? If a college professor like me can't figure out whether his son can vote, and if the election board and the state constitution can't entirely clarify this either, then what is an inexperienced care worker supposed to make of the law? Or an overwhelmed grandma serving as her granddaughter's guardian? Or someone who has difficulty with English? How are the intellectually disabled themselves supposed to figure this out? Recall that this dilemma comes not from asking for special rights: it comes from an *exclusion*, a singling-out, a targeted act of discrimination. If voting were treated like every other activity in Morgan's life, then whether he can have representation would not even be a question.

So why are we still being made to ask it?

Sometimes I suspect that what's really at stake was understood from the very beginning. I think of John Adams, writing from the Second Continental Congress just weeks before the Declaration of Independence was issued. His wife, Abigail, had recently pleaded with him to widen voting rights—"I desire you would remember the ladies, and be more generous and favorable to them than your ancestors"—but Adams refused. Writing to a friend, he explained why, in a tone meant to be despairing, but which today reads as one of the most hopeful statements he ever made. If voter qualifications were to be open to discussion, Adams fretted, "new claims will arise." Women would demand the vote, "lads" under twenty-one would demand it, and so, too, would "every man who has not a farthing." Such notions, he warned, would throw open the door to all sorts of equality.

And then, Adams wrote, "There will be no end of it." ★

CAROLINE ROSE

[MUSICIAN]

"IT'S A SACRED THING TO SPACE OUT."

Musical inspirations mentioned by Caroline Rose:
Erik Satie
Antonio Vivaldi
Kronos Quartet

I *have watched countless videos of Caroline Rose singing live. She isn't some-one who mimics herself night after night. She has an almost intoxicating way of being present—an intuitive connection to the moment—and because of this, every performance is uniquely embodied. Sometimes she cries, some-times she takes her clothes off, often she dances—and always she stares absorbedly into the beyond while singing, her gaze solidly present, grounded, and focused, yet somehow otherworldly. Some musicians I just listen to, but Rose is one to watch. She looks kind of possessed by the music, as if she were giving her whole self to it—or it to her. And her gift for reinventing herself and experimenting from album to album—moving between genres—underscores a pure love of singing, songwriting, and producing.*

Reviewers tend to focus on how different Rose's albums are, but I would say that what distinguishes her as an artist is her ability to straddle dualities, producing songs over the years that feel vast yet intimate, mournful yet danceable, fictional yet lived, naked yet dressed up, savage yet tender, silly yet serious, ironic yet disarmingly

96

forthright—I could go on. And her songs are beautifully built, both formally and emotionally. In fact, this is her genius: how the sonic structures she creates mirror what they carry inside: living feelings. A certain generosity of spirit resonates throughout Caroline's work. It is hard to explain what it means to perceive someone else's spirit. But there is a feeling of recognition: a hello *feeling; a* yes *feeling; a somehow ancient feeling; a moved, connected, and slightly bewitched feeling that is set in motion when I listen to her songs. And while it may be hard to articulate what exactly spirit is, it certainly stands out—easy to spot in these numb times. I spoke with Caroline twice by phone, for three hours total. We discussed God, self-love, nudity, grieving, heartbreak, invisible friends, and choosing art over business.*

—Leopoldine Core

I. GOOFY, FUN, AND THRASHY

THE BELIEVER: Can you talk about the process of producing and then touring *I Will Not Be Afraid* back in 2014—your first nationally distributed album? What inspired the record, and what was it like performing the material live for the first time?

CAROLINE ROSE: To be honest, I have regrets around that album. I had a vision and it just ended up being so different. I was really young and new at the time and I was talked out of making it more of a pop-style folk album. And what ended up kind of transpiring was—to me, it fell a little flat. I didn't feel like I was fully formed and pretty much immediately after putting it out I was like, This isn't right. [*Laughs*] But, yeah, I don't think I toured very much around *I Will Not Be Afraid*. It was probably empty bars at that point.

BLVR: So what is that experience like, when you're getting talked out of your vision? Was it just your age that made it hard to advocate for yourself, or were you being told you had to do certain things in order to put the record out?

CR: It was less about age and more about self… worth. [*Laughs*] When you're green or when you're feeling a moment of insecurity or something like that, it's hard to have the wisdom to know what will benefit the project or not.

BLVR: How did you evolve as an artist in the time after that album, during the shift to your next album, *Loner*, four years later, in 2018?

CR: I grew up as a theater kid, so I had this whole side of myself that I wasn't expressing. I wanted to figure out what type of artist I wanted to be onstage, and that took some time, to just grow the confidence to be more myself—like be more weird and goofy and fun and at the same time more thrashy onstage.

BLVR: I love that song "Cry!" on *Loner*. What were you feeling when you wrote that?

CR: Probably feeling like I wasn't being taken seriously as a young woman in a pretty male-dominated industry. I was kind of beating my head against the wall at the time because I really believed in my work. The vision I had for it was becoming more and more fully formed, and the more I thought it was fully formed, the less the people I worked with understood what I was trying to do. It was really frustrating. I had this power inside me and this wisdom inside me that people didn't see.

BLVR: There's a live performance of that song online—I think you were in Germany—and at the end you hit this crazy note and sustained it for a very long time. I recorded it on my phone—just that part—because it moved me. It felt like it was coming from the deepest part of you.

CR: Yeah, I guess so. I don't know. It's God's work. [*Laughs*]

BLVR: [*Pause*] Do you believe in God? How do you define God?

CR: I think the idea of God and patriarchy are so linked that you have to seriously separate the two—like there should be another word. I remember reading this book about the Lakota—they use the term *the Great Spirit* for God and I thought that made much more sense. It's not a father—it's not a father figure. Which, in Christianity, I always found *so* weird.

BLVR: You are often asked about your shifts in tone and style from album to album. Why do you think the ways you change are seen as strange?

CR: I truly don't know. So many artists throughout history have *dramatically* changed. And no one batted an eye.

BLVR: It seems sort of objectifying. It's like asking: *Why are you alive?*

CR: We should be living in a time where you never know what you're gonna get—and I feel like in a way it's sort of the opposite. I guess it's easier to sell music by an artist when it sounds the same—more understandable. And that's fine—I'm not upset by it—but it's not me.

II. EVERYDAY COSTUMES

BLVR: I watched a show of yours online where you flashed the audience and then I saw a picture of you naked in your recording studio and I thought, They look happy. Then I was thinking that there's an exposing of oneself that comes with being an artist but specifically a performer, because your body is there. So I'm curious about the relationship between the exposure of your ideas and the exposure of your body. Is it comforting to be naked?

CR: [*Laughs*] Maybe using my body is an act of rebellion against being uncomfortable with it. It gives me a power and makes some of the shame I have disappear. I am in control of how I use my body, how I move—and what I'm comfortable revealing has definitely expanded. I actually don't feel sexualized at all. If anything, it feels more like performance art.

BLVR: You've had a lot of looks over the course of your career. Is wearing a costume or having a persona a form of nudity? A revealing of oneself?

CR: I have always tried on different costumes, versions of myself that highlight different aspects of my personality. And this is partly why it makes a lot of sense to me that more and more people are coming out as nonbinary. Because I've always had this feeling that I'm this personality with all these different sides that was just plunked into a body—like this is just the one I got. And I've never felt like, Oh, this body really represents me as a person. It's just what I landed in. It's the vessel that I have. And I can dress up my vessel however I'm feeling. Sometimes I'm feeling like I wanna be

a shadow. And other times I feel like a flamboyant gay man, you know? And what I wear and how I act and how I present myself reflect that.

BLVR: Yeah, costumes are so personal. They're part of the inside. I feel they're misunderstood. [*Pause*] Maybe the anxiety around change we were talking about earlier is connected to anxiety around gender.

CR: Yeah, it's easier to just be like: *Man, woman—here are your parts. This is what you do in life. You fuckin' make babies.* It's so much easier to rationalize that than to say that actually there's a very complex spectrum, that we could be a host to different things at once.

BLVR: I feel like whatever you're wearing… there's something shining through the trees that's kind of collaborating with the costume—it's your gaze, it's your aura—like whether you're wearing lipstick or… There's always a gender that's your own, and I guess that's true of everyone—but maybe with you more apparently so. It's a compliment—

CR: No, no, I take it as one. I think that's true. I feel that way. And I also think everyone every day is wearing a costume.

BLVR: Yes, yes.

CR: We're presenting our personality to the world or to whoever's gonna see us that day, and some costumes are just more detailed than others. But we're always presenting something.

III. "IT'S LIKE A PARTICLE ACCELERATOR"

BLVR: Your latest album, *The Art of Forgetting*, deals so frankly with heartbreak. Did you plan to tell this story, or did it wind up being a surprise to you?

CR: It was definitely a surprise, kind of a left turn. I had put out another album [*Superstar*] pretty much right as the pandemic started, and we got maybe four shows in before the entire tour was canceled. It definitely knocked me down a peg [*laughs*]—or twelve. A loss of self is the best way to describe what I felt—and that was coupled with a breakup. She and I weren't speaking when I was working on *The Art of Forgetting*, and I really wanted to speak. The process of grieving isn't linear. Somebody described it to me as climbing a mountain, where some moments you'll be going up and then you go down and then you'll go sideways and then you'll go the other direction. But ultimately you will make it to the top. It's a good description of grief—because sometimes you'll be really angry and then sometimes you'll be really soft and gentle and be like, *No, I really fucked up.* And other times you're just gonna wanna go out and hook up with someone. You're constantly going—it's like a particle accelerator—you're just bouncing off all these different feelings.

BLVR: Voicemail messages and conversations with your grandmother appear on the album. Why did you choose to include them?

CR: Because I was talking to her every day. She was losing her memory—she's since passed away—so these are like little relics in time. She would leave me a message if I didn't pick up, so I collected these voice memos from her. And over time, if you play them all in a row, you can really hear her aging and changing. My grandma was so obsessed with family and wanted nothing more than to be there for my sister and me—to be involved in everything that was going on. And meanwhile I was so depressed, I could barely get out of bed. You know, I was just really not doing well. [*Laughs*] She would call me and be so happy to hear me and I was just struggling to find *any* joy. And, you know, here I was trying to forget as much as possible—all this pain that I was feeling—and she's losing her memory and all she wants to do is remember *everything.* And every time we would talk, it was this sort of slap from reality that was like: *Wake up! There's life to live!*

BLVR: Listening to the album reminded me of going to the opera. There are hooks but there's also a weird breathability—time structures that are not predictable and that feel somehow living. Can you talk about how you constructed time within these songs?

CR: You're definitely hitting the nail on the head. I wasn't listening to opera but I was listening to a lot of classical music, and if you listen to Satie or even if you listen to *The Four Seasons* by Vivaldi, he was really—I mean, that's pop music.

BLVR: Totally!

CR: [*Laughs*] He was like a pop icon for God, you know, so I'm all about that music because the motif is really important—and the melody. I find when I put on an average album, I generally want more, and I keep that in mind for my own work *constantly.* Like, are my ears still intrigued after listening to this for an hour? We really only have so many tools to work with: we have tempo, time signature, and a handful of chords. And it always amazes me what people are able to come up with. Everyone's always making something different, and that is a huge inspiration to me: that you can go from song to song and give it breathability and air just by changing the time signature, or just by taking out that chord that's not really necessary.

BLVR: I read that you have a background in architecture, and that made sense to me. It seems like your songs have a spatial element. Like you somehow create rooms with sound—songs that *surround* the listener.

CR: Yeah! A lot of that is frequency space too. I am also a mix engineer so I'm constantly thinking about how much space things are gonna to be taking up in a mix—and the way recording is evolving is *so* cool because it's getting more and more 3D.

BLVR: What effects, if any, were used on the album to create the sense of memories surfacing?

CR: The thing I used to create the feeling of memory glitching was this little modular rack that is mostly based on granular synthesis. It's this one particular company called Mutable Instruments—they came out with a modular unit called Clouds. They've since updated it—it's now called Beads—but the basic idea is that you can take what is called a grain of audio, just a little grain of sound, and you can chop it, smear it, bop it, twist it, pull it—do whatever you want with it. And it is a totally different type of synthesis. It's a way of treating audio digitally rather than analog. But it sounds

Photo by Jenny Alice Watts

really organic to me. I also used a lot of tape loops—I became kind of obsessed with loops. I was trying to get this human-like quality to everything that was on the album. And so even with all the granular synthesis stuff, I'm using audio from acoustic instrumentation to kind of give it more of a natural feel.

BLVR: Can you explain what exactly a tape loop is?

CR: It's literally just splicing a loop of tape, so that if you put any sort of sound on it—it could be a voice or it could be an instrument, and I was doing tape loops with my voice a lot, where I would just sing a note and then I would make a loop of it—and if you put it into a cassette player or a tape machine or whatever, it'll just play that same loop over and over and over again. But

what's *cool* is if you play it long enough, you'll hear it start to decay. And I just thought that was the coolest way to use an effect to show memory failing. Or just this idea of time passing.

IV. "I'M NEVER GONNA BE A McDONALD'S HAMBURGER"

BLVR: There's a theme of self-love on the album—realizing it's missing, wanting it, recognizing how essential it is—and that's so relatable. Though I think the quest to love oneself is always unique, and so I wonder: What does it mean to you? How do you define self-love?

CR: The best way I can describe it—at least the thing I *need* the most—is just being gentle with myself. That's the biggest difference when I'm talking to a friend rather than myself.

I'm always really gentle and kind with other people—and understanding—and I don't know why it's so much harder to be that way for ourselves.

BLVR: Yeah, it's so important to ask yourself, like, How would I treat my dog? How would I treat my sister? Because you probably wouldn't yell at them or shame them or think of them as *bad*, you know.

CR: It really is that simple. But for some reason it's just really hard sometimes.

BLVR: How important is being alone to your ability to be creative?

CR: It's extremely important because I tend to be way more open when I'm alone—and that could even just be if I'm writing in my journal or sitting in the park and *thinking* about things. That's when I'm the most intimate. When I'm alone I'm always exploring. I'm always a little kid that's sort of wandering into a new space. And I have yet to find that in a setting with people around. My initial ideas really always come from having this childlike sense of wonder at things that either pop into my head 'cause I'm daydreaming or because I'm out wandering.

BLVR: Spacing out is so creative. It's such a creative state.

CR: I think spacing out is a form of meditation.

BLVR: Yeah, it's spiritual!

CR: [*Laughs*] I think so too. It's a sacred thing to space out. Because if you think about it, people don't space out as much as they used to. Everyone's looking at their phone all the time. As soon as we have a *moment* of boredom or, you know, free time, we're pretty much always looking at a screen. And so to just sit and stare into space and think about stuff—to allow your brain to think about whatever it wants to think about—I think that's really important. I'm all about spacing out.

BLVR: I feel like the internet stole the medium of a dream, in a way, and it's necessary for us to have our *own* dreams—our

own consciousness inside—the psychic space that is animal. Which is not to say there's nothing good about the internet. But, yeah, I hate everyone looking at their screens on the train—it makes me lonesome.

CR: This brings up a good point that ties back into why being alone is so important. I'm always trying to place why I feel that way, because ultimately I do want to collaborate with more people. But I'm constantly learning new things from the internet and books and movies—and at the end of the day we need time alone to process those things or else we're just these… encyclopedias. I'm always gonna be the type of person that if I meet someone, I don't really believe in small talk. I think it's a waste of time. And if I were gonna get in the room with someone to make music together, it *needs* to be deep—it needs to go really deep, 'cause when I'm in the room alone, like, I'll make myself cry. I'll just sob making something, and I have to be comfortable enough with someone else in order for them to push me—to get to a new emotional level.

BLVR: I wanna talk more about sobbing. At the live shows you often break into tears mid-song. How does it feel to cry in front of an audience?

CR: Well, at first it was kind of embarrassing. But then I was like, All right, I've gotta accept that this is happening pretty much every night. And it's weird because I used to be not much of a crier but I guess I've changed. The material is also just—it *still* hits me. I mean, some of these songs I wrote in 2020, but they still bring me right back to when I was *completely* raw. I get so emo.

BLVR: Maybe that's love for yourself—when you cry.

CR: Yeah, just letting it happen.

BLVR: Or feeling compassion for that person who felt those things: that's *you*. In the videos of live shows I've seen, people cheer when you cry—they seem into it.

CR: People are sweet. I think they like seeing a human being. I always make this joke that I'm never gonna be a McDonald's hamburger—I'm never gonna be the same every time, at every show. As much as I *try* to maintain a level of professionalism by delivering a similar show each night, I personally am always gonna be different. My moods change. I'm not a robot. And maybe in the age of AI, I'm gonna find that's actually a huge asset—that my albums sound different enough that AI cannot reproduce them fast enough. [*Laughs*]

BLVR: I haven't been into any of the AI songs I've heard. I find they are entertaining but not exactly pleasure-causing… because consciousness is missing.

CR: Yeah, I kind of hope it's just having a Bitcoin moment and then people will eventually be like: *Actually, I do prefer humanity.*

BLVR: Is there an artist whose work makes you cry?

CR: One that comes to mind—it's one of my favorite pieces of music *ever*—is the Kronos Quartet playing this Philip Glass piece called String Quartet no. 5. There's a moment in it when there's this huge crescendo and then right when you think it's gonna explode—it's gonna be this climax of sound—it actually goes back *down* and you're like, *No!* [*Laughs*] He kind of fucking makes you wait for it, and by the time this big sonic release happens, it's such an overwhelm of emotions for me, I can't help but cry. It's that tension-and-release feeling—it feels like a warm bath or like a really amazing vista where you're climbing and climbing and you finally see this beautiful expanse—and it makes you feel so alive and makes you feel so grateful for *being* alive and having vision and having ears to hear.

BLVR: Can you talk about the confluence of humor and sorrow in your work?

CR: I'm always injecting humor into stuff, but it doesn't always translate. In music, especially, it's really hard to translate humor unless you're being really over-the-top with it. I think a lot of my fan base knows I'm funny—they can pick it out easier—but with this album, there were a lot of people that were like: *It's not as funny.* But there are actually moments of humor peppered throughout the album. It's just very dark.

BLVR: I think it's *so* funny. I would say it's one of your funniest.

CR: Oh, I love that. I *love* that.

BLVR: What kinds of things make you laugh?

CR: I definitely have a pretty dark sense of humor. I'm not really a slapstick kind of person. I like dark, cerebral humor because it says something about humanity. When people go really deep and they're being vulnerable with what they're joking about, it almost acts as an antidote to the darker elements of life—it's like an antidote to oppression. Or, you know, satire is an antidote to all sorts of isms, like racism and sexism—all the things that normally cause us a lot of pain. If you have the ability to turn those things into humor, then it's really like a sword that you can wield and this incredible tool that makes you feel better about something that's horrifying. It makes me feel powerful when I can find the humor in a dark situation. And this was a really dark situation for me. Every day I would have a moment where I was like: I *know* this is comically sad. Like, I *know* I'm very close to the bottom and I have this beautiful view of the sky! [*Laughs*] You know? 'Cause you've gotta find a way to laugh. It's the only way to get through the *hell* that is life on Planet Earth.

V. "THE SUCCESS STORY"

BLVR: How has religion or spirituality influenced your work—or has it?

CR: Well, I think it's important to differentiate between religion and spirituality. I've always found myself to be a pretty spiritual person. I think there's something about songwriting that's spiritual—it's the antenna, you know—the antennae are out. You're channeling something into music. You're channeling emotions and feelings into something that's tangible and listenable. There's *gotta* be something spiritual about that, 'cause not everyone can do it.

BLVR: There is, there is.

CR: I'll have these moments of inspiration and think, Whoa, where did that come from? It feels spiritual. Anything that is inexplicable has an element of some sort of spirit. I can't comprehend it but I embrace it. I'm like: I don't understand this but I'm just gonna accept it.

BLVR: Believe in the unknown.

CR: Yeah, and believe in feelings—that they're real or that something happens and then there's a reaction in us that moves us. Like, what *is* that? I don't know. I think it's the same type of thing when you go to some sort of revival and everybody's singing and shouting on their knees. There's a spiritual element to that. There *is* an overlap with the arts and *that*.

BLVR: Yes.

CR: And I think that's why it's so important to differentiate between spirituality and religion, because, like, they do not always go hand in hand. But there are oftentimes moments of spirituality in things like religion because it's deep… And when you accept the unknown and open yourself up to it, something wild happens.

BLVR: I don't know if you've ever had this experience of being alone and creating something but feeling—feeling a sense of collaboration—feeling that you are collaborating even though you're by yourself.

CR: Yeah, I've felt that for sure. It's like when you say, *OK, I'm gonna write today* and then you sit down and write and it's completely mediocre. But then something happens: you'll be driving down the highway or something and you're struck with this feeling and you're like, I gotta write this down. And then you write down all this stuff that's been channeled into you and it's *so* much better.

BLVR: Yeah, or even sometimes I'll have words enter my mind when I'm writing and I'll think: I don't even totally know that word—but then it winds up being the right word.

CR: [*Laughs*] I *so* understand that. I *so* feel that.

BLVR: It's coming from elsewhere, and I like that—that doesn't scare me, I'm like: *Haunt me*, please.

CR: Yeah. [*Laughs*]

BLVR: You made a short film called *The Art of Forgetting* using three songs from the album. How did it feel to work with an actor who was playing your ex? And how did it feel to play yourself—or a version of yourself? Was it healing? Was it strange?

CR: Both, both. It was kind of bizarre because the album is obviously autobiographical and the film is too—but I think it's also important to note that it is fiction. When the other actor and I were working out the characters, we had different names for them. I would talk about my character as someone else, not me or any particular person. That was important because it was already borderline creepy how close to home I was getting. The director, Sam Bennett, he's one of my oldest friends, and we very much speak the same language artistically. We ran with this idea of using the past and the future to create a sense of anxiety. When you're grieving, you oftentimes feel *crazy*. You're constantly creating stories in your head, and we were trying to get that idea across of how, you know, when you start creating stories, it's really hard to get in touch with what you are actually feeling and what you actually need, which is just to be still and let life go on. You can think about the other person as much as you want, but at the end of the day, you have to try to turn all that energy around and put it back into yourself. I was having such a hard time doing that. I'd have these moments of clarity where it felt like I was back in my body, but then anxiety would creep back in and I would start telling stories again. [*Laughs*]

BLVR: I really hear your singing voice in your laugh. I love that.

CR: [*Laughs*]

BLVR: When did you first know you could sing?

CR: Probably in school chorus. Everybody

was kind of forced to be in the chorus, but I liked it. I was like, *Oh*, I can harmonize and make melodies. It became a fun thing for me to do.

BLVR: What were you like as a child?

CR: I was actually really quiet. I was a loner and loved playing by myself if there was no one around. I also liked other kids—I had my best friends, but I acted a lot like an only child, which I wasn't. I've always been able to be alone and be content—just writing or drawing or zoning out, or, you know, I had imaginary friends and I'd build forts. I was kind of like a little dirt child, always outside, always running around with my shirt off.

BLVR: Tell me about one of your imaginary friends.

CR: I feel like his name was Bill. Yeah… Bill. And I remember pushing him around on the… There was a little swing, a rope swing that hung from a tree in my family's backyard. I remember pushing him around on it. [*Laughs*]

BLVR: What was the first song you wrote and what was it about?

CR: It was about time.

BLVR: Oh!

CR: It was called "Out of Time." I remember thinking kind of existentially about these big subjects that baffled me, like the scope of the universe or how time works—how it's stretchy—how it can move forward and backward. I found that so intriguing. I also had a lot of anxiety around time—I still do—just feeling like I have to make the most of it. So it was probably a mixture of both anxiety and wonder at, um, you know, moving through time.

BLVR: How old were you?

CR: I was fourteen or so.

BLVR: I wanna hear it.

CR: I'm sure there's a recording of it—it's probably *so* cringe.

BLVR: No, I bet it's good. I bet you'd be surprised to find it's really good.

CR: [*Laughs*]

BLVR: How do you define success?

CR: I think it's always changing. Success could feel very different from one album to the next. I made *The Art of Forgetting* knowing it wasn't gonna be as received as the catchier, poppier, albums but it was important to me to make it—and make it be exactly what I wanted to hear. And to me that was a huge success. I really adhered to that constitution I had written for myself.

BLVR: What was the constitution?

CR: That I wasn't gonna make any choices for business over art. I thought: I have to put my blinders on and just really tune in to how this album makes me feel, and I really adhered to that.

BLVR: What gives you hope?

CR: There's so many things that give me hope. There's also so many things that destroy my hope, but sometimes I'll be walking down the street and I'll see a honeybee and I'm like, Oh, that's the whole purpose of life right there—there's the success story. [*Laughs*] Just watching things—it's our job to pay attention, and I think that's why I've ended up gravitating toward… I call it taking my meds. Where I'll sit and meditate or walk around and look at things: be an observer. So I don't know. I actually think I'm more optimistic—well, maybe *optimistic* is not the right word. [*Laughs*] Let me make it clear: everything's going to shit, but I think there will always be moments of beauty constantly, everywhere, and that brings me hope. ★

OLÚFẸ́MI O. TÁÍWÒ

[PHILOSOPHER]

"WHEN I SAY WE SHOULD CHANGE THE WORLD, I MEAN IT LITERALLY.
I'M TALKING ABOUT A LITERAL CONSTRUCTION PROJECT."

Things we need to change, according to Olúfẹ́mi O. Táíwò:
The number of trees that are planted now
The quantity of organic matter in the soil
The amount of food that's going to this city rather than to that city

O lúfẹ́mi O. Táíwò is a philosopher by training and a public intellectual by vocation. He writes about climate and racial justice from his office at Georgetown University, where he is an associate professor. His widely acclaimed work focuses on reparations and elite capture, a term that describes how those perpetuating racial capitalism will co-opt the critique of it—by misusing the term identity politics, for example—to pit people against one another and further harm marginalized groups. Táíwò's combination of depth and range is rare in the academy.

He was born in the Bay Area to Nigerian immigrants who'd moved there for graduate school in the late 1980s. They later relocated to Cincinnati, where Táíwò spent part of his childhood in an active Nigerian American community, and the other part in mostly white institutions. He went to white schools and Sunday churches, but also attended entirely Black African Bible study groups and discovered a social scene of African Americans and African immigrants. Those contrasts marked the Midwestern

Illustration by Kristian Hammerstad

childhood of a self-described nerd. His upbringing was framed by questions of belonging, as he navigated spaces of bigotry daily. He then majored in philosophy at Indiana University, and went on to pursue his graduate studies at UCLA, but not before taking a year off to try to become a professional musician. The saxophonic life didn't pan out—he credits failing as a musician for its character-building success—but his studies of freedom, colonialism, and political philosophy earned him a PhD in 2018.

In the mere half decade since, we've seen many so-called racial reckonings and one full-blown global pandemic. During that time, Táíwò's voice has become increasingly forceful, establishing him as one of the leading contemporary thinkers to consider racial and climate justice together. That voice is above all clear and evocative. Another interviewer once characterized him as relaxed and unpretentious. Readers will notice those qualities in all his works: Elite Capture: How the Powerful Took Over Identity Politics *(Haymarket Books, 2022),* Reconsidering Reparations *(Oxford University Press, 2022), articles in a dozen-plus academic journals, and a score of essays published in mainstream venues.*

—Benjamin R. Cohen

I. LOST IN ABSTRACTION

THE BELIEVER: Climate justice, racial capitalism, reparations, identity politics, standpoint epistemology: this is not light material. But I'm reading your work in *The New Yorker*, *The Atlantic*, *Al Jazeera*, *The Nation*—places I don't often see this kind of philosophically informed broad engagement with such topics. What draws you to write for the more mainstream cultural, political, and literary forums? How does it fit into your work life?

OLÚFẸ́MI O. TÁÍWÒ: You know, in a lot of ways it's just a function of the kinds of things I work on. There's a place for philosophy that's more esoteric, I don't know what kind of conversation you could get going at *Teen Vogue* about mereology or the philosophical problem of what constitutes a "heap" or something. But the topics I work on—like reparations, like the change of our literal physical and political infrastructure in response to the climate crisis, like the goals of racial justice—I don't think there's even the presumption that those intellectual questions are purely technical. They're

clearly of some public import, even if researchers talk about them differently than the general public does.

BLVR: They're not of interest only to technical logicians or something.

OT: Right. On my part, there's never been the presumption that the only people I should be talking to are academics. For better or worse, we all live in these structures and have to figure them out together. I've been asked before why I talk about these things in public venues, but from my perspective, the thing you'd have to explain is *not* doing that.

BLVR: Even so, not all philosophers or academics write fluidly for different audiences. Did you cultivate that skill or did you just always feel it?

OT: It's definitely something I work on, and, you know, there's so much hidden labor that goes into a lot of these publications. One of the things I've been fortunate about is having good experiences with editors at various publications, people like my editor Jen Parker at *Hammer & Hope*, or Shuja Haider at *The Nation*, to name two that jump right out. People talk about publishing as if it's the work of the one person whose name is in the byline, but in my case, I've been lucky to work with editors who are good at helping me and other writers speak to different audiences.

BLVR: We tiptoed onto the topics of invisible labor and concealed structures, which I wanted to ask about more fully. Both these things happen beneath or before us. Some people—like colonizers, settlers, capitalists, industrialists—are responsible for their existence, and others bear the burden of it.

OT: Hidden infrastructures.

BLVR: That's it: hidden infrastructures. The hidden parts of publishing are a small example, I know, but it got me thinking about larger problems. You take the word *structure* seriously, not just as a metaphor but as a practical point about how people build things. *Elite Capture* and *Reconsidering Reparations* had me thinking that you're a very architectural philosopher. You talk about construction, reconstruction, foundations—the tactility of building, like, you need a hard hat to get the work done.

OT: I do talk about building often.

BLVR: There's a fable that comes up in some of my classes, about these people on the side of the river who see a baby floating in the current, so they all, quite sensibly, jump into the river to save the baby, only to find more floating down the river, and more. And they keep saving them, until someone on shore says, "Hey, we should go upriver to find out who's putting babies in the water." I mean, you don't stop getting the baby that's right there out of the river; it's not an either/or scenario. But you have to understand why this is happening if you want to truly address it. If we're talking about how to think about the big issues—justice, climate, identity—and I don't mean to get us bogged down in the place of metaphor, but how do you think through the ways our current problems are coming from upriver?

OT: I would say my writing is actually an effort to *avoid* metaphor, maybe even more than to use it. So there's an abstract, philosophical commitment—in particular a form of materialist thought—that emphasizes these kinds of broader ecological arrangements of power. These social and political relationships are the context in which we make our individual, or organizational, collective choices about what to do, what to pursue, how to pursue it. It's about these ecological relationships that load the deck in favor of some people and places and things, and against other people and places and things. In the midst of that highly abstract explanation of the way I think about politics, one of the things I fear being lost is: I'm *not* speaking metaphorically. When I say we should change the world, I mean it literally. I'm talking about a literal construction project. When I say we should change the world ecologically, I'm saying the number of trees that are planted now, the number of actual trees with roots in the actual ground, needs to be a larger number—

BLVR: A whole reality. Building gardens, forests, farm stands, community centers.

OT: Exactly! The quantity of organic matter in the soil, the amount of food that's going to this city rather than to that city, and at this price. Those are the things we need to change. And it's very easy for the concreteness of that project to get lost in the necessary abstractions we use to talk about that project at scale, and to talk about that project across domains. Sometimes we're worried about where funding is going, about where food is going, and so to talk about that on a planetary scale, you need to make abstractions. But for me, I want to speak in terms of construction projects because I'm trying to consistently emphasize that, despite the abstractions, the things I'm talking about are real, tangible flows of capital, of food, of soil, of waste. It's those distributions of political power—which are just as real as any of the things I've mentioned—that we have to do something about.

BLVR: You talk about Flint, Michigan, in *Elite Capture*. The point of the Flint water crisis being: *We want clean water, not talking points about clean water justice. We want actual clean water.* All the political work around that takes effort, we get it, but it's all so we can have actual clean water in our cups and in our sinks.

OT: That's right, and I think, at bottom, the hope is that you find a way of thinking through abstractions that makes them *aids* to thinking about concrete political decisions, as opposed to being alternatives to concrete solutions.

II. "WELCOME TO POLITICS. ARE YOU NEW HERE?"

BLVR: I wanted to get into another part of *Elite Capture*, because there's a complicated phrase you unfold in the book, "the deferential applications of standpoint epistemology," and it feels key. Could you say more about that passage?

OT: Basically, standpoint epistemology is the idea that what people know depends on who they are. So what kind of relationship do you have to the world around you? And sometimes people talk about that in terms of social position or social identity. The basic idea is that different people have access to different kinds of knowledge about the world, based on their different experiences and their different relationships to the world. Women are going to learn things about gender that men don't; Black people are going to know things about racism that white people won't. That kind of thought. If you stare at that directly, it would be very surprising if that were not true. If the kinds of things that determine how people treat you and who you have connections with had *no* impact on the information you have about the world? That would be extremely surprising, right?

BLVR: OK, so you're talking about differences in access to knowledge, a human point of experience-based understanding.

OT: Yeah, and if you have any kind of empiricism going, it would be very difficult, at this level of abstraction, to fight that conclusion. So what standpoint epistemology builds on top of—its very accurate, very poignant insight—is just the intention to pay attention to those kinds of differences in access to knowledge. It's not just true, as a matter of fact, that some people have access to different sorts of knowledge about the world. It's that when we're doing science, when we're doing theory, when we're trying to figure out what the world is like, those are differences that we can pay attention to, and as you add flesh onto the bones of this thought, you start to see where controversies might come in. Well, pay attention to those kinds of differences how? What precise difference does it make that someone is from this group or that group?

And there's lots to get into there, but I'll just punctuate this by saying that I think the basic insight of standpoint epistemology is true and it's useful and it's important. And I say that for the sake of making it clear that what I'm about to describe is just

---

WORDS THAT ORIGINATED FROM WORKS OF FICTION

✶ *Catch-22*, from Joseph Heller's *Catch-22*
✶ *Lilliputian*, from Jonathan Swift's *Gulliver's Travels*
✶ *Utopia*, from Sir Thomas More's *Utopia*
✶ *Robot*, from Karel Čapek's *R.U.R.*
✶ *Serendipity*, from *The Three Princes of Serendip*
✶ *Pandemonium*, from John Milton's *Paradise Lost*
✶ *Big Brother*, from George Orwell's *1984*
✶ *Quixotic*, from Miguel de Cervantes's *Don Quixote*
✶ *Narcissism*, from Ovid's *Metamorphoses*
✶ *Cyberspace*, from William Gibson's "Burning Chrome"
✶ *Mentor*, from Homer's *The Odyssey*
—*list compiled by Natalia Borecka*

one way to use that insight. It's not equivalent to that insight; it's a thing to do with it, and we can and should discuss it in those terms. And that gets me further into your question—to what I've been calling "deference": "deference epistemology."

One way you could respond to the true, useful, and important fact that different people are situated differently is to say this: *I'm going to figure out what an oppressive society is like and figure out how I should respond to it by finding someone from an oppressed group and deferring to their political analysis*—describing the world as they describe the world; maybe even going further than that; maybe taking cues from them about what I should do, what constitutes solidarity, what constitutes allyship, or how I should respond to that version of oppression. I don't like that way of using the standpoint epistemology insight, and I have a bunch of criticisms of it.

BLVR: You point out that identity politics derives from the Combahee River Collective in the 1970s. Who you are influences how you walk in the world. Where you come from shapes how you experience the world. Then we find in the decades since this term's origination that those in power co-opt and abuse it.

OT: Let me say it this way. It's definitely true that the people who are best positioned to opine on identity politics across the political spectrum have done so in a way that's convenient for them and not necessarily tied to the core values that either standpoint epistemology or, much more broadly, identity politics were originally thought to describe and defend. But, I don't know, the more I talk about this, the less I understand the pushback against identity politics, and I'll be a little uncharitable about it, but—

BLVR: Go for it.

OT: [*Laughs*] People tell me that identity politics is used to pursue political agendas that aren't really about helping the marginalized, and that people use these words in ways that are disconnected from the true meaning that it might have for core activists. I listen to those complaints about identity politics and I listen and I nod and I wait to hear the important insight that is being expressed to me, and they stop talking. Then I get confused. Show me a political concept that has not and could not be creatively utilized by the people in power, or the people who are relatively advantaged over some more marginalized group of people. I don't know. I don't know what people have in mind, what the contrast case is against which identity politics has some special deficiency. There's no place to go from that basic insight—like, *Welcome to politics. Are you new here?*

BLVR: [*Laughs*] Your article "Being-in-the-Room Privilege" laid out some of these issues before you expanded on them in *Elite Capture*. You say that the rooms of power and influence are built at the end of this long process. So even if we're in the room, we would say, *Sure, let's get different voices in the room. Let's pass the mic. Let's center the most marginalized*—but what about the person who built that room? How did that room get there? Who decided that we're in *this* room? There's an entire series of events that happened historically, and it's like, OK, we're just going to accept the first ninety-nine steps and then talk about step one hundred as if it is the first one. My reading of your work on deferential politics is that it's not really so much about whether the term *identity politics* is good or bad, or if it's used or misused. It's more: *Well, there's so much shit going on that got us to this point that we're in this room talking. If we put all our work into deferring to those otherwise kept out of the room, we accept that the structure, the room itself, is fine.*

OT: And it goes back to that line from earlier: if someone finds a baby in the river, we should absolutely pull the baby out of the river, but also there are questions we should ask. And one of the ways I put it when I talk about this in public is: There are actual funding structures behind CNN and Fox News and major research universities, and those structures come with people who make decisions, and those people, as a matter of concrete fact, get to decide which version of identity politics you get to hear. It's not as if there is a lottery that decides what the media covers or what is in your textbook. And as soon as you tell the story of which people occupy those decision-making points and why, you'll have gotten some distance to answering why the version of identity politics that circulates is the one that is probably more favorable to J. P. Morgan than the one that would be favorable to people whose houses were foreclosed on. I don't think you're learning some deep fact about what is actually in the Combahee River Collective Statement, right? If you wanted a deep fact about that, maybe you should just read it, rather than trying to work backward through decades of ideological drift and propagandizing.

BLVR: Is that coverage philosophically limiting? It doesn't allow for the fuller historical and, as you say, ideological context?

OT: Yeah, and it's *practically* limiting too. It doesn't just limit the ways people theorize it. It limits how people act in the world. The reason that's important is because you have to solve proximate problems—if your house is on fire, you have to put the fire out, but if you don't want to be doing that every year, you need to catch the arsonist. To make lasting, transformative change, you have to deal with root causes, not just immediate causes. And lots of political analysis and thinking try to figure out what those root causes are and what aspects of them are tractable or changeable, and identity politics is no exception to this general rule.

BLVR: That notion underneath the "Being-in-the-Room Privilege" argument and *Elite Capture*—it hit on something that got people thinking. I kept seeing references to it in a range of conversations.

OT: One of the things I've been struck by since writing the article and book is that identity politics is just like the rest of politics. There's no special thing happening there. There's no special ideological deficiency; there's no special political deficiency. The causes of the problems in that realm are not different, as far as I can tell, from the causes of other ideological problems or rhetorical problems or communicative problems that are tied to different political concepts. There's been a very intentional effort by the right wing—but I think with some participation from the center and the left—to try to make identity politics seem special for the very simple reason that people look at you funny if you just say, *I want segregation back*. But the people who want segregation back had to figure out something else to say, so they just landed on opposition to wokeness. Even that is not particularly special. It's not the first time people have found some more polite-sounding wedge issue to use to fight for openly reactionary ideals, so we shouldn't act like it is, and we shouldn't act like there's something special happening here. This is not particularly complicated or intellectually involved; it's the right fighting the center fighting the left. And if we on the left (that's where I put myself) want to grapple with it all, it might help to have some basic clarity about what's actually happening.

III. "THE DOMAIN OF JUSTICE"

BLVR: If you don't want your house to be on fire all the time, you catch the arsonist; if you want to save the babies in the river, you find out who's putting them in the river. If we move this to the climate point, we'd say that instead of the fire, instead of the baby, we're dealing with pollution and other environmental harms. If we want to redress problems like pollution, climate change, sea-level rise, lack of access to clean water, corrupted land, and damaged food, your work pushes us to try to understand the edifice that has produced environmental damage.

OT: We should talk about climate justice. And here the pollution metaphor does justice to the basic strategy of both books, because it's not a metaphor. Climate change is driven by actual pollution, which is bound up with the role of capitalism and the role of imperialism and the role of consumerism.

BLVR: We had to reschedule our initial interview last year because smoke from Canadian wildfires overtook my hometown in Pennsylvania.

OT: I forgot about that! Confronting these broader stories means confronting more specific disasters and calamities that come with the climate crisis. Heat waves, and hurricanes, and rainfall variation, and harm to crop yields, and heightened evictions, and heightened policing within countries and at the borders—

BLVR: Those make some of my metaphors a bit thin.

OT: No, it's not as clean, unfortunately, as the baby-in-the-river metaphor. But this is just me being fair to everybody else. I mean, do we have to just destroy consumerism, this entire edifice of human behavior, to deal with one hurricane in the Gulf? What do these broader ills that are harming people have to do with more local problems?

BLVR: What is a good working definition of *climate justice*?

OT: I see climate justice less as a specific kind of justice and more as a domain of justice. There are going to be pressures on our political and economic systems that are caused by the climate crisis, and there are going to be specific actions to reconstitute our energy and food systems that countries, regions, and cities take in response to the climate crisis. In both those senses there are questions to ask about justice: Which people are empowered by the changes we make to deal with droughts? Which people are made safe by the levees and seawalls that are erected to protect them from sea-level rise? Which people are insured in programs that are put into place to give people economic security in a warming world? Those are concrete political questions.

BLVR: They raise important questions about distribution, about how harms and benefits get distributed: Why is the municipal waste dump here? Why is there more trash there? Why is there bad water here? It didn't get that way accidentally. Not to mention the process of how decisions are made, who gets to participate, whose voice is heard. How do you try to address all the questions raised by the climate crisis?

OT: The way I think about these problems is through the lens of self-determination. That's what I'm working on now: freedom and self-determination. I think many have viewed freedom *as* self-determination, and I'm trying to figure out why that is, basically.

BLVR: This feels like a good place to ask for an example.

OT: OK, so suppose you're someone who can place a big emphasis on who gets to be part of the decision-making process—procedural justice. There are all sorts of reasons why procedural justice is an important aspect of thinking broadly about justice, but what mistake would someone be making if they thought procedural justice was all there was to justice? And if they thought about procedural justice as something like inclusion in political processes? Well, you know, not all inclusion is created equal. You could include the public in an advisory role; you could schedule town halls during working hours so nobody could come to them. Here it's not even inclusion but the *possibility* of inclusion. There are all sorts of ways you could cosmetically include people in politics that would fail to do the most important thing, which is including people in the political decisions that shape their lives. I don't think that's anybody's vision of justice, procedural or otherwise.

BLVR: What's missing?

OT: Well, when you start to ask what's missing from that kind of caricature of justice, what's important, to me at least, is thinking about the direction of freedom as self-determination. That's a way of asking what justice requires of a social system: it gives people meaningful power to actually shape their own lives. That does not mean simply having the opportunity to shape their lives or to be in the room when their lives are being shaped. You'd start worrying about whether people had an actual opportunity to make the meeting, or if the meeting could be scheduled at a time when more people could come. You'd start to wonder: What's the point of this meeting? Is it just a meeting to advise the people with the real decision-making power? Are the people who make the decisions about infrastructure elected or not elected? And if they are elected, are they responsive to the people who elected them? If they are not elected, are they chosen in a way that implies genuine democratic input? All those questions, I think, are about who has the power to shape the world around us. They are not simply about whether the processes that shape the world meet the cosmetic criteria of democracy, but about who is actually doing the shaping. And that's where self-determination meets freedom.

BLVR: I talk with food-justice students about the difference between food security and food sovereignty. Food security is narrower: Do people have enough calories? Is there enough food for them? Food sovereignty is more about how people choose what they are going to eat and how they are going to get their food. Do they have the capacity to choose their diets? It's a harder thing to achieve.

OT: Right. I think the food security/food sovereignty distinction is the same as the freedom/self-determination distinction, just on the topic of food. We walk that distinction out to every aspect of social life, and it's the same thing. Are we shaping the world around one another and alongside one another,

or are some of us shaping the world for others? That's the key distinction right there.

BLVR: You've done work on justice around energy technologies—how we produce it, how we distribute it, who gets it—but it's instructive that your points about climate justice keep the interconnected environmental systems at hand. That is, the ways energy and food and water are tied together.

OT: Yeah, among other things, a food system is a set of flows and stocks of solar energy—it's all systems all the way down. I get it: it's convenient and helpful for us limited beings to sift

---

ALL THE FRUIT FOUND IN ANDRÉ ACIMAN'S *CALL ME BY YOUR NAME*

☆ Apple, grabbed by Oliver on his way out of the house
☆ "Apricot" (also: *albicocca, abricot, aprikose*), in an etymology quiz casually administered to Oliver by Professor Samuel
☆ Apricots, in Mafalda's apricot juice, served to Oliver every morning; picked by Oliver while helping Mafalda
☆ Figs, peeled by Oliver and Elio during their first night together in Rome; in a tree scaled by Vimini before dinner
☆ Lemons, in Mafalda's lemonade, drunk during a break in a doubles tennis match; in lemonade hastily left by Elio in a half-full glass atop sheet music; in lemonade, as refreshment for the cutlery grinder; in soda consumed by a drunk Elio in Rome
☆ Olives, in trees from the berm where Monet used to paint; in groves passed by Elio and Oliver on their bikes; used for a large batch of martinis served by Oliver
☆ Oranges and watermelons, in juice and slices consumed by a drunk Oliver in Rome
☆ Peach, used by Elio for sex; sensually eaten by Oliver in front of Elio; cherished in memory by Elio after Oliver's departure
☆ Peaches, bananas, apricots, pears, and dates, blended into a yogurt smoothie by Elio
☆ Raspberries, in juice speckled over chocolate cake
☆ "Ripe fruit," in small talk between Marzia and Elio
☆ Tomatoes, argued over by Manfredi and Anchise

—list compiled by Gabe Boyd

parts of this enormously complex system into buckets, to sit in a room and be like, *In this room we're going to talk about food*, and to sit in another room and say, *In this room we're going to talk about energy*. We make these problems artificially smaller and artificially contained so they are trackable, so students can have an actual amount of learnable material in front of them. But that's something we impose for trackability; it's not a real distinction.

BLVR: Can you talk about the implications of how we think about justice and equity when we pay attention to interconnected environmental systems?

OT: It's like the apple tree doesn't say, *I'm part of the food network, so it doesn't matter whether or not I get water!* That's not what happens in nature. But we're dealing with the actual movement of energy and goods and the military, and in principle anything could be relevant to that. I think, in terms of my particular political philosophy, just trying to keep that sort of thing in mind is crucial.

IV. HOBSBAWM'S HISTORIES

BLVR: How did you get to these ideas? Whose work influences you?

OT: Honestly, a lot of the core theoretical convictions I have were sparked by the anti-colonial activists of the '50s and '60s. Maybe some people got there centuries before that, but I'm really motivated by that period of political history. People like Amílcar Cabral, especially. I mean, speaking of food, in addition to being an anti-colonial materialist, he was a soil scientist.

BLVR: I learned from you that he had a keen sense of history too.

OT: Definitely, and that's another thing: historians are huge influences on how I think. I think few other disciplines encourage, maybe even require, the kind of breadth that I aspire to as a political philosopher. Like, think of Eric Hobsbawm's histories. With equal fluency, this guy is talking about the rates of technological adoption across centuries in Europe and the artistic movements of the US and the intellectual progression of different elites in different parts of the world. And he's trying to tell a story that encompasses all those things. I don't know that any one person can do the complexity of the world justice, but I think that's what we should be trying for as research communities. And in the field of history it's nice to see people trying to do that. I mention Hobsbawm as an influence because he has the most comically large stories to tell. But also C.L.R. James, Robin Kelley: this could be a long list—

BLVR: We're here for it.

OT: [*Laughs*] I was about to add heterodox economists to the mix too. It's fashionable now to shit on economics, and I get why, but I think there's a lot to learn there, especially from a materialist perspective. I think some economists, like Daniela Gabor, are trying to ask and answer the kinds of questions I'm trying to ask and answer. I'm thinking of economists like Ndongo Samba Sylla and Isabella Weber. Then there are people in the intellectual journalist sphere. Tim Sahay is one. These are my contemporaries who are working on issues in ways that push me to do more.

BLVR: We haven't even touched on philosophers, though I know our time is running short here.

OT: There are people in philosophy departments, particularly in the past few decades, who have been enormously influential to me. Charles Mills is an obvious one. Plus contemporary but senior scholars that I continue to learn from—people like Lewis Gordon, Chike Jeffers, Linda Martín Alcoff. Plenty of philosophers have worked on things I'm interested in, but given how the world works, it's no surprise that someone with my interests has to read so far outside philosophy.

BLVR: We started with your own contributions to philosophy, political culture, intellectually engaging journalism, and we're ending by looking to those you've been in conversation with, the hidden infrastructure of ideas that has led you to make your own contributions.

OT: The last thing I'd say, then, is that I invest in what our contemporaries are doing, obviously, but I really don't get the sense, especially in the humanities, that the right way to think of the passage of time is as a progression. I think things are cyclical. Sometimes things regress very noticeably. Whether it was written fifty years ago or fifty seconds ago, there's potentially something to learn there. Just be open-minded. ✶

THE WAY BACK

A NEW ROTATING GUEST COLUMN OF WRITERLY REMEMBRANCES.
IN THIS ISSUE: TÍA AMELIA'S HOUSE

by Julia Alvarez

When I was growing up, in a large extended family in the Dominican Republic, one of the things that distinguished me from that indistinct mass of siblings and cousins was that mine was the best godmother.

Her name was tía Amelia, and in her youth she had been a legendary beauty. Even as an older woman, which is how I remember her, she was beautiful. Her skin was dramatically pale in contrast to her black hair, which was, by then, streaked with silver threads; her eyes were an astonishing sky blue. I say "astonishing" because I had never known a Dominican with blue eyes. I thought of blue eyes as a trait of Americans, like speaking English, freckling, and sounding silly speaking Spanish.

She had been born into a poor family, but she was so beautiful that one of the richest men in the country married her. Tío Felipe, who was sixteen years older, doted on his young bride, spoiling her with trips; expensive gifts; a big, fancy house. That's another thing that made her a fairy-tale character: hers was a fairy-tale life. Up to a point, I should add: she was widowed young and lived alone in her enormous mansion, surrounded by spacious grounds, with a swimming pool she never used and a chapel where, every day, tía Amelia said a rosary, surrounded by her numerous staff.

Tía Amelia was not just rich; she was generous. Several times a year, her chauffeur would drive over to our house to deliver a beribboned box. My cousins and sisters would flock around me, eager to see what I'd gotten. The gifts were often disappointing, though I tried not to let on in front of everyone. They were an adult's idea of what a child would like: a tasteful ring, nothing glittery or pretty I could trade for something more fun from an older cousin; an Easter bonnet trimmed with a clutter of flowers—I would have preferred ribbons riding down my back; a diary in which to write down my thoughts—"thoughts" to write down at age seven or eight? One gift I did love was a pink taffeta dress with lots of flounces, which I was allowed to wear to Sunday Mass. I felt like a gift myself when I wore it, with its big bow tied at the back, its sash that held me so tight I could never forget I was all dressed up and on my best behavior. But what I most loved about this dress was its noise. The flounces rustled luxuriously each time I knelt or sat or filed down the aisle to the altar. Any benefits that might have accrued to my soul by going to communion were rendered naught by this gift, as all I could think of as I received the body and blood of Our Lord Jesus Christ was how dazzling my rustling dress was and how all eyes were on me for once.

My godmother was also not one of those titular godmothers, who might as well have been plain and simple tías. She took her godmothering duties seriously. She traveled a lot: to Rome for an audience with the pope, to Paris to buy perfume, to New York to check with her bankers. But whenever she was in country, she would send her chauffeur over with an invitation for me to come spend Saturday at her mansion.

I don't think I was ever consulted about whether this was something I would like to do. There was no question that I would accept this incredibly kind invitation. Besides, my cousins and sisters were full of envy at my good luck. All they had ever seen of tía Amelia's house was the high wall that spanned several city blocks, and it was only through my stories that they knew what lay on the other side: the swimming pool, shaped like a giant kidney bean; the chapel, with rosaries from all over the world; a house full of hallways and winding staircases and so many parlors, dining rooms, sunrooms, and bedrooms that it always seemed like the house was a living thing that had spawned more rooms since the last time I'd visited.

The Saturday following the midweek invitation, with my bathing suit wrapped in a towel and many admonitions from my mother that I was to behave myself, I'd climb into the

Illustration by Rich Tommaso

black car my godmother had sent for me. At the front gate a uniformed guard would raise a hand in salute as we drove in. Tía Amelia was in her dressing room, sitting at her vanity, still involved in getting dressed, which seemed to be an all-morning affair. She would give me a kiss and ask me a few questions about my family before she lost interest and sent me out to play. Her affection was genuine but impersonal, except for those few moments when she trained her eyes on me and asked what I wanted to be when I grew up. I never seemed to think up a suitable enough answer to detain her astonishing blue gaze.

It was a long, empty day at my godmother's house. A maid was assigned to take care of me, with strict orders not to leave me alone. She was a tired old woman who had been with my godmother forever and no longer had any specific duties, so she was free to attend to this untoward child in the household. I'd change into my suit and wade into the pool while she sat nearby under the cabana, dozing off, no doubt as bored as I was. For how much fun could it be to have a whole swimming pool to myself with no one to splash

---

MICROINTERVIEW WITH DEVON PRICE, PART VIII

THE BELIEVER: Your work seems to both refute and substantiate some of the labels that Western psychology works through. How do you relate to the language of diagnosis?

DEVON PRICE: We're still in a place where we emphasize individual identity rather than naming social conditions and experiences that bind almost all of us. I hope we move to a paradigm where people realize that every personality disorder—so many things in the *DSM*—they're all different manifestations, slightly different takes, on how people respond to trauma and attachment distress. The need to separate them out into separate diagnoses and separate labels makes us miss the actual core experiences that give birth to them. We're treating it as: *You have evil-person disease or crazy, overly attached person disease.* No, both of these people have attachment trauma. Let's talk about the different behaviors we reach for when we have attachment issues and when we're seeking attachment. I hope this is the paradigm we get to. ✶

and jump with, no one to scream with when a boy cousin grabbed at our legs underwater, pretending to be a shark? The old woman did not want to toss a ball or play tag. In fact, she got cranky if I wandered around too much in the hot sun, tiring her out.

We ended up in the dark, cool chapel, where she'd let me play with my godmother's collection of rosaries while she sat in a pew, resting. Or she'd lure me to the kitchen with a promise to show me "el dumbwaiter," which I'd heard my godmother refer to often at lunch: "Súbalo con el dumbwaiter." Send it up with the dumbwaiter. Thanks to my English lessons, I could decode simple words and phrases. I would wait for a large, bald, stupid man dressed in a uniform to walk in with a silver tray of crystal bowls filled with wobbly flan or melting scoops of ice cream. But he never materialized. Instead, a slot opened in the wall, and inside was a shelf that was raised from the ground-floor kitchen by pulleys, with glasses of water or platters full of vegetables or the salt and pepper shakers. That was "el dumbwaiter," my godmother explained, after the nursemaid had successfully tricked me a number of times. Fiction, I was learning, was a lot more exciting than the facts.

Which was why at the end of my long and lonely visit, when the big car drove me home and my sisters and cousins rushed to the door the chauffeur was opening for me, I told them all about my fabulous day at tía Amelia's house. The swimming pool shaped like a valentine with red-colored water; the chapel with jeweled rosaries from all over the world; the large, bald, stupid waiter in a gold-and-crimson uniform. But when I saw their eyes fill with longing and their faces turn pale with envy, I felt a pang. Where was the feeling of power and specialness I had expected to feel?

It was not enough to be a storyteller to suit myself, I was learning. What good was a story that made others feel left out? The minute you used a story for an outside purpose, it lost its true usefulness of belonging to everyone and no one, of stirring the winged life inside all of us, of allowing each one to become someone else.

I did not know how to tell that kind of a story yet. The story that would allow my cousins and sisters to become the lucky girl invited to spend the day at her godmother's mansion. The story that would make it interesting to be that lonely girl, bored with treasure she couldn't share. The story that might detain the blue gaze of my fairy-tale godmother. The story I still yearn to tell. ✶

A REVIEW OF

THE COIN

BY YASMIN ZAHER

The unnamed narrator of *The Coin*, Yasmin Zaher's debut novel, is afflicted by filth. Filth is an environmental hazard of city life, evident in the "dead rats, diapers, toothpicks, and drug baggies" strewn on the sidewalk. In the spectacle of filth, what most unnerves her is poverty, as poverty begets filth, and filth besmirches character. Cleanliness, then, becomes a moral imperative for the narrator—the daughter of wealthy Palestinian parents—who protects her purity through obsessive rituals like exfoliating her entire body with a Turkish loofah (which she dubs "the CVS Retreat") and covering her back with Cattier toothpaste. "You will see that I'm a moral woman," she says, "that all I want is to be clean." Her affliction reaches an unbearable apex in New York, where she recently immigrated from Jerusalem. There, she feels her body "beginning to rot." This disorientation is a symptom of a family curse, which is traced back to a small silver shekel that she swallowed as a child. She is convinced the coin is embedded in her back, in a spot that's impossible to clean. The shekel, an unsubtle metaphor for intergenerational wealth and trauma, belies her Janus-faced fate in the US: "America was both the key and the curse," she says. And again, later: "In my family, the curse was also the key." But the narrator, unlike most body-horror victims, is not besieged by an existential fear of her accursed flesh. She is, on the contrary, calm and methodical about her ritual. Eventually, she even tries to "create a new natural order" in her apartment, hoarding dirt and plants to simulate a wilderness that she can control.

Told in a detached first-person narration, *The Coin* is composed of short chronological vignettes detailing the narrator's eight months in New York. She spends most of her time teaching at an all-boys middle school; cleaning herself, her classroom, and her home; and avoiding her long-term boyfriend, Sasha. Interspersed throughout are dreamlike sequences that recall her tragic but materially comfortable childhood. At a young age, she and her brother had survived a car accident that killed her parents. "Redeemed by a good inheritance," she lives off a substantial monthly allowance that she carries in cash in her mother's hand-me-down Birkin. Still, the undisclosed amount is not enough to sustain her spending, and she's annoyed that it is being withheld from her by her brother. "I was simultaneously rich and poor," she says. Reminiscent of Moshfegh's impudent protagonist in *My Year of Rest and Relaxation*, Zaher's narrator is mannered and mildly self-aware, more dissociative than deadpan about her recherché wealth and "exotic beauty."

Because the novel's events are recounted from a not-so-distant future, suspense is established through what the protagonist chooses to withhold from us. The narrator speaks to "you," an unidentified confidant who is eventually revealed to be another "I," a figment of her own psyche. This disjunction reflects the growing rift between her body and mind. Compulsive actions are addressed coolly, and psychosomatic aberrations are attributed to the coin's tautological presence. A proclaimed hedonist, she is "always ready to fuck" but speaks of sex with pleasureless remove: "He fucked me until I blacked out, not alcoholically, but in the sense that I had transcended the present." *The Coin*, like its narrator, is surprisingly minimalist, sedate, and clean, for a story about the squalor of mania and the profound fear of an incurable filth that torments the flesh. Stripped of the traditional conventions of character, Zaher's narrator is a spirit possessed by surfaces: a free-floating shade clad in designer goods, porous as the scent of her expensive French perfume. A semblance of emotional solidity is attained through her relationship with Trenchcoat, a homeless con man with whom she travels to Paris to partake in a Birkin resale scheme. Even so, Trenchcoat offers a short-lived return to glamor, a temporary distraction from a persistent curse. This excursion only strengthens the coin's hold on her psyche. In the end, there is no escape, only a return to the self.

—*Terry Nguyễn*

Publisher: *Catapult* **Page count:** *240* **Price:** *$27.00* **Key quote:** *"Nature is clean. It's civilization that's dirty."* **Shelve next to:** *Agustina Bazterrica, Ottessa Moshfegh, Chelsea G. Summers* **Unscientifically calculated reading time:** *Four hours at a Turkish hammam before a full-body scrub*

Illustration by Pete Gamlen

ELEVATOR IN SÀI GÒN

BY THUẬN

How to make sense of your mother's life when she dies after falling several flights from the top floor of her son's, your brother's, defective home elevator? This absurd incident, which opens Thuận's *Elevator in Sài Gòn*, occasions the narrator's return from Paris, where she has lived in exile for fifteen years. At the funeral in Sài Gòn, her brother has arranged for their mother's portrait to be placed side by side with their father's, but she finds the suggestion of them reuniting in death implausible, and fails to recall any "family scene" from her past. Instead of summoning fuzzy memories from her childhood, she spends the funeral musing on how her mother has managed to keep her face intact while her body has become unrecognizable. She calls her brother the "producer-cum-director" of their mother's funeral-cum-movie, and credits their mother for her excellence in playing the part.

Back in France, she embarks on a quest to track down a certain Paul Polotsky, who appears with her mother in a mysterious old photograph, and might have been her mother's lover. She deduces that her mother, a loyal Việt Minh apparatchik, would have met him while under interrogation in a Hà Nội prison. The narrator is dogged about following Polotsky, and meets a bizarre cast of characters along the way.

She seems comfortable being a voyeur. Much like the narrator of Thuận's Anglophone debut, *Chinatown* (2022), she often finds herself carried away by flights of fancy, so much so that it can be hard to tell what information she's gleaning from her interlocutors and what she's making up. On matters of love, she has a penchant for imagining melodramatic, grandiloquent narrative arcs. Watching Polotsky shop with his wife from afar, she imagines "a romance à la Stendhal," though nothing about the scene invites the comparison. Some of her fantasies are still more hyperactive. She teaches a Vietnamese class, and imagines the circumstances behind one student's prickliness: He must be getting a divorce. A divorce, specifically, from a wife wearing a light gray dress that shows off a "fleshy pair of thighs." He was at court just this morning, she surmises, where he would have exclaimed to the judge: "I'm so done with that rule of yours, that once a man and a woman get married, they have to spend a lifetime together!" There is a vertiginous, far-sighted quality to the prose, owing to the shaky line between empirical observation and creative invention, and also to the fact that we learn more about errant strangers than we do about her son and his father.

Her basic paranoia is that everything in life is staged. In a ten-minute meeting with a prostitute whom Polotsky regularly visits, she draws the conclusion that the stray cat in the apartment is a prop. Soon she's asking herself why this woman feels "the need to display her capability and desire to caress in front of me." Her theories solidify into facts so quickly that it's hard to keep track of reality. If appearances are unreliable, anything can be true.

Perhaps her distrust of the phenomenal world comes from her childhood, when she had to watch her mother perform the part of "Mrs. Socialist New Wife" day in and day out—which would explain her fixation on Polotsky, who symbolizes unruly desire, something her mother was never allowed to express in the role society assigned to her. Perhaps she also feels betrayed by the rapid, radical changes all around her. A communist country turned capitalist; loyalists turned opportunists. Polotsky eventually triggers a memory of the narrator's ex, who was terse in daily life but affectionate while making love. As she dwells on these thoughts, her most unguarded voice emerges: "My own desire to make love to him stemmed from my wish to discover the human he aspired to be, the dream he hid deep inside himself, a dream known only to the two of us." In *Elevator in Sài Gòn*, there are no resolutions, only points of departure; her investigation into her mother's past life turns up only cryptic clues and red herrings. Love is an escape from the phoniness she is mired in, the stage play she has been cast in against her will, but it is spare.

—*Jasmine Liu*

Publisher: *New Directions* Page count: *192* Price: *$16.95* Key quote: *"Deep in my heart, I felt that I, like all the others, was there only in order to act."* Shelve next to: *Jhumpa Lahiri, Catherine Lacey* Unscientifically calculated reading time: *A distracted evening observing neighbors' lives from a rear window*

Illustration by Pete Gamlen

MOUTH

"**I** thought we were happy, until the wolves came." This line from one of the stories in Puloma Ghosh's debut collection reads almost as a logline for the rest. These unsettling fictions are often set after minor apocalypses, the protagonists standing in the aftermath and facing the mismatch of who they once were and who they are now. In this way, *Mouth* is a welcome book for our post-COVID era, though what gives the collection its power is the dissemblance of Ghosh's worlds to our own.

In "Leaving Things," a onetime veterinarian scours the emptying shelves of her local bodega, ignoring the owner's advice to leave town. Wolves have taken over; women are disappearing in the night. In an alleyway, she finds one wolf panting, near death, her belly swollen in pregnancy. She brings the wolf home to try to heal her, and when the wolf dies, she tries to save the pups—but it's not pups she's been carrying: "I watched small limbs kick and tear out of the wolf's womb, teeth gnashing through her skin. At last, a human infant with open eyes reached for me through the carnage." Now she's a kind of mother, but as he grows rapidly in a few days, she becomes something even more intimate, with more potential for damage.

"Natalya" takes the form of an autopsy report, performed by a pathologist on the corpse of a woman she loved decades prior. As she slices open Natalya's body, she recalls their years together, when the pathologist was a teen girl with a cutting problem. Natalya was the only one she could share this with. Now, as she writes in her notes, "no matter how I touch you, you remain still, peeled apart like a pithy citrus."

These are stories concerned not so much with recovery after loss as with preservation, how the woman at each story's center can stay whole when so much of her has been stripped away. This drive for wholeness gives Ghosh her collection's title and central metaphor: the mouth as an organ for consumption. Pritha, an ice-skating rival of the protagonist in "Desiccation," is discovered "crouched against [a] gray wall, her teeth deep in a crumpled rodent"; later, she sucks lightly on the protagonist's wounds. In "Supergiant," an international pop star sits calmly as her makeup artist digs deep into her mouth, unhooking the seams of the "celebrity skin" that forms her public self. Many of Ghosh's characters at one point get their necks and shoulders bitten, some of them benignly, but one to the extent that she's left bleeding everywhere, "and I leaned into it, longing to let all of my writhing insides spill forth at last."

Consumption, in its way of transforming the body from a container of the self to food for someone else, is in Ghosh's fiction an erotic act. That shattering of the ego. So many of these characters long to be eaten, swallowed whole, and transformed into something else. The tone Ghosh favors in these stories—cool, almost clinical—serves her well when writing about sex, bringing readers close to sex's effect on the psyche as much as on the body. "It was a strange way to come," she writes in "In the Winter" as a man (who may also be a wolf) works his fingers into the protagonist, "treated a bit like a fleshy little vegetable that had to be held down and scraped clean of seeds."

It's that tension between becoming an object and a subject that sets these characters on their journeys. In "Anomaly," time agents from the future have created rips in the fabric of space-time, one of which our protagonist visits while on a first date. Couples can pay to step through the anomaly, dissolve molecularly into one another, and fall out somewhere in Indiana. In a field, the anomaly gleams and shimmers. It is another mouth, another hole to fall into. Ghosh deftly delivers each of her protagonists to these kinds of precipices. The pleasure throughout *Mouth* lies in watching each of them jump.

—Dave Madden

Publisher: *Astra House* **Page count:** *224* **Price:** *$26.00* **Key quote:** *"I wait for her teeth, but they never come."* **Shelve next to:** *J. G. Ballard, K-Ming Chang, Kelly Link, Carmen Maria Machado* **Unscientifically calculated reading time:** *Twenty-two games of Hide-and-Go-Seek*

Illustration by Pete Gamlen

THE PUZZLE OF INCREDIBLY WIDE AND DEEP KNOWLEDGE

IF YOU COMPLETE THIS PUZZLE, YOU ARE A GENERALIST OF BROAD SKILL AND GREAT RENOWN

by Wyna Liu; edited by Benjamin Tausig

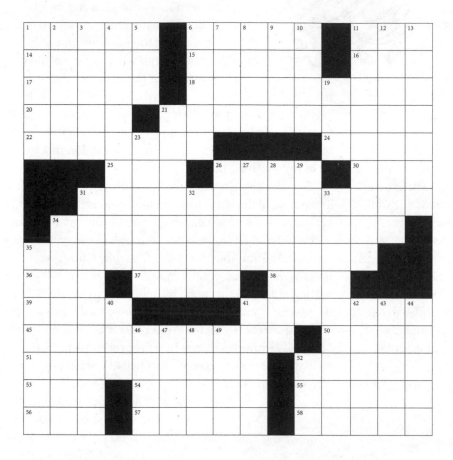

ACROSS

1. Concert ephemera
6. Softens, as a certain cube
11. Letters after a year
14. Stay away from home?
15. Clips before a new episode
16. Exclamation while pointing up, perhaps
17. Lot calculations
18. They may be blown across the room
20. "___, A Tale" (Byron narrative poem)
21. Online degree?
22. Overly eager
24. Moved effortlessly
25. Chew ___
26. General equivalents: Abbr.
30. Hosp. section
31. Open challenge for kids?
34. Compliment to the gifted
35. Kitchen hand-me-downs
36. Not just intimate
37. Spanish pronoun
38. Peace sign shape
39. Sweet ingredient in some vegan baking
41. Likely scoring position
45. They may be analyzed in genealogy research
50. Genesis figure
51. Woman with the most Oscar wins in history (eight)
52. Word with false or flying
53. "TV Funhouse" show, familiarly
54. Words under a coat of arms
55. Sensitive topic to discuss with one's manager
56. Clock-stoppers: Abbr.
57. Street in New York's Lower East Side named for an English county
58. Giant meanies

DOWN

1. Word after "thou"
2. Text which by law must be written on parchment
3. A female kangaroo has two
4. Iconic sitcom star who said "I think we made television a little more adult"
5. Rocket in the Artemis mission: Abbr.
6. Spencer who was the first person to win two consecutive Academy Awards for Best Actor
7. Next in line
8. Land unit
9. Ship's trail
10. Barre alternative
11. Features of ancient Roman architecture
12. Descriptor for all elements
13. Softened
19. Sides of a city block: Abbr.
21. Slender probing devices
23. Swanky shindig
26. Condition treated with a CPAP machine
27. Universal Studios sucker, familiarly
28. Drivers
29. Turbo-charged, with "up"
31. Old fashioned and sour
32. Concave kite, in geometry
33. Game where you have to stop if caught
34. "It's complicated ..."
35. Most blue
40. Contractor's fig.
41. Reaction where electrons are exchanged
42. Recording sign
43. Like the gods Vili and Ve
44. Blues musician Sleepy John ___
46. "Alas"
47. Units replaced by siemens
48. Strokes lovingly
49. Stuck in traffic, perhaps, or claiming to be
52. Ticket spec

(answers on page 124)

10 ERRORS HAVE BEEN INSERTED INTO THIS PASSAGE. CAN YOU FIND THEM?

by Caitlin Van Dusen

MIDDLEMARCH (1871)
by GEORGE ELIOT (MARY ANN EVANS)

Dorothea rose to leave the table and Mr. Casaubon made no reply, taking up a letter which laid[1] besides[2] him as if to reperuse it. Both were shocked at their mutual situation—that both[3] should have betrayed anger towards the other. If they had been at home, settled at Lowick in ordinary life among their neighbors, the clash would have been less embarrassing: But[4] on a wedding journey, the express object of which is to isolate two people on the ground that they are all the world to each other, the sense of disagreement is, to say the least, confounding and stultifying. To have changed your longitude extensively and placed yourselves in a moral solitude in order to have small explosions, finding[5] conversation difficult and to hand a glass of water without looking, can hardly be regarded as satisfactory fullfillment[6] even to the toughest minds. To Dorothea's inexperienced sensitiveness, it seemed like a catastrophe, changing all prospects; and to Mr. Causabon[7] it was a new pain, he never having been on a wedding journey before, or found himself in that close union which was more of a subjection than he had been able to imagine, since this charming young bride not only obliged him to much consideration on her behalf (which he had sedulously given), but turned out to be capable of agitating him cruelly just where he most needed soothing. Instead of getting a soft fence against the cold, shadowy, unapplausive audience of his life, had he only given it a more substantial presence?

Neither of them felt it possible to speak again at present. To have reversed a previous arrangement and declined to go out would be[8] a show of persistent anger which Dorothea's conscious[9] shrank from, seeing that she already began to feel herself guilty…. she was inwardly seeing the light of years to come in her own home and over the English fields and elms and hedge-bordered highroads; and feeling that the way in which they may[10] be filled with joyful devotedness was not so clear to her as it had been. But in Dorothea's mind there was a current into which all thought and feeling were apt sooner or later to flow—the reaching forward of the whole consciousness towards the fullest truth, the least partial good. There was clearly something better than anger and despondency. *(answers on page 124)*

Follow The Chicago Manual of Style, *17th edition. Please ignore unusual spellings, hyphenations, and capitalizations, and the that/which distinction. All are characteristic of the author's style and time.*

JACKET CAPTCHA

CAN YOU IDENTIFY THESE NINE BOOK COVERS?

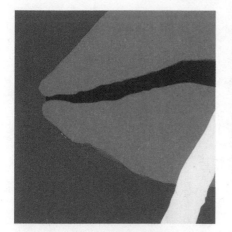  

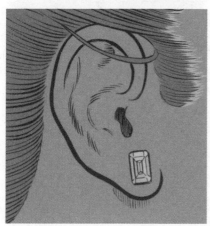  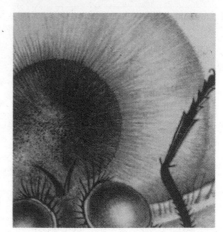

INTERNATIONAL BESTSELLER LISTS

See what the rest of the world is reading in this regular feature, which highlights a rotating cast of countries in each issue.

COMPILED BY JASPER CERONE, ACCORDING TO 2023 ANNUAL LISTS

AUSTRALIA

1. *The Bookbinder of Jericho* by Pip Williams. *Twin sisters working as bookbinders at Oxford University Press amid wartime struggles discover the ways they are different.*

2. *Lola in the Mirror* by Trent Dalton. *In an attempt to escape the grips of one of Brisbane's crime bosses, a girl and her mother seek out a mysterious woman named Lola.*

3. *Homecoming* by Kate Morton. *A journalist returns home to Sydney and uncovers a personal tie to a murder that occurred in 1959 in the South Australian town of Tambilla.*

4. *Dictionary of Lost Words* by Pip Williams. *A young girl covertly assembles a book of words that were overlooked by the men responsible for creating the Oxford English Dictionary.*

5. *Mr. Einstein's Secretary* by Matthew Reilly. *On her journey from Berlin to New York, an aspiring physicist works as a secretary for an array of historical figures.*

6. *Black Sheep* by Judy Nunn. *In this historical novel about the the Great Shearers' Strike, a wealthy sheep-farming family adopts a resilient teenager.*

7. *The Seven* by Chris Hammer. *In the fictional country town of Yuwonderie, detectives investigate a murder that targeted one of its seven founding families.*

8. *Darling Girls* by Sally Hepworth. *Three sisters still haunted by their strict foster mother become suspects in a murder case after police find a body in their childhood farmhouse.*

9. *Exiles* by Jane Harper. *One year after a new mother disappears, her family draws the attention of an investigator, who joins their gathering in South Australian wine country.*

10. *Before You Knew My Name* by Jacqueline Bublitz. *A lonely young woman finds the dead body of a Jane Doe and becomes obsessed with discovering her identity.*

POLAND

1. *Langer* by Remigiusz Mróz. *Lawyer Joanna Chylka defends a wealthy sadist from Mokotów who has been accused of murder.*

2. *Dawno temu w Warszawie (Long Ago in Warsaw)* by Jakub Żulczyk. *This novel considers Warsaw's most vulnerable citizens as dark forces rise to power during the COVID lockdown.*

3. *Seria z komisarzem Forstem (Series with Commissioner Forst)* by Remigiusz Mróz. *In these collected volumes of an eight-part novel series, Commissioner Forst struggles to find an ally in his fight against various bad actors.*

4. *Kabalista (Kabbalist)* by Remigiusz Mróz. *In the city of Opole, journalist Małgorzata Rosa enlists the help of a clairvoyant as she looks into a neglected sexual assault case.*

5. *Zarzut (Allegation)* by Remigiusz Mróz. *Lawyer Joanna Chyłka questions the innocence of her client, a priest accused of pedophilia, to whom she is indebted.*

6. *Światła w popiołach (Lights in the Ashes)* by Remigiusz Mróz. *Newly discovered human remains challenge a closed case in which two teenagers were said to have been killed in a fire.*

7. *Nie mylić z miłością (Not to be Confused with Love)* by Nosowska Katarzyn. *This is a book-length meditation on the divine power of love and radical self-acceptance.*

8. *For Sure Not You* by Weronika Ancerowicz. *A long-standing feud between a high-performing student named Natalie and her rebellious classmate takes an unexpected turn during their senior year at Westwood Academy.*

9. *Maybe You* by Weronika Ancerowicz. *In this sequel to For Sure Not You, the two protagonists reconsider their hostile relationship during their final semester of high school.*

10. *Mitologia (Mythology)* by Jan Parandowski. *Published to international success in 1924, this collection of ancient myths focuses on Hellenism.*

INDIA

1. *The Hidden Hindu* by Akshat Gupta. *This first book in a trilogy follows the young Prithvi on his search for Om Shastri, an Aghori Hindu who is marooned on a remote Indian island.*

2. *The Hidden Hindu 2* by Akshat Gupta. *The trilogy continues as Om and two enigmatic warriors travel to procure a hidden verse and are pursued by a former foe.*

3. *The Hidden Hindu 3* by Akshat Gupta. *The trilogy ends with a battle between Prithvi and a group of gods over Om, whose epoch-spanning secrets could alter the future.*

4. *War of Lanka (Ram Chandra series book 4)* by Tripathi Amish. *The fourth book of this series based on the ancient epic the Ramayana takes place during a bloody war.*

5. *You Only Live Once: One for Passion, Two for Love, Three for Friendship* by Stuti Changle. *A YouTube sensation, a stand-up comic, and the quirky owner of a beach shack join forces to locate their missing friend in Goa.*

6. *That Night* by Nidhi Upadhyay. *Twenty years after a game of Ouija among hostel mates left one of them dead, a menacing figure upends the lives of those who survived.*

7. *One Day, Life Will Change: A Story of Love and Inspiration to Win Life When It Hits You Hard* by Saranya Umakanthan. *In the wake of a traumatic relationship, Samaira falls in love with a successful and tender man named Vivian.*

8. *The Immortals of Meluha (Shiva Trilogy book 1)* by Amish Tripathi. *In 1900 BCE, Suryavanshi rulers pin their hopes on the prophesied hero Shiva to save their empire.*

9. *The Bird with Golden Wings* by Sudha Murty. *This collection of whimsical tales is illustrated by Ajanta Guhathakurta.*

10. *The Palace of Illusions* by Chitra Banerjee Divakaruni. *This feminist retelling of the ancient epic the Mahabharata takes Panchaali's perspective.*

SPAIN

1. *Las hijas de la criada (The Maid's Daughters)* by Sonsoles Ónega. *An act of revenge indelibly alters the future of two girls born on the same night in February 1900.*

2. *El problema final (The Final Problem)* by Arturo Pérez-Reverte. *In a storm-trapped hotel on the island of Utakos, an actor tries to solve the mystery behind the recent death of a tourist.*

3. *El cuco de cristal (The Crystal Cuckoo)* by Javier Castillo. *A heart transplant recipient visits Steelville, Missouri, at the urging of her donor's mother, but a disturbing incident soon occurs.*

4. *El ángel de la ciudad (The Angel of the City)* by Eva García Sáenz de Urturi. *After a Venetian palazzo burns down during a booksellers' meeting and bodies are missing from the rubble, one detective finds himself confronted by his family's past.*

5. *Esperando al diluvio (Waiting for the Flood)* by Dolores Redondo. *In this novel inspired by true events, a Scottish detective tracks the elusive Glaswegian serial killer Bible John to Bilbao.*

6. *El viento conoce mi nombre (The Wind Knows My Name)* by Isabel Allende. *This novel follows a man fleeing Nazi Austria on a Kindertransport and a woman escaping El Salvador.*

7. *Cómo (no) escribí nuestra historia (How I (Didn't) Write Our Story)* by Elísabet Benavent. *Faced with unshakable writer's block, Elsa Benavides debates killing off the character that brought her wealth and fame.*

8. *Maldita Roma: La conquista del poder de Julio César (Accursed Rome: The Conquest of Julius Caesar's Power)* by Santiago Posteguillo. *In 75 BCE, the exiled Julius Caesar sets the foundation for his rise to power by acquiring the oratory skills necessary to challenge Cicero.*

9. *Hijos de la fábula (Children of the Fable)* by Fernando Aramburu. *Two young men arrive at a chicken farm in France in hopes of joining Euskadi Ta Askatasuna, only to learn that it has ceased operations and they must create a seperatist group of their own.*

10. *El infierno (Hell)* by Carmen Mola. *During a political revolt in Madrid, Leonor and Mauro becoming embroiled in a murder and flee to Havana's sugar plantations, where they encounter a cruel system of enslavement.*

NOTES ON OUR CONTRIBUTORS

Julia Alvarez is the author of six novels, three books of nonfiction, three collections of poetry, and eleven books for children and young adults. *In the Time of the Butterflies*, which has more than one million copies in print, was selected by the National Endowment for the Arts for its Big Read program, and in 2013, President Obama awarded Alvarez the National Medal of Arts in recognition of her extraordinary storytelling. Her most recent novel, *The Cemetery of Untold Stories*, has just been published.

Andrea Bajani is an award-winning Italian novelist and poet. His novel *If You Kept a Record of Sins*, translated by Elizabeth Harris and published in the United States by Archipelago Books, won the Super Mondello Prize, the Brancati Prize, the Recanati Prize, and the Lo Straniero Prize. His latest novel, *Il libro delle case* (*The Book of Homes*), was a finalist for the Strega Prize and the Campiello Prize, and is being published in more than seventeen countries, including in the United States by Deep Vellum. He is currently the distinguished writer in residence at Rice University in Houston.

Taneum Bambrick is the author of *Intimacies, Received* and *Vantage*, winner of the 2019 *American Poetry Review*/Honickman First Book Prize. Their work can be found in *The New Yorker*, *The Nation*, *American Poetry Review*, and elsewhere. She lives in Los Angeles and is a Dornsife Fellow at the University of Southern California.

Pablo Calvi is an Argentine American writer and journalist. He is the author of *Latin American Adventures in Literary Journalism*, a cultural history of literary journalism in the Americas. Calvi's work appears in *The Nation*, *Jacobin*, *Guernica*, and *El Mercurio*. His work has received honorable mentions in *The Best American Essays*, *The Best American Travel Writing*, and *The Best American Nonrequired Reading*. He teaches journalism at Stony Brook University. He can be found on X at @plcalvi.

Benjamin R. Cohen lives and works in Easton, Pennsylvania. He is a former film critic for *The Granville Sentinel* and a current professor at Lafayette College.

Paul Collins is the author of ten books of non-fiction. A newly revised edition of his collection *Banvard's Folly: Thirteen Tales of People Who Didn't Change the World* is now available as an audiobook. He is a professor in the creative writing program at Portland State University, in Oregon.

Andrew Lewis Conn is the author of two books, *O, Africa!* and *P*. He recently finished his third novel, *The Freedom Tower*.

Leopoldine Core is the author of the poetry collection *Veronica Bench* and the story collection *When Watched*.

Elisa Gabbert is the author of seven collections of poetry, essays, and criticism, most recently *Any Person Is the Only Self*.

Jasmine Liu is a writer living in New York.

Dave Madden is the author of two books. Recent essays have appeared in *The Guardian*, *Defector*, *Harper's Magazine*, *Zyzzyva*, and *Literary Hub*. He teaches nonfiction in the MFA program at the University of San Francisco.

Ruth Madievsky is the author of the bestselling novel *All-Night Pharmacy*, a finalist for the California Book Award and the Lambda Literary Award, and the winner of the National Jewish Book Award for Debut Fiction. Her work appears in *The Atlantic*, *The Los Angeles Times*, *The Cut*, and elsewhere. Originally from Moldova, she lives in Los Angeles, where she works as an HIV and primary-care clinical pharmacist.

Laura Marris is a writer and translator. Her first collection of essays, *The Age of Loneliness*, is forthcoming from Graywolf Press in August 2024. She teaches creative writing at the University at Buffalo, in New York.

Lane Milburn is a cartoonist in Chicago. He is published by Fantagraphics Books.

Ahmed Naji is a writer, journalist, documentary filmmaker, and criminal. His novel *Using Life* made him the only writer in Egyptian history to have been sent to prison for offending public morality. His published novels in Arabic are *Tigers, Uninvited*, and *The Happy End*. He is also the author of the memoir *Rotten Evidence*, which was a finalist for the National Book Critics Circle Award in Autobiography. For more about his work, visit ahmednaji.net.

Terry Nguyễn is an essayist, critic, and poet from Garden Grove, California. She lives in Brooklyn, New York.

Niela Orr is a story editor for *The New York Times Magazine* and a contributing editor at *The Paris Review*. Her writing has appeared in the *London Review of Books*, *BuzzFeed*, *The Baffler*, and *McSweeney's Quarterly*, among other publications.

Monica Sok is the author of *A Nail the Evening Hangs On* (Copper Canyon Press, 2020). She has received fellowships from Hedgebrook, Kundiman, MacDowell, the National Endowment for the Arts, the Poetry Society of America, and other organizations. Her poems have appeared in *The American Poetry Review*, *The Paris Review*, *Poetry*, *The Kenyon Review*, and *The Washington Post*. She lives in New York City.

Jude Stewart is the author of three books, most recently *Revelations in Air: A Guidebook to Smell*. She has written about design, science, and culture for *The Atlantic*, *The Wall Street Journal*, *Quartz*, *Wired*, *Fast Company*, and many other publications.

Alejandro Varela is based in New York. His work has appeared in the *Boston Review*, *The Yale Review*, *The Georgia Review*, *The Point*, *Harper's Magazine*, and *The Offing*, among other publications. His debut novel, *The Town of Babylon*, was a finalist for the National Book Award for Fiction. His short-story collection, *The People Who Report More Stress*, was one of *Publishers Weekly*'s best works of fiction in 2023, a finalist for the International Latino Book Awards, and long-listed for the Story Prize and the Aspen Words Literary Prize. Varela is an editor at large of *Apogee* journal, and he holds a master's in public health from the University of Washington.

Emerson Whitney is the author of the critically acclaimed titles *Heaven* and *Daddy Boy* (McSweeney's 2020 and 2023, respectively), and the forthcoming experiment in memoir, *Haunt Me, Please*, to be published by McSweeney's in 2026.

James Yeh is a writer, editor, and journalist living in Brooklyn, New York. His fiction and nonfiction appear in *The New York Times*, *New York* magazine, *The Guardian*, *McSweeney's Quarterly*, *NOON*, and elsewhere. He teaches writing at Columbia University.

IN THE NEXT ISSUE

Not all contents are guaranteed; replacements will be satisfying

SOLUTIONS TO THIS ISSUE'S GAMES AND PUZZLES

CROSSWORD
(Page 118)

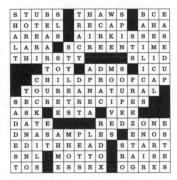

JACKET CAPTCHA
(Page 121)

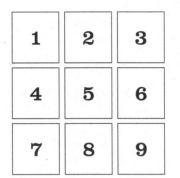

1. *The Woman Destroyed* by Simone de Beauvoir
2. *All Fours* by Miranda July
3. *How to Do Nothing* by Jenny Odell
4. *Real Americans* by Rachel Khong
5. *Big Swiss* by Jen Beagin
6. *Charlotte's Web* by E.B. White
7. *Monica* by Daniel Clowes
8. *The Heaven and Earth Grocery Store* by James McBride
9. *The Fly* by Richard Chopping

COPYEDITING THE CLASSICS (Page 119)

Dorothea rose to leave the table and Mr. Casaubon made no reply, taking up a letter which laid (1) besides (2) him as if to reperuse it. Both were shocked at their mutual situation—that both (3) should have betrayed anger towards the other. If they had been at home, settled at Lowick in ordinary life among their neighbors, the clash would have been less embarrassing: But (4) on a wedding journey, the express object of which is to isolate two people on the ground that they are all the world to each other, the sense of disagreement is, to say the least, confounding and stultifying. To have changed your longitude extensively and placed yourselves in a moral solitude in order to have small explosions, finding (5) conversation difficult and to hand a glass of water without looking, can hardly be regarded as satisfactory fullfillment (6) even to the toughest minds. To Dorothea's inexperienced sensitiveness, it seemed like a catastrophe, changing all prospects; and to Mr. Causabon (7) it was a new pain, he never having been on a wedding journey before, or found himself in that close union which was more of a subjection than he had been able to imagine, since this charming young bride not only obliged him to much consideration on her behalf (which he had sedulously given), but turned out to be capable of agitating him cruelly just where he most needed soothing. Instead of getting a soft fence against the cold, shadowy, unapplausive audience of his life, had he only given it a more substantial presence?

Neither of them felt it possible to speak again at present. To have reversed a previous arrangement and declined to go out would be (8) a show of persistent anger which Dorothea's conscious (9) shrank from, seeing that she already began to feel herself guilty…. she was inwardly seeing the light of years to come in her own home and over the English fields and elms and hedge-bordered highroads; and feeling that the way in which they may (10) be filled with joyful devotedness was not so clear to her as it had been. But in Dorothea's mind there was a current into which all thought and feeling were apt sooner or later to flow—the reaching forward of the whole consciousness towards the fullest truth, the least partial good. There was clearly something better than anger and despondency.

1. lay. *Laid* is the simple past tense of *lay* (the transitive verb meaning "to put or set down"), but, maddeningly, *lay* is also the simple past tense of *lie* (the intransitive verb meaning "to be or to stay at rest in a horizontal position"), which is what is meant here.
2. beside. *Besides* ("other than") and *beside* ("next to") are often confused.
3. each. Because their individual—rather than their collective—actions are emphasized here by "towards the other," *each* rather than *both* is called for.
4. but. Per *Chicago* style, the first word after a colon is lowercased unless it is a proper noun, or the colon introduces more than one sentence, a question, speech in dialogue, or a quote.
5. to find. For parallelism with "To have changed" at the start of the sentence: "To have changed…, to find…, can hardly be regarded…"
6. fulfillment. A frequently misspelled word.
7. Casaubon. Names are frequently misspelled, as the reader's eye tends to gloss over them once the name is recognized.
8. would have been. A tense fix to follow "To have reversed" at the start of the sentence.
9. conscience. *Conscience* and *conscious* are sometimes confused with each other.
10. might. *Might* is the simple past tense of *may*.